Senses of Vibration

A History of the Pleasure and Pain of Sound

SHELLEY TROWER

continuum

The Continuum International Publishing Group
80 Maiden Lane, New York, NY 10038
The Tower Building, 11 York Road, London SE1 7NX

www.continuumbooks.com

Library of Congress Cataloging-in-Publication Data
A catalog record for this book is available from the Library of Congress.

1006726705

ISBN: HB: 978-1-4411-6197-0
PB: 978-1-4411-4863-6

Typeset by Fakenham Prepress Solutions, Fakenham, Norfolk NR21 8NN
Printed and bound in the United States of America

CONTENTS

Acknowledgements vii
Introduction: Hearing Vibrations 1

1 Nervous Motions 13
2 Psychophysical Sensations and Spiritual Vibrations 37
3 Wires, Rays and Radio Waves 73
4 Pathological Motions: Railway Shock, Street Noises, Earthquakes 94
5 Sexual Health: Sewing Machines, Bicycle Spine, the Vibrator 126

Afterword 151
Notes 155
Bibliography 193
Index 211

ACKNOWLEDGEMENTS

This project has been in interrupted progress for about ten years, and in this time quite a number of people have helped it along its way. I must firstly thank Nicholas Ridout, for his brilliant intellectual input, his generosity and support throughout a great deal of the process. Much of the research was completed during my Ph.D. studies, and I am very grateful for funding from the AHRC, and for Steve Connor's excellent supervision. I would also like to thank Brandon LaBelle, in particular, for making it possible to transform all that into a book. For valuable insights and encouragement at different stages I am grateful to Jude Allen, Isobel Armstrong, Anthony Enns, Marion Gibson, William Hughes, Mary Lindsey, Kaye Mitchell, Phil Mollon, Laura Salisbury, Justin Sausman, Graham Smith, Chris Stuchbery, and Peter Trower.

A version of Chapter One was originally published in *Romanticism and Victorianism on the Net* (2009), part of Chapter Four was published in *Senses and Society* (2008), and part of Chapter Five was published in *Neurology and Modernity*, edited by Laura Salisbury and Andrew Shail (Palgrave, 2010). Thanks are due to these publications for permission to reprint.

INTRODUCTION
Hearing vibrations

Sound, at its lowest and loudest, begins to break down into separate, palpable vibrations. Bass notes in the ground, underfoot, in our bones. Slow the sound down further and each vibration might be separated out, counted, added up; there is no more sound, just individual shocks, one at a time. The research that led me to this book arose out of my experience of this phenomenon of sound breaking down in the clubs and parties of the 1990s, and my desire to understand and gain some historical perspective on the feeling that sound was composed of repeated physical sensations. In that decade, it was easy to become aware of the vibrations that make up sound, at a time when bass vibrations had taken on new prominence as an essential element of most forms of dance music, and when subwoofers became a standard part of sound systems both at home and in clubs and other public spaces. Music seemed no less palpable than audible, and sometimes almost as painful as it was intensely pleasurable.

Many commentators describe the experience of the bass in dance music as an 'extra-auditory' experience – not just heard by our ears but through our whole body. Derek Walmsley, for instance, claiming in a piece in *The Wire* that 'the true low end experience' can only be appreciated with the right kind of sound system in clubs, describes how bass 'pulses through your body, prickles the skin, presses upon your face, confounds sensations of distance and depth'.[1] Subwoofers are designed to transmit sound through air and also to vibrate floors and furniture, to increase the impact on our bodies as a palpable as well as audible phenomenon. At some clubs, like *Fabric* in London, bass speakers are mounted in the 'bodysonic dancefloor', so that dancers are vibrated through their feet along with the rest of the body.[2] Speaker technologies continue to be developed for multisensory purposes, such as the 'ButtKicker' brand of subwoofers which allows you to 'Feel Bass Without Volume', according to the advertising, as its low frequency transducers 'shake' your sofa 'in sync with your movie, music or game'. This ability to 'shake' the body seems to result in sound that is experienced as both more intense or loud and also quieter, that is felt rather than heard: 'Now you can enjoy powerful bass, realistic special effects and concert quality music without disturbing the neighbors or waking the kids'.[3]

The vibratory quality of sound can be experienced as palpable and audible and also visible. We can feel, hear and see a subwoofer vibrate, and see its effects on other bodies or matter: on the glass that bounces its way gradually across the top of a speaker and smashes on the floor, on the cat that attempts to pretend nothing is happening[4], and on potato starch.[5] The cultural prominence of vibrating speakers seems evident in the multiple ways in which they continue to be adapted for musical, commercial and artistic purposes or other forms of entertainment. 'White Lives on Speaker', an art project designed by Yoshimasa Kato and Yuichi Ito, demonstrates the mediation of sound vibration into other forms. Liquid potato starch is placed on a speaker; when stimulated by vibrations it jumps about and becomes solid, forming many different shapes as a kind of moving sculpture. The artists explain that two modes of vibration are used to stimulate the starch: a constant sound frequency which they produce themselves, and the changing frequencies of viewers' brain waves, captured by means of an encephalograph, and transformed via a laptop into further and unpredictable sonic vibrations. As the sculpture can also be touched – viewers can insert their fingers into the starch – this becomes, they suggest, a new way to experience and interact with one's own brain waves.[6] Their work thus exemplifies one of the central themes of this book: the idea that there is an intimate connection between the external world of objects in motion and an internal world of mental activity. Vibration provides the connection between the science of energies and bodies in movement – physics – and a whole range of sciences (or would-be sciences) of minds in action – neurology, psychology, spiritualism. In 'White Lives on Speaker', it turns out, Kato and Ito are reviving, repeating even, an older fascination with the capacity of the material world to vibrate the mind and that of the mind to vibrate the world.

As I started to explore the physics of vibration, in my attempt to understand the sense of being bombarded by music in the 1990s, it soon became clear that split seconds of sound had emerged into public consciousness long before late twentieth-century speaker technologies. This book, then, despite its origins in the relatively recent past, maps out an earlier historical period when new technologies and scientific theories heightened awareness of the physicality of sound as vibration. In the late eighteenth and the nineteenth century physicists, philosophers, poets, physiologists, medical writers, patients, inventors, geologists, engineers, mathematicians and novelists developed a preoccupation with those different speeds of vibration known as frequencies. Measurements ranged from the number of sound vibrations in a second to the frequencies of such extrasensory phenomena as radio waves, from the number of vibrations undergone in a railway carriage, or delivered by medical instruments like the percuteur (sometimes seen as an early version of the vibrator), to the frequencies at which telepathic and spiritual communications were imagined to operate.

Concerning the slowest end of the musical scale, for instance, in a public lecture delivered in 1857 the physicist Hermann Helmholtz described the lowest notes produced by pianos and organs – two of the key technologies of sound production most obviously available to him at the time. Near the limit of audibility, he explained, is the deepest C note available on most pianos, which 'makes thirty-three vibrations in one second of time'.[7] Large organs make available a whole octave below this C note, 'reaching to the next lower C, with 16½ vibrations in a second'. The tones in this octave reach beyond the limits of audibility; the hearer no longer experiences a single tone but multiple separate impulses. Helmholtz explained that all musical instruments have a similar limit to the depth of tone they can produce, due not to the impossibility of producing slower vibrations but to the limits of the ear, which 'hears slower impulses separately, without gathering them up into single tones'.[8]

So there is a consciousness here of what usually lurks inaudibly within sound, of the multiple vibrations which join together into apparently singular tones. Numerous physicists, medical writers and other kinds of commentators in the nineteenth century drew attention to what I think of as an auditory form of the 'optical unconscious', as Walter Benjamin first put it. Benjamin, analysing technologies that he found central to the experience of modernity, proposed that photography and cinema brought to consciousness that which previously escaped us: 'the dynamite of a tenth of a second' – that is the moment of a person's walk captured in a frozen image.[9] Without the camera, 'Even if one has a general knowledge of the way people walk, one knows nothing of a person's posture during the fractional second of a stride. [...] The camera introduces us to unconscious optics as does psychoanalysis to unconscious impulses'.[10] Bringing split seconds of sound to consciousness much as photography did to the moving image, auditory technologies, from the phonograph to subwoofers, made it possible to detect vibrations of sound, to see and to feel them as never before. Railway trains and other technologies also intensified awareness and experiences of vibration, which corresponded with scientific interest – as indicated by Helmholtz's study – in detecting and calculating vibrations that might otherwise escape consciousness. One of the main arguments of this book is that the numerous attempts to detect, to count and to analyse vibrations formed part of a struggle against the increasing speeds that characterize modernity, at which things move too fast to be consciously registered, like ultrasound. In short, they were attempts to bring to light that which lurked just beyond consciousness, or, perhaps more appropriately, to make audible the silent vibrations that were shaping the experience of modernity. It was important to retain awarenesss of vibrations in order to manage them, because while vibrations could be stimulating, therapeutic, and even life-giving, they were increasingly felt to be a dangerous force, or a kind of noise, causing pain and nervous illness.[11] Further, physicists and others used sound – known as a vibratory or wave-like phenomenon since antiquity – as a model for other forms of vibration which normally escape consciousness, including light, heat, electricity, X-rays, and nerve impulses in the body. Sound, in other words, became a way of making manifest for the senses those vibrations that exist beyond the limits of sensitivity. It is crucial to this book, then, that sound is the experience through which the conceptualization of vibration more generally is made possible, and the means by which it is dangerous and beneficial, and painful and pleasurable (or even is dangerously pleasurable) manifestations could begin to be managed. To hear vibration is perhaps to understand it, to control it.

The seventeenth-century experimental philosopher Marin Mersenne was one of the first to attempt to calculate the number of vibrations in a period of time that constitute a musical tone (now known as frequency).[12] Sound had long been thought of as vibratory, and the alternative theory that it consists of particles or 'corpuscles' began to die out in the seventeenth century.[13] Natural philosophers increasingly investigated sound as vibration, taking sound as an object in itself rather than in terms of particular forms such as music. Thus sound was readily available as a basis for the study of other kinds of vibratory activity. It was not until the eighteenth and nineteenth centuries, though, that the emphasis shifted towards human consciousness of sound, towards the body's capacity to receive vibrations, and especially towards the limits of consciousness, as observed by Helmholtz.[14] In Helmholtz's description of the lowest octave on large organs, the ear can no longer hear the impulses as a tone, but gains consciousness of the vibrations that make it up. The lecture goes on to discuss frequencies of audible vibrations at more length (measured using an instrument called the siren, of which we will hear more later), and to explain that the frequencies heard as sound by the ear range 'from about 20 to about 32,000 in a second'.[15] While we lose the sense of sound below a certain frequency range, then, we are unconscious of the vibrations sensed as sound above it. Physicists like Helmholtz in the nineteenth century developed an awareness of vibrations which usually lie beyond consciousness, and yet amount to sensation itself.

Toward the end of the lecture Helmholtz compares the ear to the eye, explaining that light, like sound, consists of frequencies of vibration.[16] Frequencies of light are visible as different colours, much as sonic frequencies are audible as musical tones, while the vibratory consistency of light and sound itself tends to escape consciousness. Sound became a model for a new way of comprehending the workings of energies both in the outer world and within the human body. As Gillian Beer has put it, regarding the outer world, ' "Things" themselves proved to be modes of motion rather than stable entities. Instead of being described as material particles, light, like heat and sound, was newly understood as a mode of motion'.[17] Similarly the theory that superfine particles (or 'animal spirits') flowed through the nerves in the body was replaced by the idea that vibrations transmit sensations to the brain – vibrations which cannot themselves be sensed.

Many historical and cultural analyses of sound, and of sensory experience more generally, have emphasized the contingent, constructed, ever-changing quality of human experience and of the ways it is understood.[18] Among such analyses, those developed by media theorists like the influential Marshall McLuhan and Walter Ong present the most extreme historical shifts in sonic experience, arguing not only for changes in a particular kind of sensory experience but for an epochal shift away from sound altogether with the onset of print culture, in place of which vision took on greatly increased importance.[19] Vibration, in contrast, provides a basis for thinking about relations between the senses, moving beyond the differences between sound and vision emphasized in accounts such as Ong's of the shift from orality to literacy that are now extensively criticized.[20] Vibration crosses sensory thresholds in so far as it can be simultaneously palpable and audible, visible and audible. The increasing preoccupation with vibration in the eighteenth and nineteenth centuries corresponds to a particular mode of engagement with sensation as such, rather than any particular sense. It corresponds to an intensified focus on the nervous system[21], understood to be at least as important as the individual sense organs. The vibrating ear, along with strings and wires, as we will see, thus become a model for the mechanics of the nerves in general.

So although sound in a sense is central to the vibratory paradigm it is also key to understanding the role of sensory experience in general and how it was rooted in the human body and technologies.[22] Sound was used as a model for the movement inside our own nervous systems as well as for universal energies and technological vibrations. Vibratory technologies also provided models for the nervous body, a body conceived of in turn as especially sensitive to those technological vibrations. Auditory technologies in particular, including musical strings and telephone wires as transmitters of sonic and electrical vibrations, were used as an image for the vibrating nerves that were so crucial to the idea of the sensitive body which developed in the eighteenth and nineteenth centuries, a body that is especially sensitive and responsive to the vibrations of the external world – from light and other forms of ethereal energy to the more palpable, painful and pleasurable vibrations of technology and industry, including the 'shocks' produced by railway trains and the therapeutic motions of the percuteur. All such technologies – exploring, exploiting, directing, and harnessing the potential of vibration, and seeking to manage its movement between pleasure and pain – may be seen, therefore, as antecedents of the subwoofer. Although it is primarily a history of vibration between the eighteenth and early twentieth centuries, this book might also be read as a sort of prehistory of the vibrating floor of the 1990s nightclub.

Materiality of vibration

Material culture has made an important contribution to much recent work in nineteenth-century literature and culture. One thing that some material culture studies seeks to do is to get beyond the critical framework of 'discourse', beyond language and texts and narrative, by attending primarily to material objects or things. As Bill Brown has put it: 'Where other critics had faith in 'discourse' or in the 'social text' as the analytical grid on which to reconfigure our knowledge about the present and past, I wanted to turn attention to things – the objects that are materialized from and in the physical world'.[23] Rocks are one of the kinds of material objects studied in this context. Even if the focus on the materiality of rocks is not always intended to move beyond discourse-based approaches, the decision to start from the object and the material practices it implies, rather than work from the discursive towards the object it supposedly constructs is likely to result in different kinds of knowledge and understanding. Adelene Buckland points out that while literary criticism has focused on nineteenth-century geology's production of narratives of the history of the earth, and on the related development of evolutionary narratives, elite practitioners of the science (with an interest in its economic uses, for example in locating valuable minerals) were most centrally concerned with stratigraphy: the study of the order and structure of the layers of rocks and fossils. The project of stratigraphy focused 'on the material structure of the earth, rather than its story', and was rooted in material objects: in minerals, museums, collections and exhibitions.[24]

Material culture is to a large extent a consequence of the collecting traditions of the nineteenth century, along with growing consumerism. From the early work situated in archaeology and anthropology to more recent developments in literary criticism, material culture studies has maintained its interests in a variety of collectable and consumable objects. Buckland's interest in collections of rocks, mineral and fossils, is thus quite typical of work in the field, although recent work has also engaged with other kinds of materiality including less determinate substances. Vibration, in contrast, is not a commodity or object or even substance in the same way as rocks or glass, or gas or dust, or, as Kate Flint puts it, 'things that Victorians sat on or ate at or read or wrote on or wore; things that they consumed, inhaled, or became addicted to; that they smelt and touched and saw and heard'.[25] Vibration is not itself a material object at all, but it is bound up with materiality: vibration moves material, and moves through material. Rocks are among the most solid, the most palpable and stable of objects, yet in an earthquake they are of course subject to vibratory movements. In one sense this book is about the dissolution of matter, or a process of dematerialization, as 'things' themselves were increasingly understood to consist of modes of motion, as Gillian Beer has observed, but in another it is about sensory experiences of things which vibrate. Much of this book is thus concerned with the vibratory movements of various material objects, including musical strings, telephone wires, railway trains, sewing machines, and medical instruments. Vibration is also bound up with different kinds of materiality beyond objects, including the air and ether (a nineteenth-century notion of space as vibrating matter[26]) through which light and sound waves, rays and radio waves travel. So although vibration is not itself an object or any other kind of material thing, we can consider vibrating objects or materials among those reflected on by scholars of material culture (from rocks and fossils to ether). I am keen to emphasize, like Buckland, that the meaning of material objects, and in this case physical movements, is not just dependent on texts – on lectures and novels, on scientific and artistic representations – but on other kinds of practices: on the operation of musical and scientific instruments, travel by train or by bicycle, the use of sewing machines and auditory technologies. 'What the fossil [or vibration] means for the Victorian', writes Buckland, is dependent on a whole range of 'practices and discourses which make it available as a cultural artefact'. The study of the object also makes possible an approach that works beyond disciplinary confines from the outset:

> In examining the meanings of the material object as produced in tandem by a range of practices and discourses, rather than starting out from the disciplinary formations 'literature' and 'science', we are less likely to constrain ourselves to thinking within these disciplinary parameters. In doing so we are therefore more able to register the multiplicity of meanings proliferating around an object.[27]

Multiple meanings can of course proliferate around any number of material objects, and also around physical movements and other kinds of phenomena. Rather than focusing primarily on a particular author or on a literary period such as 'the Victorian', then, I attempt to track how a wide range of different kinds of texts and practices make sense of vibratory movements from the eighteenth to the twentieth centuries.

Further, vibration allows me to move beyond the category of the material object and to resist its distinction from the human subject. Much of the work in material culture creates space for thinking about how objects or things interact with humans in ways that supposedly move beyond clear distinctions between them. For Brown, 'things' are what seem to assert their presence in their own terms (like 'when you cut your finger on a sheet of paper'), making the human body a 'thing among things'. In contrast, 'we look *through* objects (to see what they disclose about history, society, nature, or culture – above all, what they disclose about *us*)'.[28] The focus on things, then, can provide an alternative not only to discourse-based

approaches but also more generally to the prioritization of humans, of
'*us*', or to what David Miller calls 'the tyranny of the subject'.[29] Brown
and Miller among other material culture scholars resist the distinction
between human subjects and inanimate objects; the false distinction which
Bruno Latour has argued was made by modernity. Latour himself takes
up Michel Serres' concept of 'quasi-objects', to instead provide means of
acknowledging how objects can be both material and social or discursive:
'Quasi-objects are much more social, much more fabricated, much more
collective than the "hard" parts of nature', but at the same time 'much more
real, nonhuman and objective than those shapeless screens on which society
– for unknown reasons – needed to be "projected"'.[30] Vibration, similarly, is
neither wholly material nor wholly discursive: it has physical existence but
cannot itself be perceived except through its effects.

Material culture scholars continue to assert how objects are not simply
shaped by human discourse or society, placing more emphasis on how
objects have 'agency', and how humans are in turn material, or 'thing-
like'.[31] Jane Bennett perhaps takes this furthest with the concept of 'vibrant
matter' which she develops as a means to oppose the 'habit of parsing the
world into dull matter (it, things) and vibrant life (us, beings)', a habit
bound up with common fantasies of 'escape from materiality, or of mastery
of nature'. The concept of vibrant matter is applied to things which have
an active power and even life of their own. Instead of focusing on '*human*
designs and practices ("discourse")', Bennett highlights 'the active role of
nonhuman materials in public life'. Humans, in turn, of course, are constituted as vital materiality rather than just passive beings under the direction
of a nonmaterial soul or mind.[32] Bennett is interested in materiality that
has an intrinsic vitality, that is distinct from 'figures of passive, mechanistic
or divinely infused substance'.[33] She is more concerned with matter, in
other words, than with the movement of vibration, whereas I am of course
specifically preoccupied with the vibratory aspect of vibrant matter – taking
into account the definition of vibrant as 'moving or quivering rapidly;
vibrating'[34] – and with its emergence and meanings in a particular historical
moment.

Vibration commonly provides a means of conceptualizing resistance to
boundaries and identities in contemporary theory, which we might begin
to trace back to the eighteenth and nineteenth centuries. 'Vibrations are
becomings that undermine stable forms and identities', notes David Bissell,
following Gilles Deleuze and Felix Guattari.[35] For Jean Luc Nancy, 'The
sonorous [...] outweighs form. It does not dissolve it but rather enlarges it;
it gives it an amplitude, a density and a vibration or an undulation whose
outline never does anything but approach'.[36] For Latour, vibration provides
a model for 'entities with uncertain boundaries, entities that hesitate, quake,
and induce perplexity'.[37] Vibration, not itself a thing or matter, can move
simultaneously through subjects as well as objects, bridging internal and

external worlds. Indeed, vibration was key to the increasing understanding that mind itself is material, as Enlightenment thinkers had begun to shift attention from the transcendent soul to the mechanics of physical form.[38] In particular, eighteenth-century associationism began to theorize that the external world vibrates the nerves; vibrations in the nerves transmit sensations to the brain; vibration-sensations generate ideas, feelings, memories, thought, imagination.

Vibration plays a part in the history of the 'material imagination', a concept which also collapses or indeed makes meaningless the distinction between subject and object. As Steven Connor puts it, this term describes 'two intersecting things: firstly, the ways in which the material world is imagined'. The conventional move here is 'to doubt whether one can ever look steadily at anything other than one's own conceptions or categories', but Connor goes on to point out, leading us to the second aspect of the material imagination, that:

> there is no way of imagining the nature of the material world which does not draw on and operate in terms of that material world, its spaces, substances, stresses, processes. Imagination is itself always prepossessed by the world that it attempts to imagine, made up, like the gingerbread-man enquiring into the question of his dough, of what it makes out. So the phrase 'material imagination' must signify the materiality of imagining as well as the imagination of the material.[39]

Beginning with the work of the eighteenth-century associationist David Hartley, my first chapter examines a materialist account of mind that is inseparable from the body and material world. The Romantic image of the aeolian harp provides an early case in my study of how the vibrating body was conceptualized, in a way that is comparable with the use of musical strings as an analogy for nerves in physiological and medical theories of the time. The harp thus operates not only as a vibrating object, to which the neurological self sensitively vibrates in response, but also as a model for the vibrating subject himself. The harp's vibrations generate thought, feeling, imagination; the possibility of imagining oneself to be a vibrating harp. In Samuel Taylor Coleridge's 'The Aeolian Harp', on which part of the chapter dwells, the harp figures as 'vibrant matter' in the literal sense, as the wind makes it tremble, bringing it to life like a 'maid half-yielding to her lover', while its sound vibrations are themselves described as the fluttering motion of birds. The harp's production of musical vibrations in turn provides a model for the poet's creation of the sounds and rhythms of poetry; the poet's reception of vibrations provides a model for that of his ideal reader or auditor. The poet, in other words, draws vibration right into and through his work, through the materiality of language. Coleridge's work ties in with a wider poetic fantasy of instantaneous, universal communication: the vibratory substrate of his mental life being directly perceptible as sound, collapsing the distinction between inner and outer, subject and object, self and text and reader.[40]

This first chapter builds on the work of critics who focus on the body in Romanticism, which tended to be overlooked in the canonical understanding that Romantic poetry sought, through the creative power of the mind, to transcend the material body and world, to reach an ideal or spiritual realm. As Sibylle Erle and Laurie Garrison observe, Romanticists who have developed a growing interest in the period's materialist tendencies have focused on the interaction between literature and scientific accounts of mind, and on the concept of the 'creative mind' as embodied, while 'Victorianists have leant more toward explorations of the period's material culture, focusing on the ways in which the results of scientific studies have migrated into everyday consciousness via the means of optical toys, stimulating literatures and other popular commodities'.[41] Erle and Garrison go on to say that Victorian scholars have most directly focused on the influence of technologies on perception, but rather than emphasize the differences between Romantic and Victorian studies I want here to identify a point of continuity between the two periods: to situate the prominence of the aeolian harp in my first chapter in relation to material objects and subjects in later chapters.

The second chapter incorporates further discussion of technological objects which on the one hand produce vibration-sensations (which in this chapter include tuning forks and the siren) and on the other provide a model for the sensitive human body (piano strings and other musical strings). By the mid-nineteenth century, physicists were using technologies to produce controlled, measurable frequencies of vibration in order to calculate corresponding intensities of sense experience, quantifying the connection between the external and inner realms. Nerve impulses were still considered to be vibratory, but were by now understood to be just one among a number of universal kinds of energy, including light, heat and electricity, all conceived of as modes of vibration, like sound. Physicists also emphasized, however, that some frequencies extend beyond the sensory thresholds (such as ultrasound and infrared). According to the law of the conservation of energy, light becomes extrasensory, but continues to exist in the form of radiant heat, contributing to what I have termed above the 'auditory unconscious'. Spiritualists took this first law of thermodynamics to support their claims that vibrations in the nerves also continue to exist indefinitely, conceiving of life itself as a form of vibrant energy that radiates out of the body – as sound radiates out of a stringed instrument – even after death.

In this scenario the distinction between object and subject, or between world and self, again totally collapses. Objects in the external world vibrate the sensitive self, the very sensitivity of whom in the form of vibrations radiates outwards, as the sound of an instrument, to become part of that world. There is a two-way process, in other words, whereby external vibrations seem to set the matter of the body into a kind of sympathetic vibration; vibrations in the body then radiate outwards into the world beyond, in turn potentially vibrating another sensitive person. This dual movement of 'invasion' and 'escape' is one way in which vibration contributed to anxieties about the permeability of the body, about its lack of fixed, secure borders, while it also played into the fantasy of direct, unmediated communication (a development of Coleridge's late eighteenth-century version).

Among Victorian scholars who have attended to materialist theories of human nature in the period, particularly theories of mind as embodied, William Cohen focuses on the role of the senses in conceiving of the interior self in relation to exterior materialities.[42] Human interiority, Cohen observes, is permeable. Senses are vehicles for 'alien' matter to enter the interior. Cohen also considers the relation between interiority and the surface of the body, especially the skin – which can project inner states of subjective being – and further, we can explore the sense of movement from the interior outwards beyond the skin.[43] Anxieties about such permeability were intensified by spiritualist theories and by communication technologies which made intimate contact across distances possible in fantasy and reality.[44] As wires increasingly took over from strings as a model for the nervous system, my third chapter explores the idea that the nerves could be connected to a vast telephone network through which neuronal vibrations from one's inner self could be transmitted directly to others – and received from others – across great distances. This chapter takes up the case of the psychotic Daniel Paul Schreber, whose memoirs set out his belief that his nervous system was linked into a vast network, and ultimately to God. By means of this network of nerve-wires the distinction between inner and outer reality, or object and subject, again collapses: voices from far distances seem intimately connected to oneself; voices originating in oneself seem to come from far distances (in the form of hallucinations, or what psychiatrists and telecommunications engineers called 'noise').

My final two chapters look more closely at how technologies impact on the body that is itself conceived of as technological, ranging from railway trains and their allegedly damaging effect on the nervous body, to medical instruments used to harness the power of vibration for therapeutic and pleasurable purposes. These chapters consider further the various attempts to register and to control vibration, from practices of counting and otherwise documenting its presence to the invention and use of instruments that can deliver exact frequencies. It seemed that female nerves, in particular, were most sensitive to vibrations of all varieties – both spiritual and mechanical – and that their exposure to vibration should thus be managed, even more than that of men. The sensitively vibrated figures of my first four chapters are mostly male, but they tend to have feminine characteristics, or to consider themselves to be female in some way, while my final chapter focuses on the widespread view that women were especially sensitive to vibratory communications, much as they were considered to be over-stimulated by certain kinds of reading material, including sensation novels. Spiritualist mediums were usually female, as the female nerves were apparently most 'finely strung'. Doctors also considered female nerves to be most sensitive to mechanical vibrations. Some doctors advised women not to travel by train or by bicycle, and warned of the dangers of working at sewing machines in factories (run by treadle, rather than electricity), as such practices could apparently not only cause medical complaints like railway spine and bicycle spine, but also over-excitation and masturbation. Such medical opinions thus helped to support the domestic ideal whereby women should be protected from the masculine worlds of travel and industry, city life and work. One kind of attempt to manage the new forms and quantities of vibration in general was by registering and measuring it, as I have said, while the development of medical vibrating instruments – for application particularly to the female body – was another way of attempting to control, even to counteract the vibrations of the modern world. In other words, sensitive women were to be subjected to even more vibration, the crucial aspect of medical vibrations being that these were carefully measured and their application controlled. Katie Fox provides a case study in this final chapter, a well-known spiritual medium whose sensitivity to the uncontrollable world of vibratory communications seems to have been managed by the medical application of vibrations. Fox was a patient with the physician George Henry Taylor, a specialist in such vibratory techniques. As vibration was understood to be a form of energy, indeed as a life-force, its potential ability to heal the matter of an ailing or even inanimate body – or to bring machines to life – seemed almost limitless. Women and feminine men, then, with their finely strung nerves, were most likely to figure as passive mechanical objects, sensitive to vibrating machines.

CHAPTER ONE

Nervous Motions

The aeolian harp (also known as the 'wind-harp'), a technology which turned wind into sound[1], was first described in poetry in 1748, in James Thomson's *Castle of Indolence*, where it is said to have an almost magical effect on the human body and mind. The sounds of the harp's strings, blown by the wind, 'Lulled the weak bosom, and induced ease. [...] Here soothed the pensive melancholy mind'.[2] By the end of the century the harp had its dedicatory poems and appreciative descriptions in numerous prose works, from novels to scientific analyses of acoustics[3], and had become renowned not only as an instrument that influences body and mind, as in Thomson's poem, but as a way of explaining their workings.

This chapter examines the use of the aeolian harp as a model for human nerves, corresponding with a shift in the understanding of the physical basis of human sensitivity. By the end of the eighteenth century a new understanding of the nerves as solid, like musical strings, began to replace the earlier idea that nerves are hollow, and that animal spirits flow through them (superfine fluids, almost immaterial, were thought to flow between soul and body). Vibrations in solid nerves delivered sensations to the brain, according to an increasing number of philosophers, anatomists, neurologists and medical practitioners like David Hartley who made a major contribution to this new theorization in his *Observations on Man* (first published in 1749). Followers of this theory began to see the aeolian harp as a model for a human mind/body conceived as a machine for translating sensory vibrations into consciousness. It became an image of the doctrine of association. The aeolian harp did more, though, than provide an image of passively vibrating 'nerve-strings': it was creative as well as sensitive, transforming the force of the wind into harmonious sounds. Focusing initially on Coleridge's 'The Aeolian Harp' (first composed in 1795), I track how the harp as a metaphor for the sensitive *and* imaginative, creative poet, corresponds with Hartley's materialist account of both perception and creativity, of receptive and responsive motions, or 'incoming' and 'outgoing' vibrations. Hartley claimed that vibrations travel along the 'motory' as well as 'sensory' nerves, leading to muscular action, whether that is walking, writing, or reciting poetry. The harmonious vibrations of 'The Aeolian Harp', however, are subsequently transformed into the screaming noises of 'Dejection' (1802) and the trembling bodies of Gothic novels. As medical writers increasingly viewed nervous vibrations as a cause of pain and illness, sensitivity and harmony began in literary descriptions around the turn of the century to give way to trembling and convulsions, the vibratory movements of nervousness and suffering. But some medical writers also viewed painful, violent vibrations, at least within certain limits, as a powerful, even life-giving stimulus. Vibration, in other words, could be experienced as both painful and pleasurable, as a dangerous and as a healing force.

Many historians and critics have looked at theories of mind developed by the 'sensualist philosophers' who conceived of it as a mechanical, passive receiver of sense data.[4] More specifically, critics have frequently compared the mechanism of the harp to the passive mind as conceived by Hartley, and as depicted in Coleridge's poetry prior to his maturer engagement with idealist philosophy[5], while I, by contrast, will develop a more detailed comparison between physiological and medical theories – focusing initially on Hartley's – and poetic descriptions of the harp. This chapter provides a materialist account of mind, emphasising its inseparability from the body and physical world, as a corrective to the tendency in past criticism to overemphasize the transcendental aspect of the Romantic worldview and its attendant poetics. The extent of Hartley's influence on Coleridge has been a subject of quite lengthy debate[6], but a key limitation in much of this discussion is that critics tended to rely upon a disembodied version of the theory of associationism. As Alan Richardson points out, in a study of 'neural Romanticism', analyses of the Romantic mind tended to ignore its material support – the brain, even though historians of neurology and psychology viewed this period as crucial for the emergence of theories and discoveries concerning the brain and nervous system – increasingly viewed as the seat of consciousness.[7] Critics have recently intensified their focus on the body in Romanticism, previously often overlooked in the canonical understanding that Romantic poetry sought, through the creative power of the mind – of thought, memory, imagination – to transcend the material body and world, to reach an ideal or spiritual realm.[8] My aim here is thus to identify a materialist, vibratory undercurrent through neurological and medical theories and poetry of the era. By viewing the Romantic mind as embodied I am by now predictably engaging with that trajectory of work that has developed and critiqued Jonathan Crary's insights about the role of the body in perception, where he argues that the empirical sciences and new technologies between 1810 and 1840 'severed' sensory experience from any direct relation to an external world. Vision, the sense on which

Crary focuses, was 'relocated in the human body', and thus 'knowledge was accumulated about the constitutive role of the body in the apprehension of a visible world'.[9] For Crary, there is a sharp break between classical models of vision and the 'subjective vision' developed after 1810, when sensations were no longer seen to originate in the external world but in the body. Crary focuses on optical instruments like the camera obscura and magic lantern, whereas the aeolian harp provides an earlier, acoustic model of embodied consciousness, which could serve as a bridge between the 'classical' and 'modern' accounts of sensitivity. This model presents sensations as originating in *both* an external stimulus and the body, especially the nervous system. Further, the aeolian harp also allows me to introduce the role of technology in mediating information. Both Crary and Friedrich Kittler have identified a historical shift toward an understanding of perceptual processes as unconscious and automatic, or mechanical, but where Crary focuses on bodily perception, Kittler goes further with his argument that media – ranging from the wax slate or book to the gramophone and digital technologies – are also capable of registering and storing sensory information. According to Kittler, 'we knew nothing about our senses until media provided models and metaphors'.[10] By taking the aeolian harp as a model for sensory perception, this chapter works toward an understanding of vibration as the force that is imagined to stimulate the human mind and body – both conceived as matter – into mechanical life and consciousness.

'The Aeolian Harp' and 'Dejection' draw on the physiology of vibrations and sensations set out in *Observations on Man*, though they may also be seen to question it. It was just when Coleridge was most explicitly devoted to Hartleyan doctrine (as a result of which he had named his son Hartley in 1796) that he wrote 'The Aeolian Harp'.[11] It was only later that Coleridge's extensive criticism of Hartley appeared in *Biographia Literaria* (1817), in which he argued that associationism is unable to account for active and creative mental faculties such as will and imagination, as it renders the mind passive and mechanical, determined by the 'despotism of outward impressions'.[12] Coleridge's denunciations have often been taken to support the idea of Hartley's theory as a mechanical and sterile system, utterly incompatible with the creative mind of Romanticism, but there is much debate regarding Hartley's influence, which others have explored in more depth with respect to Coleridge's ambivalence, for example.[13] Coleridge became an influential critic of associationism and supporter of Kantian philosophy, but the physiological approach to psychology was by no means abandoned, as both Richardson and Rick Rylance, in his history of Victorian psychology, have observed. Writers such as George Henry Lewes and John Stuart Mill, Rylance notes, 'championed Hartley as a pioneer of the physiological psychology of the 1860s and 1870s'.[14]

Nerves vibrate, like strings

'The doctrine of vibrations' as set out in Hartley's *Observations on Man*, asserts that vibrations in the nerves transmit sensations.[15] Sensations generate ideas, which in turn generate thought and feeling, memory and other aspects of mental life. 'The doctrine of association' explains how increasingly complex ideas are built up from sensations by means of association, a process through which ideas are combined. As many historians have observed, Hartley's work was probably the first comprehensive attempt to integrate associationist philosophy with Newtonian physics, to ground mental processes in the physical. Drawing on the work of John Locke and others who developed associationist theories, Hartley sought to ground philosophy of mind in corporeal foundations: the anatomy and motions of the nerves and brain.[16]

Drawing on Newton's *Principia* and the 'Queries' to *Opticks*, Hartley proposed that 'motions' from the external world cause vibrations to run along the 'medullary substance' of the nerves, which consists of particles small enough to transmit rather than interrupt the vibrations, the pores or spaces between which are filled with even smaller, 'infinitesimal' particles of ether. This understanding of the nerves differed from the alternative theory that the nerves are hollow, through which animal spirits flow (superfine fluids were thought to flow between soul and body). Hartley writes that 'the nerves are rather solid capillaments, according to Sir *Isaac Newton*, than small *tubuli*, according to Boerhaave' (*OM*, 17). While earlier philosophers including Descartes and Malebranche had claimed that animal spirits flow in a vibratory or wave-like manner, for Hartley vibration itself is transmitted along the nerves. Rather than a stream of spirits running through the tubular nerves it is solely the motion that is transmitted, triggering further vibrations ('vibratiuncles') in the medullary substance of the brain.

In the seventeenth century, the theory of animal spirits was occasionally challenged. Penelope Gouk notes that from the early 1700s Boerhaave's physiology was taught in medical schools throughout Europe, but the structure of the nerves was debatable: 'Some physicians conceptualized them as small pipes through which the animal spirits flowed like a fine liquor. Others claimed the nerves to be more like strings that communicated their effects through elastic, vibrative motion'.[17] Gouk also observes that doctors were beginning to use acoustic technologies in the seventeenth century to explain how the eardrum resonates with vibrations of the air. The anatomist Joseph Du Verney employed the image of sympathetic resonance between lute strings to explain the ear's response to sound: 'these vibrations were then transmitted to the cochlea and labyrinth by means of the auditory ossicles in the same way that the vibrations of a string on one lute were transmitted to a string on a neighboring lute via their bodies and the table'.[18] These vibrations often came to a halt, however, as many doctors still thought that the sounds were then carried by animal spirits along the nerves to the brain.[19] Hartley in contrast used the understanding of the anatomy of the ear to support his claims that much smaller or 'more subtle' vibrations are transmitted through the ether, though these cannot themselves be sensed:

> As sounds are caused by pulses or vibrations excited in the air by the tremors of the parts of sounding bodies, they must raise vibrations in the *membrana tympani*; and the small bones of the ear seem peculiarly adapted, by their situation and muscles, to communicate these vibrations to the cavities of the *vestibulum*, semicircular canals, and *cochlea*, in which the auditory nerve is expanded; *i.e.* to the nerve itself. Now these are gross vibrations, in respect of those which we must suppose to take place in the ether itself, yet they prepare the way for the supposition of the more subtle vibrations of the ether. (*OM*, 26–7)

The use in the seventeenth century of that other sonorous mechanism – musical strings – as a model for human sensitivities indicates that there is no sudden shift to a completely new paradigm, but it was not until the late eighteenth century that the theory of animal spirits was giving way to the understanding of vibrating nerves being more like the ear or strings than pipes. Hartley's work can be seen as an early and speculative line of investigation into this area. The debate around whether nerves are string-like or tubular is discussed in many historical accounts of neurology, which generally agree that around the turn of the century anatomical discoveries with microscopes began to establish the solidity of the nerves. Edwin Clarke for example shows that the idea of tubular nerves 'endured virtually intact throughout the seventeenth and eighteenth centuries', but not into the nineteenth. He claims that it was only at the turn of the eighteenth century that the nerve fibre began to be recognized.[20] Beyond the scientific debate, however, the increasing use in the eighteenth century of musical strings as an image of nerves conveyed the idea of their solidity, and capacity to vibrate, to a wider public.

During the eighteenth century strings increasingly provided a model of the nerves, along which vibrations convey sensations to the brain, including sensations of sound, light and heat, and pleasure and pain. It is in this context that Joseph Roach, tracing the relations between scientific ideas of the body and theories of acting, writes that while 'seventeenth century authors favored images of bodily and vocal eloquence based on wind or brass instruments, those in the eighteenth century showed a decided preference for strings – violins or harpsichords'.[21] Roach examines the move from animal spirits to sensibility, from the idea that the soul governs the body to the idea that humans are sensitive and responsive to external stimuli. 'Animal' refers to the soul or *anima*; it was thought that the spirits were governed by or *animated* from within, by the soul or 'ghost in the machine', rather than the later idea that mental life is determined by vibrations. The spirits conveyed information about the world to the soul, and conveyed from the soul to the body information or directions for movement, for muscular action. Roach identifies the change in theories about the body to explain why actors were increasingly advised in the eighteenth century to cultivate their sensibility, which 'grants organs the capacity to register an external impression and to move in response to the intensity of that impression', according to the physician Fouquet whose work was taken up by the actor Garrick.[22] But it was not only the actor who should cultivate his sensibility, his ability to move in response to an external impression; the audience should respond to his response, feel moved by his movements. The sympathetic vibration of strings provided an image of the relation between actors and audiences, an image supported by 'the widely held opinion that all sensation is caused by acoustical vibrations in the nerves'.[23]

Roach points out that Hartley's *Observations* provided one of the main sources for such 'acoustical vibrations', though Hartley's own response to the idea that nerves are like strings was to distinguish between them because vibrations travel *along* the nerves whereas in the case of strings it is the whole string itself that vibrates. He writes that the idea that 'the nerves themselves should vibrate like musical strings, is highly absurd' (11–12). However, he did use strings elsewhere as an explanatory model, for example, to argue that the nerves similarly return to their former condition after vibrating, rather than being permanently altered (62). He also used sound and the ear to explain the vibratory activity of the nerves and other phenomena. As sonorous or 'gross vibrations' are more evidently vibratory than the 'subtle' ethereal vibrations, sound is used as a model to explain light and electricity, for example, as well as nerve impulses, while electricity vibrating along hempen strings is used to explain the sensory function of the nerves (26–7, 28, 88, 231–2). Later in the century, in his popularized edition of Hartley's theory, Joseph Priestley developed an explanation of vibrating nerves in terms of the sympathetic vibration of strings:

> For what is more natural than to imagine that the tremulous motion of the particles of the air, in which sound consists, must, since it acts by successive pulses, communicate a tremulous motion to the particles of the auditory nerve, and that the same tremulous motion is propagated to the brain, and diffused into it? It is not necessary to suppose that the vibrations of the particles of the air, and those of the particles of the nerves, are *isochronous*, since even the vibration of a musical string will affect another, an octave above, or an octave below it.[24]

For this introductory essay to *Hartley's Theory of the Human Mind, on the Principle of the Association of Ideas*, entitled 'A general view of the doctrine of vibrations', Priestley omitted much of the detail of the doctrine as it was considered outdated in the light of new understandings about electricity, and in order to present a more accessible version, as Hartley's work was not widely read. The doctrine of vibrations is omitted altogether from the main text, which is instead an attempt to clearly explain the doctrine of association for a wider public.[25] Whether or not Hartley himself approved of the analogy, his work appears to have supported the idea of string-like nerves for many people without direct access to his original *Observations*. Robert Miles suggests this in an account of how responses to popular forms of Gothic literature were explained in terms of eighteenth-century associationism, which 'increasingly relied on the figuration of the mind as a kind of vibrating machine, where the 'nerves' stood as the individual strings'.[26] Like the image of the actor's audience as a set of sympathetically vibrating strings, the reader of popular novels, Miles observes, was described as 'a detached observer waiting for her receptive mechanism – her "nerves" – to be played upon'.[27] For the critic Nathaniel Drake for example, 'sublime events "wrought up" in a masterly manner, cause every nerve to vibrate "with pity and terror."'[28]

Hartley's *Observations* contributed at least indirectly to the idea of the self as a sensitive, responsive, and automatic kind of mechanism in the eighteenth century, as Roach and Miles have suggested. As well as actors, novelists and poets, their audiences and readers were described as strings that responded to vibration. Toward the end of the century, as I will next show, the strings of the aeolian harp became a model for such registrations and expressions of sensitivity and sympathy, and the harp itself an embodiment of suffering.

Sensitivity and harmony

What distinguishes the aeolian harp from other musical instruments is that nobody plays it. Most people who write about the instrument observe that it is unique in its capacity to respond to nature, to be moved by the wind, to play 'Nature's Music'[29] (though there are one or two other exceptions, like wind-chimes). Thomas Hankins and Robert Silverman have studied a range of instruments invented by natural philosophers in the seventeenth century, which were later taken up in art and popular culture, among which the aeolian harp was distinctive: 'It was sensitive – listening and responding to nature, rather than invading and dissecting nature. Its appeal was quasi-magical. Its music brought to the senses a wonder or harmony of nature that was not otherwise perceived'.[30] The magic of the harp was in its capacity to be both sensitive and sonorous, to hear and be heard. Its very sensitivity, or its nerve-strings, it seems, yields the sounds to which hearers are sensitive.

The vibrating strings of the aeolian harp brought nature's music to the senses, and provided a model of sensitivity. In the early lines of Coleridge's 'The Aeolian Harp' the poet's sensitivity to the sounds of the harp prefigures the lines in which he becomes the harp itself. This sensitivity is multisensory. Vibration moves through all matter, exciting every sense. As well as sound, the first verse of the poem describes senses of touch, sight, smell, and possibly taste. Sara's 'soft cheek' reclines on the poet's arm, while it is 'sweet' to sit beside their home, to see flowers, clouds, and a star, the colour white, shapes, and light, to inhale the 'scents' of the bean-field, and to hear the 'stilly murmur' of the sea.[31] The sound of the sea waves seems then to flow into the 'surges' that 'sink and rise', as if figuring the fluidity of the 'soft floating' sound of the harp (AH, 19–20). While water waves provide a way of visualising the vibratory nature of sound, another image is then found in the motion of birds:

> [...] Melodies round honey-dropping flowers,
> Footless and wild, like birds of Paradise,
> Nor pause, nor perch, hovering on untamed wing!
>
> (23–5)

Senses are compounded, the fluidity of sound becoming feathery, an almost palpable, visible thing. The vibrations of sound accelerate as we progress from the gentle 'sink and rise' of the waves to the rapid motion of hovering, pauseless, untamed wings. As Timothy Morton has observed, the descriptions of ambient sounds encourage us to hear the environment as a kind of music, along with the sounds of the harp, which he calls an 'environmental instrument' as it is seen to respond directly to nature. Morton briefly notes that the nervous organism as conceived in this period was comparable to the harp, before moving on to consider it as a model for human response to the environment in light of current ecological concerns.[32] Hearing is only one way of sensing the environment, though, as I have shown, while the surrounding sounds become almost an environment in themselves, the poet being immersed in the sea waves, which then take on another texture, of the softness of feathers, recalling Sarah's 'soft cheek' in the opening line, and how the harp is 'caressed' by the breeze which generates the very sounds which in turn, being feathery, could lightly caress.

Sight and sound, especially, become increasingly interchangeable, as the light which earlier in the poem has shifted from the sun behind clouds to the star of eve then appears to become itself sonorous, with the line that refers to 'A light in sound, a sound-like power in light' (28, line 28). The sources of this idea of light in sound and sound in light, which Coleridge added to the poem in 1817, have previously been identified as the sixteenth-century mystic Jacob Boehme and Friedrich Schelling's theories of gravitation[33], but beyond these specific references the analogy between sound and light was frequently drawn by natural philosophers in the seventeenth century and Hartley and others in the eighteenth and nineteenth centuries. In the seventeenth century the harp's inventor Athanasius Kircher is thought to have influenced Isaac Newton with regard to his analogy between tones and colours.[34] Newton's proposition that 'different rays excite vibrations of different bignesses, as different vibrations of the air excite different sounds' was later taken up by Hartley and by Priestley in his edition of Hartley's work and in *The History and Present State of Discoveries Relating to Vision, Light and Colours*.[35] The idea of vibratory light appears again in Priestley's *Experiments and Observations on Different Kinds of Air* where wave motions provide an analogy for knowledge, 'which, like the progress of a wave of the sea, of sound, or of light from the sun, extends itself not this way only, but in all directions'.[36]

Vibrations in the nerves are the cause of all sensations which, by means of association, produce thought, or, in Hartley's words, both 'ideas of sensation' and 'intellectual ideas', or 'simple' and 'complex ideas' (56–114). In this way it seems that the waves of the sea, fluttering of birds, sound and light in 'The Aeolian Harp' vibrate the nerves or strings of the sensitive, responsive poet, resulting in mental activity: 'Rhythm in all thought' (28, line 29). Like the sound in light, the rhythm in thought is vibratory. This seems to be a crystallization of Hartley's speculations that ideas, as well as sensations, are caused by vibrations. He writes, for example:

Since therefore sensations are conveyed to the mind, by the efficiency of corporeal causes upon the medullary substance, as is acknowledged by all physiologists and physicians, it seems to me, that the powers of generating ideas, and raising them by association, must also arise from corporeal causes. [...] And as a vibratory motion is more suitable to the nature of sensation than any other species of motion, so does it seem also more suitable to the powers of generating ideas, and raising them by association. (72)

'Rhythm in all thought', however, seems to take Hartley's theory further, suggesting not only that vibration causes thought, but that it is in thought, or even is thought. This sense of thought as vibration would correspond with Coleridge's account of thought in his letter to Robert Southey in December 1794, where he wrote that 'I am a compleat Necessitarian – and understand the subject well almost as Hartley himself – but I go further than Hartley and believe in the corporeality of thought – namely, that it is motion – ' (137). With this motion in mind, in 'The Aeolian Harp' the distinction between subject and object, between the poet and the vibratory world of nature in which he is situated, to which he is sensitive, begins to fade. The sensitive person seems to become what he is sensitive to, vibration echoing through the physics of thought.

The rhythmic motion of light is again followed by thought, and phantasies, in the following verse:

> The sunbeams dance, like diamonds, on the main,
> And tranquil muse upon tranquility;
> Full many a thought uncalled and undetained,
> And many idle flitting phantasies,
> Traverse my indolent and passive brain,
> As wild and various as the random gales
> That swell and flutter on this subject lute!
>
> (28, lines 37–43)

The rhythm of thought seems echoed through the sound of the poem itself, its sense of rhythm being created through metre, rhyme and alliteration. 'Full many a thought' and 'many idle flitting phantasies' are generated in the poet by the wind, much as sound is generated by the gales that 'flutter', like the 'footless' birds earlier in the poem, on the 'subject lute' (Coleridge used the word 'lute' and 'harp' interchangeably). George Dekker, who argues that the preoccupations of the 'Age of Sensibility' continued to function in Coleridge's work, writes that the harp in this poem is 'a metaphor for passive reception of the influxes of thought, feeling and sensation'.[37] But while most analyses of this poem agree that the harp is passive, this instrument is at the same time active in that it is not only sensitive but sonorous, it hears and is heard, receives and transmits. For the opposition between passivity and activity, M. H. Abrams has examined the well-known images of the mirror and lamp, using the shift from eighteenth-century associationism to Kantian idealism to explain how the neoclassical ideal of poetry as a reflection or imitation of the natural world was replaced by the Romantic emphasis on the creative imagination and spontaneity of the poet himself. For the projection rather than reception of light, the lamp, in contrast to the mirror, is an image for the mind as 'active rather than inertly receptive, and as contributing to the world in the very process of perception'.[38] The use of the aeolian harp as an analogue for the mind is understood to derive from Coleridge's early interest in associationism, from which he turned in the nineteenth century toward Kant, but unlike the visual images of the mirror and lamp the strings of the harp are both passive and active, receptive and responsive, not just reflecting but harmonizing the forces of nature which they transmit, or 'hear-speak', like nerves that are at the same time vocal cords. As Jonathan Crary has observed, 'subjective vision' has long been explored in Romantic criticism. Abrams in particular has mapped out the shift 'from conceptions of imitation to ones of expression, from metaphor of the mirror to that of the lamp'.[39] Crary goes on to add, however, that such explanations centre around the idea of 'a vision or perception that was somehow unique to artists and poets, that was distinct from a vision shaped by empiricist or positivist ideas and practices'.[40] The connections between the harp and Hartley's theory (to be further developed here shortly) demonstrate that the responsive poet is not physiologically unique, and that the nineteenth-century shift from passive 'imitation' to creative 'expression' is less clear cut than Abrams and Crary consider, as the pre-Kantian harp both receives and harmonizes, hears and speaks.

Mechanics of voice

The harp becomes a metaphor for the poet, and the sound of the harp for poetry, which corresponds with Hartley's account both of receptive hearing and responsive motions, or 'incoming' and 'outgoing' vibrations. The first sections of *Observations on Man* explain how vibrations transmit sensations and how sensations develop into ideas, and later sections explain how people learn to do things like walk and speak a language. The arguments of the first two sections, 'which prove the performance of sensation and intellectual perception by means of vibrations of the small medullary particles', lead to the claim that 'muscular motion is performed by vibrations also', as vibrations travel along both sensory and motory nerves: 'Vibrations descend along the motory nerves, *i.e.* the nerves which go to the muscles, in some such manner as sound runs along the surfaces of rivers, or an electrical virtue along hempen strings' (86, 88). These vibrations underlie two sorts of muscular motion: 'automatic', which includes the beating of the heart, respiration, and the crying of new-born children, and 'voluntary', which includes speaking, writing, and playing a musical instrument, activities which in the first place have to be learnt, but which may then be converted into 'secondarily automatic motion' (103–9). To learn to speak, for example, children must form associations between the sounds they hear and the creation of sounds, between 'impressions made on the ear' and 'actions of the organs of speech', and between sounds and other things in the world including objects and actions (106–7, 268–77). After much repetition and practice, speech finally becomes an automatic action, as does playing a musical instrument. Automatic motions, according to Hartley, 'of which the mind is scarce conscious, and which follow mechanically, as it were, some precedent diminutive sensation, idea, or motion, and without any effort of the mind, are rather to be ascribed to the body than the mind' (104). The aeolian harp provides an image of this mechanically automatic body, which both receives and transmits vibrations. Much as sound provides the model for nerve impulses earlier in *Observations on Man*, as sound is more evidently vibratory than the ethereal motions, the speaking body seems to make audible or to amplify the vibrations of the 'motory nerves', while it shapes them into words. Several times in *Observations* speaking is described as primary and embodied, and thus distinctively vibratory:

> Since not only the parts about the throat, but those of the mouth, cheeks, and even of the whole body, especially of the bones, vibrate in speaking, the figure of the vibrations impressed upon the air by the human voice will be different from that of the vibrations proceeding from a violin, flute, &c. provided the distance be not too great. (228–9)

Among the vibrations received by humans, then, are those produced by other humans, 'by the human voice'. In his discussion of poetry, Hartley suggests that the voice has a special kind of effect on its hearers, unlike the written word: 'Verses well pronounced affect us much more, than when they merely pass over the eye, from the imitation of the affections and passions represented, by the human voice' (431).

Like Hartley, and like many Romantic and other poets, Coleridge valued the orality of poetry over its written form.[41] Poetry was the art of the speaking body. In *Biographia Literaria* he distinguished between the publication and recitation of poetry because the latter offers a certain stage presence in which the sound of the voice plays a part. He referred to 'the sympathy of feeling' produced in an audience by the recitation of a poem, which can be seen as a form of 'animal magnetism, in which the enkindling reciter, by perpetual comment of looks and tones, lends his own will and apprehensive faculty to his auditors'.[42] Animal magnetism was a topic of general interest in the Romantic period, believed to allow the magnetizer to influence the body and mind of his patient. Founded in the eighteenth century by Franz Anton Mesmer, this practice was rooted in the theory that a vital electrical energy flowed through the nerves, transmitting the will from the brain to the limbs. Mesmer claimed that he could channel this energy with healing effects on his patients, transmitting it from his own body to others', which according to contemporary reports often induced trance-like states or convulsive fits, which Mesmer saw as healing 'crises'. Though theories of magnetism usually assumed the nervous energy to be a fluid, there are some similarities between Hartley's ideas and those of such physicians. For one thing, the energy was often described as travelling in a vibratory manner.[43] Further, both Hartley and Mesmer built on Newton's hypothesis that ether pervaded outer spaces as well as the nerves in the body. This ether, as Tim Fulford puts it, 'explained action at a distance – gave a material medium for the influence of one body on another across space'.[44] A magnetist might thus transmit energy from his body to another's, and, further, Mesmer described how planets could influence the body, which he conceived of as sonorous and vibratory, writing of 'the ineffable effect of

UNIVERSAL GRAVITATION by which our bodies are harmonized, not in a uniform and monotonous manner, but as a musical instrument furnished with several strings, the exact tone resonates which is in unison with a given tone'.[45] Fulford explores how ideas of mesmerism were applied widely, far beyond the relationship between the physician and his patient, as a way of explaining the power not only of the speaking poet, but also of politicians, for example, including the Prime Minister William Pitt, whom Coleridge saw as having a dangerous influence over the ignorant and superstitious English population. On the one hand Mesmer's theory was blamed for influencing the masses and infecting them with fanatical, irrational beliefs; on the other, it held out the promise of a more harmonious, united society, in which people are in sympathy with each other through the intimate connections in ethereal space.

To describe the speaking poet or politician (or whoever) as a magnetist, then, was to ascribe to him an intense power over the nerves/strings of his audience (whether for good or ill). The poet should be a sensitive instrument, but his listeners, too, were expected to be sensitive, like the mesmerist's patient, or Roach's theatrical audience or Miles's reader of Gothic novels 'waiting for her receptive mechanism – her "nerves" – to be played upon'. Vibration and related sonorous terms, like reverberation, were frequently used by eighteenth- and nineteenth-century literary critics, such as Josiah Conder who argued that 'the only converse to be held with a poet's mind is that of sympathy. The feelings of the reader must be strung to a pitch in unison with those of the poet himself, or they will not vibrate in reply'.[46] Such vibration will be at its most intense when the transmission takes place directly between human bodies. Poetry spoken aloud vibrates between the bodies of the poet and the listener. It may even vibrate between a multitude of bodies.

'The Aeolian Harp' moves from individual experience, from the sensitivity of the poet to sound and light and so on, toward communication and a sense of universal harmony. According to Hartley, as we have seen, sensations develop into ideas and thought, and voluntary actions develop into automatic or unconscious actions. *Observations on Man* moves on from the sense of hearing to the act of speaking, while the strings of the harp provide an image of hearing that *is* speaking, of nerves that are vocal cords, collapsing the distinction between inner and outer, subject and object, self and other, producing, for Coleridge, a kind of universal communicativeness:

And what if all of animated nature
Be but organic harps diversely framed,
That tremble into thought, as o'er them sweeps
Plastic and vast, one intellectual breeze,
At once the Soul of each, and God of All?

(28–9, lines 44–8)

Once again, the nervous vibrations of Hartleyan doctrine seem to echo through the poem, through the sonorous thought of the harps as they 'tremble into thought'. These lines are among the most heavily interpreted in English poetry, and while they are usually thought to reflect Coleridge's pantheist speculations they are also compatible with Hartley's religious system.[47] The second volume of *Observations* develops the argument that as sensations become thought, and actions become mechanical, the mind is freed from direct and material concerns, so that experience leads us toward the immaterial and spiritual, toward God. Nature is divinely designed so that humans continue to improve and find happiness.[48] But while the ideal relation between each Soul and God as described in 'The Aeolian Harp' is harmonious – the self vibrates in sympathy with the universe – this can also be seen as a fragile, precarious state, dependent upon an 'attuned' nervous system. Universal communicativeness might be a vision of utopic harmony, as it is for other poets of the period[49], but it is also a vision of the dissolution of the self.

In the nineteenth century, then, vibration continued to be considered the source of sensations, of ideas and thought, and poetry, but, as medical science increasingly presented nervous vibrations as a cause of pain and illness, the harmony of the harp gives way to pain and the screaming noises of 'Dejection'.

Suffering noises

In 'Dejection', Coleridge again personifies the aeolian harp. The wind retains its power over the nerves of the sensitive self, though it treats them differently than did the Godly breeze in the earlier poem. In 'The Aeolian Harp' the harp is 'caressed' by the gentle wind, and is like 'some coy maid half-yielding to her lover' (14–15). It responds to the wind's touch with 'sweet upbraiding', 'delicious surges' (16, 19). In 'Dejection', instead of pleasurable sensations and sounds, there is

> [...] the dull sobbing draft, that moans and rakes
> Upon the strings of this Aeolian lute,
> Which better far were mute.[50]

The wind in this opening verse seems to drag and scrape the strings of the harp, and its 'dull sobbing' to echo the poet's own sense of 'dull pain'. The verse ends with the poet's desire for, or feeling of a need to feel, the sounds of a storm to 'startle this dull pain, and make it move and live!' (*D*, 114, line 20).

To attempt an understanding of why Coleridge would have wanted a storm to intensify his pain, in this section I will first consider Hartley's account of painful sensations and vibrations as a materialist precursor to

Edmund Burke's theory of the sublime. Burke claimed that the sublime –
with its capacity to vibrate or shake the body – could be a kind of medical
treatment for disordered nervous systems. Burke, along with medical
writers, also perceived violent vibrations, at least beyond certain limits, as
potentially dangerous, however. I will explore the sublime as both medicinal
and pathological, and then go on to further develop an understanding of the
harp in Coleridge's poetry in the context of the physiological and medical
theories of its time.

Along with sensations of sounds and colours and so on, 'pleasures and
pains' are related to the doctrine of vibrations. 'The most vigorous of our
sensations,' Hartley explained, 'are termed sensible pleasures and pains'
(34). He proposed that pleasure and pain are not essentially different, that
they are not different qualities but rather quantities, existing on a continuum
or single scale: 'The doctrine of vibrations seems to require, that each pain
should differ from the corresponding and opposite pleasure, not in kind,
but in degree only; *i.e.* that pain should be nothing more than pleasure itself,
carried beyond a due limit' (35). According to this conceptualization, then,
pain is in a sense *an excess of* pleasure. It is at least an intensification of
sensation, which generates ideas, phantasies, feelings, and poetry.

Pain, then, may counteract the deficiency of sensation, and corresponding
lack of poetic creativity or expression, experienced by the poet in his state
of dejection. He suffers

A grief without a pang, void, dark, and drear,
A stifled, drowsy, unimpassioned grief,
Which finds no natural outlet, no relief,
In word, or sigh, or tear. (114, lines 21–4)

In a similar way to Hartley, Burke in *A Philosophical Enquiry into the
Sublime and Beautiful* (1757) argued that 'pain is stronger in its operation
than pleasure,' and that 'pain can be a cause of delight'.[51] Anything that
produced a sense of the infinite and powerful could have the painful and
terrifying effects of the sublime, including aspects of nature such as thunder,
earthquakes, and oceans, while the ultimate sublime object was God. In an
encounter with the sublime the individual, feeling threatened by his own
smallness and mortality, his own obliteration, could experience a terrifying
thrill, a form of delight. Hartley's account of the pleasures to be gained from
beautiful things in the natural world similarly indicates that the vastness of
nature, as opposed to 'pleasant tastes, and smells, and the fine colours of
fruits and flowers, the melodies of birds,' and so on, may be experienced as
both horrifying and pleasurable:

If there be a precipice, a cataract, a mountain of snow, &c. in one part
of the scene, the nascent ideas of fear and horror magnify and enliven

all the other ideas, and by degrees pass into pleasures, by suggesting the security from pain.

In like manner the grandeur of some scenes, and the novelty of others, by exciting surprize and wonder, *i.e.* by making a great difference in the preceding and subsequent states of mind, so as to border upon, or even enter the limits of pain, may greatly enhance the pleasure. (419)

Burke went further than Hartley, however, in his claim that the sublime can provide a beneficial kind of exercise for the nervous system. Too much rest and inactivity, according to Burke, can produce a state in which the nerves are liable to 'horrid convulsions', a state which results in 'dejection, despair, and often self-murder'.[52] The sublime may on the one hand be detrimental to health, and on the other beneficial to the nervous and muscular tissues. 'If the pain and terror are so modified as not to be actually noxious', Burke claims that the sublime can restore the health of the nervous system, as well as being experienced as delightful. Though the therapeutic quality of the sublime derives in part from its ability to unblock the nerves, thereby aiding the flow of animal spirits, according to the earlier understanding of nervous activity, its vibratory nature makes it adaptable to the idea of string-like nerves. In cases of dejection and melancholy the nerves should be vigorously vibrated, or, in Burke's words, 'shaken and worked to a proper degree'.[53]

Coleridge, who notoriously suffered from a range of medical complaints, which he considered at least in part to derive from his disordered nervous system, tried various forms of treatment, including 'horse-exercise' and opium, and was interested, precisely in this context, I will argue, in the therapeutic effects of the sublime. In *Coleridge and the Doctors* Neil Vickers shows that Coleridge had a good understanding of the medical systems of the late eighteenth and early nineteenth centuries, which had seen the rise of the view that disease may be caused by a disorderly or 'untuned' nervous system. Many doctors, including Albrecht von Haller, John Brown, and Coleridge's own physician Thomas Beddoes, held that stimulation of the nerves could be a beneficial treatment, prescribing exercises such as horse-riding and walking, exposure to extreme temperatures, alcohol and opiates, oxygen, and 'the exciting passions of the mind'.[54] The sublime, with its capacity to excite terror, could be seen as a most powerful stimulant, along with the opium which Coleridge took initially for his gout. That terror may have been experienced by Coleridge as pleasurable, although beyond certain limits harmful, as Burke had suggested, is indicated in his review of Matthew Lewis's *The Monk*: 'To trace the nice boundaries, beyond which terror and sympathy are deserted by the pleasurable emotions, – to reach those limits, yet never to pass them, – *hic labor, hic opus est* [This is the effort, this is the work]'.[55] According to Coleridge, it is because *The Monk* goes beyond the limits, is improbable, and immoral, that it is a 'poison', '*pernicious*', having harmful effects on its readers, especially young people and women.[56] The view of terrifying novels as potentially harmful also accords with medical concerns that while the nerves of some patients required stimulation, others were over stimulated, and that mass culture – including sensation novels – tended in this way to have pathological effects.[57]

Coleridge's attempt to distance his own work from Gothic novels is associated with the denigration of sensibility around the turn of the century as pathological and effeminate. Robert Miles, following his account of how readers' nerves were described as strings which in response to 'sublime events [...] vibrate with "pity and terror"' (above, p. 19), goes on to explain how sensibility was increasingly reviled: 'Where it was a compliment to call someone "nervous" in 1790 (the term suggested one was robustly yet finely strung, in the manner of a well-tuned instrument), by 1810 it had taken on its overtones of being fractiously "highly-strung."'[58] The denigration of sensibility as 'highly strung' was connected with the sharp rise in the number of diseases thought to originate in the nervous system. Sensitive or over-stimulated nerve-strings were increasingly seen to underpin pathological and feminine conditions. Medical literature frequently reported and classified the pathological equivalents of delicate quiverings and tremblings as shaking, twitching, paroxysms, spasms, convulsions. According to nerve doctors such as Robert Whytt, such vibrations were contagious, as the sympathy between the nervous systems of different people meant that 'various motions and morbid symptoms are often transferred from one to another, without any corporeal contact'.[59] Whytt observed that it is usually women who are seized with convulsive fits. Hysteria, that especially female disease, became prominent in the eighteenth century. In the Royal Infirmary, frequently, 'women have been seized with hysteric fits, from seeing others attacked with them'.[60] That it is women who suffer such fits is apparently due to the fact that 'Women, in whom the nervous system is generally more moveable than in men, are more subject to nervous complaints, and have them in a higher degree'.[61] Conditions of tremor appear to rely on this 'moveable' nature of the nerves, to be manifestations or amplifications of nervous vibrations. Violent vibrations may be triggered in the more sensible nerves of women by a noise for example, as many physicians reported, or even a blister, causing the whole body to shake. 'Some adults have so delicate and sensible nerves,' explained W. Smith, 'that a vomit, smart purge, blister, sudden fright, & c. will throw them into convulsion fits. Women, whose nerves are generally more delicate and sensible than those of men, are most subject to nervous complaints'.[62]

But Smith also suggested that while the nerves of women are especially 'delicate and sensible', so are the nerves of a genius. 'People of weak nerves', he claimed, are 'quick thinkers, from the delicacy of their sensitive organs'.[63] Such medical views presumably contributed to Coleridge's desire to define the qualities of male genius as including 'a feminine Ingredient', while carefully distinguishing the feminine from the pathologically effeminate: 'N.B. By *feminine* qualities I mean nothing detractory – no participation of the *Effeminate*'.[64] Coleridge's discussions of genius in his *Biographia Literaria* were an attempt to negotiate the transition from sensibility as a trait of genius to its increasing associations with illness and femininity. As George Rousseau comments,

> the more you were afflicted by nerves – as in so many ailing artists – the greater your talent with a price to be paid either in chronic ailment or abbreviated life. It was only a short step from this neural sensibility to Coleridge's poetry as madness of a higher type, and then to Nietzsche's Apollonian/Dionysian divide and Thomas Mann's visionary tuberculars. [...] A weeping or blushing male becomes the signifier of extraordinary delicacy and exquisite sensibility, in the Enlightenment thought to be quasi-hermaphroditical, in the nineteenth century evidence of dandyism or decadence.[65]

But while sensitive or over-stimulated nerves increasingly seemed to underpin pathological and feminine conditions (which we will see more of later), stimulation – within limits – also seemed to retain some medicinal qualities. In his medical account, for example, Smith went on to claim that for the 'dejected ideas' often suffered by geniuses, music could be helpful, because it vibrates the hearer: 'by the oscillatory motion of the air, vibrating against the tympanum of the ear, there is such an impulsive motion given to the finest fibres of the brain', which restores their 'tone'.[66] The understanding that an external stimulus was required for medical disorders, and that mental states like 'dejection' could be affected by physiological conditions, was developed both by Burke and in the medical literature with which he engaged. Aris Sarafianos has considered how Burke, along with Haller, Brocklesby and other medical empiricists, developed a particular conception of pain as possessing therapeutic value, so that by the end of the eighteenth century it was frequently seen as a means of recovery. 'Echoing Burke's earlier propositions,' according to Sarafianos, Brunonianism in particular, named after John Brown's theory of nervous excitability, 'advocated the therapeutic properties of maximizing rather than reducing excitation'.[67] Brown's theory was that every creature has a certain amount of excitability, which is a material substance, and which allows it to live. Life depends on having enough excitability at one's disposal within his or her organism and on the availability of exciting powers in the external world, necessary as stimulation. Health and disease were seen as the result of either a lack or excess of such excitability. Theories about vitality thus influenced medical treatments including those of Coleridge's physician Thomas Beddoes, who, in his attempt to apply the Brunonian theory of excitability, had experimented with the medical benefits of air (developing Joseph Priestley's earlier findings), understood to stimulate the vital forces of life. As Neil Vickers discusses at some length, 'Beddoes saw himself as trying to refine out of common air the very essence of the exciting powers'.[68] Humphrey Davy, whose early mentor was Beddoes, in turn developed his theory that oxygen combined with light are essential to life.[69] In the course of his experiments, Davy tried out the effects of the gas nitrous oxide on Coleridge, to see if it was a powerful stimulant. Coleridge responded enthusiastically, reporting after his first inhalation 'a highly pleasurable sensation,' and on the third occasion a feeling of 'extasy'.[70] Considering the medical context of Burke's aestheticism, as Sarafianos puts it, 'as a materialist inquiry dealing with *the bodily reception of external stimuli*'[71], the wind might thus figure among the airs and gases with which later Brunonians experimented.

The storm wind in 'Dejection' has a number of the qualities that Burke ascribed to the sublime, including 'obscurity', which he says is necessary for it to have its terrifying effect. 'When we know the full extent of any danger', he continues, 'when we can accustom our eyes to it, a great deal of the apprehension vanishes'.[72] Burke goes on to suggest that rather than seeing, we might hear and be shaken by the sublime. He refers to a passage in the *Book of Job* as 'amazingly sublime', due to the 'terrible uncertainty', or near invisibility, of the object described:

> *In thoughts from the visions of the night, when deep sleep falleth upon men, fear came upon me and trembling, which made all my bones to shake. Then a spirit passed before my face. The hair of my flesh stood up. It stood still,* but I could not discern the form thereof: *an image was before mine eyes, there was silence; and I heard a voice, – Shall mortal man be more just than God?*[73]

The wind in 'Dejection' – something that cannot itself be seen but only sensed through its effects – has the 'obscurity' or formlessness and power of the sublime. The harp is an image of passivity and trembling submission, while the superior force of the wind is addressed with the kind of 'reverence and respect'[74] which Burke claims is felt for the sublime:

> Thou Wind, that ravest without,
> Bare craig, or mountain-tairn, or blasted tree,
> Or pine-grove wither woodman never clomb,
> Or lonely house, long held the witches' home,
>   Methinks were fitter instruments for thee [...]
>   Thou Actor, perfect in all tragic sounds!
> Thou mighty Poet, e'en to frenzy bold!
>   (Coleridge, 'Dejection' 117, lines 99–109)

Unlike 'The Aeolian Harp', in which the harp is the image for the poet, in 'Dejection' the wind is described as musician, actor and author. The harp is dispensable; other unstable structures, like a 'blasted tree' or 'lonely house,' would be 'fitter instruments for thee'. The active wind, as opposed to the responsive harp of the earlier poem, becomes the 'mighty Poet'. This shift from the passive poet may correspond with Coleridge's well-documented move away from the associationist philosophy of mind. In *Biographia Literaria* he went on to argue that Hartley's theory of the passivity of mental processes had been rejected, and consciousness instead considered by ex-followers 'as a tune, the common product of the breeze and the harp: though this again is the mere remotion of one absurdity to make way for another, equally preposterous. For what is harmony but a mode of relation, the very *esse* [being] of which is *percipi* [to be perceived]?'[75] This understanding of harmony may in turn be seen as a sign of Coleridge's move toward the Kantian idea of perception, in which the mind with its a priori concepts such as time and causality structures our perception of reality. Harmony and noise do not exist in themselves but are constituted in the act of listening, as 'the delicious melodies of Purcell or Cimarosa might be disjointed stammerings to a hearer, whose partition of time is a thousand times subtler than ours'.[76] The idea that perception is itself constructive seems to correspond with the notion of the poet's creative mind. Coleridge's idea in 'Dejection' that 'we receive but what we give' (115, line 47), for example, has often been taken by critics to support the argument that for Romantic poets perception was creative rather than receptive.[77] What Coleridge felt he had lost, however, in his state of 'dejection', what Abrams calls his 'death-in-life'[78], was precisely this mental creativity, his 'shaping spirit of Imagination' (116, line 86), rendering him passive and in need of powerful external stimulation. In the earlier verses of 'Dejection', before the build-up of the sublime wind, which threatens to overpower the harp's capacity to produce the regular metre and rhyme that is still evident here, the poet is distant, detached, and still, seeing rather than hearing or feeling:

> All this long eve, so balmy and serene,
> Have I been gazing on the western sky,
>   And its peculiar tint of yellow green:
> And still I gaze – and with how blank an eye!
>
> [...]
> I see them all [clouds, stars, moon] so excellently fair,
> I see, not feel how beautiful they are! (114–15, lines 27–38)

The poet's loss of creative perception is referred to here with the description of the eye as 'blank'. Looking outwards and seeing the external world – the colours and shapes of which are described in vivid detail, 'the western sky'

with its 'tint of yellow green', 'those thin clouds above, in flakes and bars'
– is not enough. Lacking creative power from within, the poet requires the
violent, bodily stimulus of the wind, or the air, as recommended by medical
writers from Burke to Beddoes.

The sublime, then, was sought as a means of recovery, of reviving the
poet's capacity for expression. More violently than in 'The Aeolian Harp',
the wind forces the passive instrument to 'speak'. The resulting sound is not
attributed to the harp but to the wind, as we have seen, which confronts the
harp's capacity to organize, or harmonize vibration. The sounds produced
by the wind, as well as the wind itself, are sublime. They resemble the
sounds which Burke describes as sublime, including the 'shouting of multi-
tudes', and sudden, loud, and 'low, tremulous' sounds[79]:

[...] groans of trampled men, with smarting wounds –
At once they groan with pain, and shudder with the cold!
But hush! there is a pause of deepest silence!
    And all that noise, as of a rushing crowd,
With groans, and tremulous shudderings – all is over –
    It tells another tale, with sounds less deep and loud! [...]
    'Tis of a little child
    Upon a lonesome wild,
Not far from home, but she hath lost her way:
And now moans low in bitter grief and fear,
And now screams loud, and hopes to make her mother hear.
                    (117, lines 111–25)

The voices communicate not through language but the texture of sound
itself, through the volume, pitch, rhythm, and tremulousness of 'groans' and
'moans', shuddering and screaming. In contrast to such sublime sounds, or
noises, in 'The Aeolian Harp' the gentle action of the breeze on the harp's
strings generates 'soft', 'sweet', 'delicious', harmonious sounds. These correspond with the 'soft', 'sweet', and 'delicate' qualities of Burke's beautiful
sounds, founded on pleasure.[80]

The various forms of the sublime tend of course to have a vibratory
effect. When the ear receives sound, the eardrum and other parts of it
vibrate, as Burke explains.[81] Like Hartley, he then uses sound to suggest
that light is vibratory, and also that certain foods have the 'power of putting
the nervous papillae of the tongue into a gentle vibratory motion'. Bitter
tastes, such as salt, are sublime. As opposed to sweetness, salt has 'vibratory
power'.[82] The harp and the poet in 'Dejection' thus seem to become increasingly vibratory as the wind builds up toward the climax, in the form not
only of sublime sounds but also the palpable vibration of 'tremulous
shudderings', which might be seen as the result of intensified vibrations
in the nerves. The body vibrates in a kind of palpable scream, much like

the numerous trembling bodies in Gothic novels by authors like Matthew Lewis and Anne Radcliffe[83], the pathological equivalent of which can be found in those variations of shaking and convulsions frequently reported and classified in contemporary medical literature. Some physicians thought that pain, excessive stimulation or shock could cause such symptoms as trembling, twitching, palpitations and convulsions – those symptoms most usually suffered by hysterical women.[84]

The aeolian harp was distinctive in being played by the wind, rather than by a person, as I have mentioned. Another, related way in which it differs from other musical instruments is in being both a stringed instrument (like a guitar) and wind instrument (like a flute). John Hawkins, one of the early commentators on the aeolian harp, whose comments are included in Robert Bloomfield's 'Nature's Music' (first published in 1808), wrote that the harp 'astonishes the hearers: for they are not able to perceive from whence the sound proceeds, nor yet what kind of instrument it is, for it resembles neither the sound of a stringed, nor yet of a pneumatic instrument, but partakes of both'.[85] In 'Dejection', however, the chaotic, formless force of the wind becomes the dominant feature, threatening to overwhelm the strings' capacity to harmonize, which in 'The Aeolian Harp' is preserved. Unlike 'The Aeolian Harp', in which the gentle breeze leads to gentle pleasures and thoughtful contemplation, in 'Dejection' the noise of the wind induces pain and passionate feelings, ranging from 'agony' to 'delight'. As stringed instruments are traditionally associated with reason and order they have long been seen, in Western cultures at least, as a means of procuring physical and mental health, while wind instruments have historically been connected with the threat of mental or physical derangement.[86] Like other stringed instruments, the harp continued in the eighteenth and nineteenth centuries to be regarded as having therapeutic value for the physical and mental illnesses caused by disordered nerves, whereas the aeolian harp, as both a stringed and wind instrument, was understood to have both soothing and disturbing effects. This instrument can thus be described as having 'soothed the pensive melancholy mind', as noted in the opening paragraph of this chapter, in contrast to the description in 'Dejection' of its 'scream / Of agony by torture lengthened out' (lines 97–8). In the case of 'Dejection', however, both effects appear to be experienced at once, as if the exercise provided by sublime kinds of disturbance were both pain and therapy. The therapeutic quality of the wind-harp may derive from the activity of turning, or tuning the disorderly or unpatterned buffetings of the wind into sounds of regular intervals, making sense out of chaos or noise. Should the sublimity of the wind exceed certain limits, however, defeating the harmonizing power of the strings, it may have dangerous or harmful effects. James Beattie wrote of a friend who 'has been once and again wrought into a feverish fit by the tones of an Aeolian harp'.[87]

The Romantic regard for the wind is perhaps epitomized by Percy

Shelley's 'Ode to the West Wind'. The hope in the last verse of 'Dejection', that 'this storm be but a mountain-birth', prefigures later ideas of the wind as a force of both destruction and resurrection, pain and rebirth. Like Coleridge, Shelley speaks directly to the invisible, audible wind:

> O WILD West Wind, thou breath of Autumn's being,
> Thou, from whose unseen presence the leaves dead
> Are driven, like ghosts from an enchanter fleeing [...]
> Wild Spirit, which art moving everywhere;
> Destroyer and preserver; hear, oh hear! [...]
> Make me thy lyre, even as the forest is:
> What if my leaves are falling like its own!
> The tumult of thy mighty harmonies
> Will take from both a deep, autumnal tone.
> Sweet though in sadness. Be thou, Spirit fierce,
> My spirit! Be thou me, impetuous one!
> Drive my dead thoughts over the universe
> Like withered leaves to quicken a new birth![88]

The violent revival of inner life is a central form of the correspondence between the wind and the poet in the works of Wordsworth, Coleridge, and Shelley. M. H. Abrams argues that it is the theological background of the wind's divine inspiration and powers of rebirth which these writers recover in 'versions of an older devotional poetry'. The Romantic wind, according to Abrams, 'is remote in kind from the pleasingly horrific storm dear to eighteenth-century connoisseurs of the natural sublime'.[89] The wind can also of course be viewed in a contemporary scientific context, however. Sharon Ruston observes that Shelley's description of the wind as life-giving shares a preoccupation with the scientific debate of the time about how life began, and about the difference between living and dead matter, while theories about vitality influenced medical treatments, as we have seen. Much like the electricity which animates dead bodies in Mary Shelley's *Frankenstein*, the wind which stimulates the harp in the poems by Coleridge and Shelley, both of whom were familiar with such theories and practices, may thus be more than just a healing force – it is a vital energy, generating life itself.[90] While Coleridge came to reject his earlier materialist views of life, as Ruston notes, 'instead arguing for a far more conservative notion of a soul, an immaterial mind and the design of an omnipotent God', Shelley continued to represent the wind in his poetry as a force or energy which could potentially animate matter.[91]

The continued use of the harp as a model for the poetic, creative self in the work of Shelley, Bloomfield and others in the nineteenth century indicates that this instrument, despite the bad reputation which theories of sensibility began to get after about 1800, was still the vogue invention for materialising the relationship between outward nature and the inner self. The harp, as both a stringed and wind instrument, provides a way of bridging what Crary has described as a historical disjuncture with the new understanding of sensations as originating in the body rather the external world. As a stringed instrument, the harp provided a model of the nerves as having a constitutive role in perception, and in the production of poetry, as earlier sections of this chapter have shown, while as a wind instrument, the harp's capacity to organize or harmonize external forces or energies may be reduced or even obliterated. Powerful, overwhelming stimuli from the external world, such as the wind, could be experienced as both painful and pleasurable, and seemed to have both detrimental and beneficial effects on bodily and mental health. The sublime force of the wind could painfully excite the mind out of dejection and inspire poetic production (within the limits beyond which it could be harmful), and further, it could become a life-giving energy with the power to reanimate life and consciousness. The Romantic mind – with its inspired thoughts, productive imagination, passionate feelings – is not conceived here as spiritually transcending the material body and world. Rather, the harp became one of the chief emblems of a culture in which new technologies helped to produce and served to demonstrate a mechanized understanding of mind in relation to the material world.

CHAPTER TWO

Psychophysical Sensations and Spiritual Vibrations

In 1801 Thomas Young first gave a demonstration of the wave theory of light. His earlier acoustical researches led him to propose that just as sound consists of vibrations in the air, so does light consist of vibrations in the ether. In his demonstration at the Royal Society that later became known as the double-slit experiment, Young split a beam of light into two using a thin card. The two beams then overlapped on the opposite wall, demonstrating the principle of interference, according to which light waves either reinforce or cancel each other to produce alternating bands of brightness and darkness, like sound and silence (sound waves similarly interfere with each other when they cross, reinforcing and cancelling each other to produce beats).[1] It took another two decades for wave theory to firmly establish itself in Britain against the corpuscular theory of light that had previously dominated, but Young's acoustic-based theory was developed and verified in France by Augustin Fresnel and François Arago, and by the mid-nineteenth century the widespread acceptance of the wave theory of light – frequently conceived of as a kind of sound – also supported an undulatory or wave theory of heat.[2]

Sound vibration thus provided a basis for explaining the vibratory activity of energies in the external world, as well as nerve impulses in the body. Wave theory began to replace the theory of light particles much as neuronal vibrations took over from animal spirits. My last chapter focused on vibrations in the nerves, while this chapter, following a brief discussion of how sound was used in physics to conceptualize vibrations more generally, will explore how physicists, physiologists, psychophysicists and spiritualists began to understand the connections between internal and external energies – all conceived of as forms of vibration. By the mid-nineteenth century scientific thinkers and practitioners were transforming speculative, theoretical modes of inquiry into experimental and verifiable techniques, in the process employing new instruments and technologies. Physicists were thus calculating how frequencies of vibration in the external world result in corresponding intensities of sense experience, quantifying the connection between the world outside and the interior mechanics of the body and mind. They also emphasized, however, that some frequencies exist beyond the sensory thresholds. According to the law of the conservation of energy, light becomes extrasensory but continues to exist in the form of radiant heat. Spiritualists took this discovery to support their claims that life continues in some form after death, by conceiving of life itself as a form of energy. Vibrations within the body – the life of the bounded organism – seem thus to become part of the external world – the eternal life of the unbounded universe, although usually at frequencies beyond the range of the senses. The work of Gustav Fechner is important to this chapter as the crossover between the spiritual and scientific is exemplified by his theological text *On Life After Death* (1836) and the results of his mathematical and experimental research in *Elements of Psychophysics* (1860). Fechner wanted psychophysics to support his earlier work, which claimed that nervous energy is one among the various forms of vibratory energy, that it radiates out of the body – much as sound radiates out from stringed instruments – it goes on after death. Although such spiritual vibrations usually exist beyond the sensory thresholds of living humans, he claimed that there are some exceptionally nervous, sensitive people who can detect those otherworldly frequencies.

Jonathan Sterne has shown how the concept of frequency as 'a way to think about sound as a form of motion or vibration' took hold in nineteenth-century sciences, which broke with older understandings of sound. 'Where speech or music had been the general categories through which sound was understood', writes Sterne, 'they were now special cases of the general phenomenon of sound'.[3] This process of generalization was also taken further so that sound, in turn, became a special case of the general phenomenon of vibration, and hearing a special case of sensation (as we saw in the last chapter where the receptivity of musical strings and the ear became a model for the nerves). Hermann Helmholtz's studies in acoustics are representative of the process by which sound frequencies were used as a way of explaining the existence of other kinds of frequencies, or 'periodic times of vibration', as in the lecture 'On the Physiological Causes of Harmony in Music', which introduces the concept of wave-motions by moving from an analysis of musical tones toward light waves: 'The motion of a mass of air through which a tone passes belongs to the so-called wave-motions – a class of motions of great importance in physics. Light, as well as sound, is one of these motions'.[4] After a detailed analysis of the motions of sound waves, the sympathetic vibration of the ear, and the sensation of musical tones, the lecture marks out a correspondance with light waves and the sensation of colours:

Light is also an undulation of a peculiar medium, the luminous ether, diffused through the universe, and light, as well as sound, exhibits phenomena of interference. Light, too, has waves of various periodic times of vibration, which produce in the eye the sensation of colour, red having the greatest periodic time, then orange, yellow, green, blue, violet.[5]

As Gillian Beer has pointed out, light and heat were no longer seen to be stable, material particles but were understood as invisible forms of motion, hence 'the performance of energies lay beyond the reach of eyesight, and even perhaps beyond the reach of any signification outside mathematics'.[6] Along with the invisible quality of light itself, wave theory also emphasized 'periodic times of vibration' beyond the colour scale. In 1800 William Herschel had found that there is no sudden break at the end of visible red light. His thermometer detected heat, which he called 'infra-red'. It became increasingly apparent that sound, light and heat differ less in quality (they are all vibratory) than quantity (infra-red has a greater periodic time than visible red). Herschel's demonstration that light becomes heat at the infra-red point on the spectrum supported the wave theory of heat, which was in turn confirmed by the law of the conservation of energy.

The first mathematical formulation of the law of energy conservation, according to which energy is transmitted and transformed rather than created or destroyed, is generally thought to be Helmholtz's 'On the Conservation of Force' (1847), which typically argues that heat can no longer be seen as a 'substance'; 'We must rather conclude that heat itself is a motion'.[7] Helmholtz went on in a later lecture to develop his use of sound as a model for other forms of vibration in terms of the law of energy conservation, comparing the radiation and conservation of heat to how 'the sound-movement of a string can leave its originally narrow and fixed home and diffuse itself in the air, keeping all the time its pitch'. The sound produced by this string, Helmholtz went on to explain, can also put another string into sympathetic vibration, as it 'starts this again or excites a flame ready to sing to the same tone'[8] (many physicists carried out experiments with 'sensitive flames', known to shrink or flare, sing or roar, in response to sound[9]). This resonates with Helmholtz's studies in acoustics which analyse the process of sympathetic vibration in great detail. *On the Sensations of Tone*, first published in 1862, explains how if the periodic time of a vibration corresponds with the tuning of a string, tuning fork, or eardrum, such objects will vibrate sympathetically.[10]

Sound, then, as this opening section has shown, became a model for energy in general, which physicists described as vibratory, imperceptible and infinite. The concept of one kind of universal energy – conserved and converted, transmitted and transformed, but with an underlying vibratory consistency – led to analyses of phenomena as quantitatively, rather than qualitatively different, as this chapter will go on to show. The identification of waves in space led to analysis of their movement in time, as physicists and other scientifically informed theorists differentiated between the various forms of energy by quantifying numbers of vibrations in a specific period. In the context of energy with its capacity to take on multiple forms, it was frequently implied that light is sound; sound is light – only light vibrates at a greater speed than sound. By the end of the century a continuum or scale of electromagnetic radiation would define the underlying unity of qualities ranging from infra-red and ultra-violet to X-rays and radio waves, all the way up to – at least according to some spiritualists – the frequencies of life itself, extending beyond death into a vibratory afterlife. The concept of a sonorous scale of spiritual frequencies will finally provide the context in this chapter for my analysis of fiction including George Eliot's 'The Lifted Veil'[11], Wilkie Collins's *The Woman in White*, and Florence McLandburgh's 'The Automaton Ear'[12], with its sensitive, first-person narrator who suffers from the voices of the dead. Through stories like these I will develop my investigation into the concern with the dangers as well as pleasures of vibratory frequencies.

Sensory thresholds

Fechner's *Elements of Psychophysics* is considered a key if not the founding text of modern scientific psychology, in its attempt to show that mental processes are related to physical phenomena and can be analysed using experimentation and quantitative methodologies as well as philosophical speculation.[13] Hartley's *Observations on Man* has its place in many histories of psychology as the earliest comprehensive attempt to integrate Newtonian physics with Locke's associationist philosophy, though the physiological basis of his observations was largely speculative. Though historians frequently claim that Hartley's doctrine of vibrations represents his commitment to a psychology grounded in the material, they have not so often observed the many later evocations of this motion in the work of the psychophysicists, neurologists, physiologists and other scientific theorists who feature on the time-line of the development of psychology. My aim here, therefore, is to show that vibration has been central to various forms of psychological theory, which can help to highlight an ongoing commitment to, and a plurality of ways of conceiving of mind as grounded in the body and the physical world, both of which were increasingly understood, as we have seen, to be vibratory.

Hartley went so far as to postulate that vibrations in the nerves correspond with sensations in the brain, whereas Fechner developed a far more exact analysis of the relation between vibrations and sensations. By calculating the relation between physical stimulation and psychological sensation ('outer psychophysics'), Fechner wanted to prove that the relation between nervous activity and sensation is also governed by mathematical laws ('inner psychophysics'). Although the bodily activity could not be directly measured, the relation between the external stimuli and sensation necessarily demonstrated the relation between body and mind, according to Fechner, as 'sensations are merely in a mediated relationship to the external stimulus, which initiates these processes [in the brain] only via the intervention of a neural conductor'.[14] For his equation between stimuli and sensation, then, in his investigation of outer psychophysics, Fechner established a zero point from which measurement could commence, and a basic measurement unit. Below a certain stimulus intensity there is no sensation. At this threshold, sensation is said to be zero. For a unit of measurement, Fechner took the notion of a 'just noticeable difference' from Ernst Weber's earlier experiments into lifted weights, extending it to the other senses. The magnitude of any sensation could then be taken as the number of just noticeable differences above the zero point. For example, among his discussions of the thresholds for the various sense domains, Fechner notes that Ernst Chladni found the lower limits of hearing to have a periodic time of 30 vibrations in a second.[15] In respect of just noticeable differences Fechner found that the ear is able to differentiate between the tones of 'two tuning forks which were almost precisely in tune, so that one vibrated at 1209, the other at 1210 vibrations per second'.[16] Starting from the observation that a just noticeable difference requires larger changes as the stimulus increases, Fechner derived the law that the intensity of a sensation varies according to the logarithm of the intensity of the stimulus.

Psychophysics can be characterized, for now, as experimental investigation into the relation between quantities of vibration and sensation. Audible and inaudible sounds, like colours and heat, are explained as different periodic times or frequencies on a continuum, rather than as different qualities. Fechner came up with the now renowned psychophysical law but a number of similar investigations were published around this time. For his study 'On the Physiological Causes of Harmony in Music', for example, Helmholtz experimented with a siren. The siren blows air at a flat circle-shaped disc with holes around its edges at regular intervals. When the disc is set into rapid rotation air escapes through these holes producing a certain tone, depending on the number of holes and the speed of rotation. So if there are twelve holes then twelve 'puffs' are produced with one rotation of the disc. If the disc is made to revolve ten times in one second then 120 puffs are produced, which generates 'a weak and deep musical tone'.[17] It is possible to establish, by knowing the number of holes and the number of rotations per second, the numbers of vibrations that produce different tones. It is only above a certain speed that the siren begins to produce frequencies perceived as musical sound:

> When the siren is turned slowly, and hence the puffs of air succeed each other slowly, you hear no musical sound. By the continually increasing rapidity of its revolution, no essential change is produced in the kind of vibration of the air. Nothing new happens to the ear. The only new result is the sensation experienced by the ear, which then for the first time begins to be affected by the agitation of the air. Hence the more rapid vibrations receive a new name, and are called Sound.[18]

The key concept for this physics of sensitivity is the threshold. Much as Helmholtz draws attention to the moment when the 'vibration of the air' is for the 'first time' perceived as sound, Fechner's system of measurement starts from the zero point below which vibrations are not sensed ('stimulus threshold'), and counts upwards with the just noticeable differences, beyond which changes in stimulus are not sensed ('difference-stimulus-threshold'[19]). Psychophysics drew attention to frequencies outside conscious awareness, including invisible as well as inaudible frequencies. As sound is the model for light, hearing is the model for sight where Helmholtz uses the musical scale to quantify the limited range of the senses: 'The ear is sensitive to about ten octaves of different tones, while the eye is sensitive to only a musical sixth. With both sound and light, however, vibrations exist outside of these ranges, and their physical existence can be demonstrated'.[20] 'Invisible light' is defined in William Thomson's 'The Wave Theory of Light' which states in the first place 'simply that sound and light are both due to vibrations propagated in the manner of waves'.[21] Described as a kind of silent sound, the quantity of the invisible is found to be three times greater than the visible, for 'we have one octave of visible light, one octave above the visible range and two octaves below the visible range'.[22] Behind all these accounts of frequencies lies the idea that it is the quantity of vibrations that underpins the qualitative difference between types of energy: thus light becomes invisible heat, and both are described as sound.

The various forms of energy in the world are also transformed in the body. Fechner held that psychophysical activity in the nerves – 'the vibrations of the ultimate particles'[23] – is one among the multiple aspects of universal energy. All sensations are mediated, so that 'a stronger sensation depends on a stronger stimulus; the stimulus, however, causes sensation only via the intermediate action of some internal processes of the body'.[24] Energy in the nerves has to rise above a threshold before a stimulus is sensed, and also an increasing number of different kinds of nerve energies were identified, each of which transmit only one kind of sense. This explains how quantitative frequencies of vibration are experienced as qualitatively different sensations. In 1826 Johannes Müller had formulated the 'doctrine of specific nerve energies', stating that there are five kinds of sensory nerve fibres with specific energies, one for each of the five senses.[25] The effects of these energies are described in the first paragraph of Helmholtz's *Sensations of Tone*, again suggesting that sound, light and heat are on the same scale or spectrum, and are experienced as different only because of the different organs that receive them:

> Sensations result from the action of an external stimulus on the sensitive apparatus of our nerves. Sensations differ in kind, partly with the organ of sense excited, and partly with the nature of the stimulus employed. Each organ of sense produces peculiar sensations, which cannot be excited by means of any other; the eye gives sensations of light, the ear sensations of sound, the skin sensations of touch. Even when the same sunbeams which excite in the eye sensations of light, impinge on the skin and excite its nerves, they are felt only as heat, not as light. In the same way the vibration of elastic bodies heard by the ear, can also be felt by the skin, but in that case produce only a whirring fluttering sensation, not sound.[26]

It is frequently observed that frequencies of vibration produce different sensations, as well as different tones, colours, temperatures. Light can be felt by the skin 'as heat, not as light', sound as 'a whirring fluttering sensation, not sound'. The human body, in other words, differentiates between 'things' that are actually the same. Whereas to the 'natural philosopher', writes Helmholtz, 'the impressions of sense are not an irrefragable authority; he examines what claim they have to be trusted; he asks whether things which they pronounce different are really different, and often finds that he must answer, no!'[27] To illustrate how all the senses are of 'force', another of Thomson's essays, 'The Six Gateways of Knowledge', notes that Beethoven, 'who was deaf for a great part of his life [...] used to stand with a stick pressed against his teeth, and thus he could hear the sounds that he called forth from the instrument'.[28] The same kind of force can be experienced in different ways, or not experienced at all. In this essay Thomson refers again to sounds beyond the range of all the senses, explaining that the lowest we can hear are at about 20 vibrations per second, while at about 400 million millions we have dull red light, below which is inaudible, invisible heat.[29]

What these accounts of thresholds and specific nerve energies emphasize is that sensory experience depends on the physiological make-up of the subject, as well as the external object. The stimulus is understood to be mediated by the nerves, and may be translated into sensations of sound or fluttering, light or heat, or not sensed at all. Psychophysics, as Jonathan Crary has argued, thus contributed to the growing awareness of the subjectivity of perception, grounded in the body. Crary argues that psychophysics contributed to the shift from the classical relation between the external object and subjective experience, replacing associationist models, for example, of the perceiver as passive receiver of stimuli, whose perceptions mirror the external world. My last chapter explored a bridge between these two models, with the mechanism of the aeolian harp (it can operate as both a passive receiver and creative, responsive perceiver of stimuli); psychophysics establishes the shift to subjective perception more completely. Crary refers to the work of Helmholtz, Fechner and others as 'one of the conditions for the emergence of notions of autonomous vision, that is, for a severing (or liberation) of perceptual experience from a necessary relation to an exterior world'.[30]

Crary focuses on the paradoxical nature of 'modern attention', arguing that this was both a condition of the functioning of disciplinary institutions, and of individual creativity and freedom. Psychophysics produces a model of attention that establishes the active, creative and autonomous power of the perceiving subject, but paradoxically also becomes the basis for disciplinary efforts to control and render this subject docile. According to Crary, psychophysics was central to the construction of the new kind of disciplined subject whose attentiveness (an elementary form of which is sensitivity) was observed and measured, quantified and controlled, though the attempts to manage attention were often contradictory. The subject began to be conceptualized in the late nineteenth century, Crary writes, 'not only in terms of the isolated objects of attention, but equally in terms of what is not perceived, or only dimly perceived, of the distractions, the fringes and peripheries that are excluded or shut out of a perceptual field'.[31] Having considered both the quantification and limits of sensory attention, I want next to consider how stringed instruments, like the aeolian harp discussed in my last chapter, continued to provide a model for the conceptualization of subjective perception.

More strings

Helmholtz extended Müller's doctrine of specific nerve energies to account for the different qualities within each sense, identifying approximately 4,500 specific auditory energies. He used an instrument to measure quantities of sound as a stimulus (the siren) and another instrument (the piano) to explain how the body sympathetically vibrates in response. The end of every 'string' is connected to a nerve fibre which is excited when the string is vibrated, generating sensation:

> If we suppose the dampers of a pianoforte to be raised, and allow any musical tone to impinge powerfully on its sounding board, we bring a set of strings into sympathetic vibration, namely *all* those strings, and

only those, which correspond with the simple tones contained in the given musical tone. Here, then, we have, by a purely mechanical process, a resolution of air waves precisely similar to that performed by the ear. The air wave, quite simple in itself, brings a certain number of strings into sympathetic vibration, and the sympathetic vibration of these strings depends on the same law as the sensation of the harmonic upper partial tones in the ear.[32]

The sense of different tones depends upon a 'purely mechanical process', automatic operations in the body. As Friedrich Kittler observes in *Discourse Networks*, 'the very channels through which information must pass emit noise. [... It] hums in the ears themselves'.[33] According to both Kittler and Crary, this kind of sensory mechanism was new to the nineteenth century. It is not only that certain frequencies of vibration were understood to exist beyond the zero point, escaping consciousness, but the process of sense-making itself also eluded the conscious operations of the mind. Crary writes that one of the ways in which attention began to be understood in this period, by Arthur Schopenhauer, Sigmund Freud and others, was as 'determined by the operations of various *automatic* or unconscious processes or forces'.[34]

But Kittler is hostile to Crary's 'over-emphasis on the body' which he sees as currently fashionable among many branches of scholarship. For Kittler, Crary's thesis would be more precise if he had spoken about 'material effects in general, which can impact on human bodies just as well as on technical storage media'.[35] Kittler argues that both human bodies and technical media process information, and that our conception of human subjectivity is based on our understanding of non-human transmission. Human subjectivity, in Kittler's analysis, is bound up inextricably with the machinery of communication technologies. Sense experience is interfered with by the noise of the medium, like the messages transmitted and stored by technologies like the typewriter and gramophone. Between input and output, the mechanical mediation of information structures the psychophysical mediation of sense. Despite their differences, however, both Kittler and Crary suggest that the objective world became newly inaccessible, that our perception of external objects or events is interfered with in the very process of our perceiving them – whether the interference is bodily or mechanical or both. The medium – nerves in the body, strings in the ear or pianoforte – was thought to contribute its own sound or 'noise' in the automatic, unconscious process of sense-making, of perceiving or interpreting a stimulus. Rather than go along with the epistemological breaks favoured by Kittler and Crary between 1800 and 1900 or between associationism and psychophysics, though, I want here to draw attention to a continuity in the use of musical strings as a model for processes of bodily perception between the earlier and later periods. My last chapter proposed that the strings of the aeolian harp, vibrated or energized by the wind, provided an image of the 'infinitesimal' nervous vibrations which, while themselves beyond consciousness, underpinned sensation itself. Its sympathetically vibrating strings were imaginable as both nerves and vocal cords, as simultaneously receptive and creative. Its ability to 'hear-speak', as I called it, to oneself as well as to others, will be developed here as a model for how processes of reception were also processes of transmission. Musical strings were used in the later nineteenth century as an image of how the nerves do not simply hear but speak information to the brain. In 'Visible and Invisible Radiation' for instance, John Tyndall used strings to model the harmonious mechanics of nerve energies. The first and last paragraphs are as follows:

> Between the mind of man and the outer world are interposed the nerves of the human body, which translate, or enable the mind to translate, the impressions of that world into facts of consciousness and thought. [...]
>
> If you open a piano and sing into it, a certain string will respond. Change the pitch of your voice; the first string ceases to vibrate, but another replies. Change again the pitch; the first two strings are silent, while another resounds. Thus is sentient man acted on by Nature, the optic, the auditory, and other nerves of the human body being so many strings differently tuned, and responsive to different forms of the universal power.[36]

The 'universal power' is sonorous, indicating that its 'different forms' are on a periodic continuum. The nerves 'translate' these forms into 'facts of consciousness and thought'; each nerve 'replies' and 'resounds'. Tyndall, who popularized Helmholtz's work in Britain, seems to adapt the latter's use of piano strings as an analogy for the hearing mechanism into the metaphor for sensation in general, much as Hartley did over a century earlier (see above, p. 17). Tyndall's *Sound* takes up the use of strings as the more specific image for the mechanism of hearing, describing the corti (the sensitive element in the inner ear, containing thousands of sensory hair cells) as 'to all appearance a musical instrument, with its cords so stretched as to accept vibrations of different periods, and transmit them to the nerve filaments which traverse the organ'. The corti is a 'lute of 3,000 strings' that has 'existed for ages, accepting the music of the outer world, and rendering it fit for reception by the human brain'.[37]

It is, of course, because the nerves were thought to vibrate that musical instruments are especially useful as models. The transition in the eighteenth century from spirits in tubular nerves to vibration itself as the way in which sensations were transmitted provided mental operations – association, thought, memory – with a revised mechanical basis. Tyndall describes the vibratory mode of transmission in the opening paragraphs of *Sound*: 'We have the strongest reason for believing that what the nerves convey to the brain is in all cases *motion* [...] the vibration, or tremor, of its molecules or smaller particles'.[38] Among many comparable accounts is Fechner's: 'The play of the nerves may be reduced to chemical or electrical processes. In either case it must be acknowledged either to consist of the vibrations of ultimate particles, or at least to be evoked by or connected with them'.[39] It is in this context then that psychophysics developed the implications of the idea of strings as receiver-transmitters, as an image of transmission within oneself, of internal as well as external communication to others (I will say more about the latter shortly).

Instruments are models for the human, which may also be brought to life and consciousness by the energy of vibration. The idea of energy is at the heart of analogies between humans and mechanisms, in Helmholtz's 'Conservation of Force' and elsewhere. In a discussion of the principle of energy conservation Fechner writes that 'no one has found reasons to doubt its general applicability in the areas of the organic and the inorganic' (*EP*, 29). He describes the human subject in these terms, as being ruled by the same forces as inorganic nature, explaining that 'the relations are like those of a steam engine with a complicated mechanism [...] The only difference is that in our organic machine the engineer does not sit on the outside but on the inside' (35). Fechner believed matter and mind to be aspects of the same reality, seeking to establish the mathematical equation between physical stimuli and subjective sensations to show that they are functionally related.

Historians tend to emphasize either the scientific ideas or the philosophical origins on which *Elements of Psychophysics* rest. I will interpret Fechner's work as a form of spiritual material, by which I mean to refer to how his religious and spiritualist beliefs were bound up with his scientific understanding of the physical world. As mind can be reduced to the physics of matter, according to Fechner, matter is mind. All nature is besouled ('beseelt'). In *Nanna, or the Soul Life of Plants*, published in 1848, he responds to the objection that plants have no soul because they have no nervous system, no strings:

This analogy is very appropriate because here we compare the means for producing objective sensations with the means for producing subjective sensations. The violin when it is played imparts a sensation to others, the body does the like to itself. But now when I see that the flute after all does actually produce tones, in spite of my pretty argument, I cannot see why the plants might not be able to produce subjective sensations without having nerves. The animals might be the string instruments of sensation, and the plants the wind instruments.[40]

As well as producing 'subjective sensations', Fechner argues that nervous vibrations radiate out of the body. Elaborating on this kind of hear-speaking, both to oneself and to others, he describes how a flower produces a 'sweet smell' for its own pleasure just as a person plays a 'sweet song' that also gives pleasure to others.[41] As an image for this sympathy between the subjective and objective world it was customary to use the sounds of musical instruments. As Gretchen Finney explains, the human body was likened to instruments which not only 'suggested sensitivity, responsiveness'; at the same time, the body 'could produce a harmony similar both to that of the universe and that of heard music'.[42]

On Life After Death was Fechner's first comprehensive account of his spiritual system, prepared during his first years as professor of physics at Leipzig University and published in 1836. This explains that 'vibrations only *seem* to die out, in so far as they spread indefinitely in all directions; or, if dying out for a time, transformed into energy or tension, they are able to begin afresh, in some form or other, in accordance with the law of the conservation of energy'.[43] There is therefore an infinite feedback loop, whereby vibrations generate sensations, sensations vibrations. Even the most subtle vibrations radiate outwards in all directions, beyond the zero point:

> However minute and gentle a vibration connected with some conscious movement within our mind may be – and all our mental acts are connected with, and accompanied by, such vibrations of our brain – it cannot vanish without producing continued processes of a similar nature, within ourselves, and, finally, around ourselves, though we are not able to trace them into the outer world. A lyre cannot keep its music for itself; as little can our brain; the music of sounds or of thoughts originates in the lyre or in the brain, but does not stay there – it spreads beyond them. (*LD*, 52–3)

Having outlined the physics of extrasensory vibration earlier in this chapter, I have gone on in this section to discuss how the objective world, as Crary and Kittler have observed, increasingly seemed to become inaccessible to direct perception, to be subject to interference in the process of perceiving it, though older mechanisms than these writers usually allow for were available for thinking this through. The medium – strings in the ear, nerves in the body – was thought to contribute its own 'noise' in the automatic, unconscious process of sense-making. Hearing and speaking, reading and writing, the reception and radiation of energy both within and out of the brain was conceived as one and the same process. Not only were people, described as mechanisms, understood to be sensitive to the various forms of vibratory energy, but energy was conceived as the driving force behind life and consciousness itself. This is a body without borders, as I discussed in the introduction, simultaneously receiving vibrations and radiating outwards, while it becomes impossible to distinguish between inner and outer reality. I will return later to the question of 'noise'; my next section firstly continues to examine the radiation of energy that 'spreads' through time and space, and never dies.

Brain waves and radiation

It is the principle of the conservation of energy that forms the basis of Fechner's argument that there is life after death, evidence of which is beyond the range of the normal sensory thresholds. *On Life After Death* explains that 'consciousness is present and awake when and where the activity of the body underlying the activity of the mind – the psychophysical activity – exceeds that degree of strength which we call the threshold'. Above this threshold, which in *Elements of Psychophysics* becomes the zero point, the 'summits of the waves of our psychophysical activity move about from place to place, though confined, in this life, to our body' (*LD*, 99). Beyond this threshold, vibrations pass beyond both the range of our senses and the confines of our body, but continue to exist.

Wave theory has temporal and spatial dimensions and implications. The idea of co-present frequencies puts time in space, in that the afterlife could be considered an area of the vibratory spectrum, the other world radiating through our world. *Elements of Psychophysics* indicates that there is no limit to the periodic time in space. 'The audibility of tones appears not only to have a lower, but also an upper, limit' which Joseph Sauveur put at 12,400 vibrations per second, William Wollaston at 19,000 to 22,000, or even higher:

> [Félix] Savart discovered in the meantime that if one generates very high tones of sufficient loudness, as he did with a toothed wheel whose teeth struck against a thin material, tones corresponding to 48,000 simple vibrations (24,000 strokes) could be heard. Also [César] Despretz concludes from experiments of his with small tuning forks that the ear can still perceive, determine, and classify (*entendre, apprecier, classer*) tones up to 73,000 vibrations. [...]
>
> One might after all pose the question whether the limit of audibility of high tones has already been reached, or if still higher tones might not be audible with greater amplification. On the other hand, it is quite possible that either the nerves themselves are incapable of perceiving tones which are too high or that the eardrum and its appendages might be incapable of receiving them. (*EP*, 216)

Cultural and literary historians and critics have quite intensively examined the connections between scientific discourses and the emergence of spiritualism in the second half of the nineteenth century, focusing particularly on the Society for Psychical Research (formed in 1882), while Fechner's attempts to give scientific valency to spiritualist concepts began earlier in the century than is usually noted, in the 1820s (until his death in 1887).[44] Though many spiritualists, like Fechner, presented their beliefs as grounded in scientific facts, spiritualism is often thought to be a result of widespread dissatisfaction with nineteenth-century science, with its materialist and determinist world view. The 'ambivalence' of spiritualists over science was, writes Janet Oppenheim, 'shared by countless other Victorians for whom it would be mistaken to assume an unquestioning and cheerful optimism about the social impact of scientific discoveries'.[45] In the 1820s Fechner similarly saw the scientific version of the universe as a bleak, godless mechanical system, and death as the brutal annihilation of self-identity. Marilyn Marshall observes that there was in Fechner's musings 'a felt paradox between the necessity of viewing the world as mechanism (to satisfy the requirements of science) and viewing the world as consciousness (to justify his idealistic premises and his moral-religious convictions)', the resolution of which he struggled to find.[46] He wanted *Elements of Psychophysics* to produce evidence in support of his religious philosophy, and although I have found little evidence that Fechner's theories directly influenced spiritualists as they did scientists such as Helmholtz and Hermann Ebbinghaus[47], many similar if not indistinguishable formulations of spiritualism were produced later in the century, indicating that Fechner did indeed help to shape the development of spiritualist ideas. Along with the quantification of sensory thresholds, the idea of psychophysical energy was frequently taken to account for how spiritual vibrations might pervade the air or ether though inaudible and invisible. In an account of Fechner's influence on Freud, Henri Ellenberger writes: 'After Fechner, the concept of "mental energy" was adopted by many authors, and by the end of the century it was quite common in European psychology and neuropsychiatry'.[48] In that energy or 'waves' were thought to radiate out of the brain this was also conceptually linked to the practice of mesmerism, often regarded as the first of the popular sciences, taking off in the late eighteenth century, popularized in England and elsewhere by Coleridge and others (see above, pp. 24–5), evolving through various forms of neo-mesmerism, hypnotism, and spiritualism in the later nineteenth century.[49] In her chapter on the rise of neo-mesmerism in *fin-de-siécle* psychiatry, Anne Harrington claims that there was nothing in the world of late-nineteenth-century physics – 'a splendid baroque world of rarefied ethers, invisible energy fields, moving lines of force, waves and undulations' – or in neurophysiology that ruled out the possibility that 'nervous energy could "radiate" out of the body'.[50] She shows that there was a move from magnetic fluids toward other theories of hypnosis, notably those of J. M. Charcot, but argues that they were dealing with the same 'phenomenological reality'.[51] Psychiatrists and others continued to draw on the vocabulary and claims of physics in order to stress how, in the words of a worker at the Charité hospital, F. de Courmelles in *Hypnotism*: 'The brain nerve cells vibrate under the influence of different causes, why should it be thought that the movement does not extend further than the cranium'.[52]

The radiation of nervous energy was represented in the work of hypnotists, spiritualists and others by the sympathetic vibration of instruments, again echoing the earlier work of Fechner. In *Phantasms of the Living* (1886) Edmund Gurney, a founding member of The Society for Psychical Research, noted that:

> The familiar phenomena of the transmission and reception of vibratory energy are ready to hand as analogies – the effect, for instance, of a swinging pendulum on another of equal length attached to the same solid support; or of one tuning-fork or string on another of the same pitch [...] So it is possible to conceive that vibration-waves, or nervous induction, are a means whereby activity in one brain may evoke a kindred activity in another – with, of course, a similar correspondence of psychical impressions.[53]

The mechanics of sympathetic vibration – the distant touch between musical strings – precede the communication technologies that are the focus of much recent work.[54] In his account of the invention of telepathy in the later nineteenth century, Roger Luckhurst argues that this form of spiritualist theory (which concentrates on extrasensory communication between *living* humans) was premised on this sympathetic resonance, deriving from scientific sources including Tyndall's lectures on sound, flames and other physical phenomena.[55] William Crookes, president of the Society for Psychical Research, developed a slightly more convoluted version of hear-speaking. This starts at a very low frequency of 2 vibrations per second, reaching 32 'where atmospheric vibration reveals itself to us as *sound*' which stops at 32,768, then moves on to ether vibrations which rise from heat to ultraviolet to the recently discovered X-rays of Professor Röentgen which extend to '2,305763,009213,693952 per second or even higher'...

> Let it be assumed that these rays [X], or rays even of higher frequency, can pass into the brain and act on some nervous centre there. Let it be conceived that the brain contains a centre which uses these rays as the vocal chords use sound vibrations (both being under the command of intelligence), and sends them out, with the velocity of light, to impinge on the receiving ganglion of another brain. In this way some, at least, of the phenomena of telepathy, and the transmission of intelligence from one sensitive to another through long distances, seem to come into the domain of law, and can be grasped.[56]

Crookes responded to the objection that 'brain waves, like any other waves [...] should die out altogether before great distances are reached', with an explanation of the conservation of energy: 'that energy is transformed and not destroyed, and that whenever we can trace the transformation we find it quantitatively exact'.[57]

Where mesmerism and telepathy seem to work with the transmission of energies through space, between living contemporaries, spiritualism works with transmission in all directions, including through time, with a geographical kind of history of all the vibrations that have ever been. Crookes wrote that 'our mundane ideas of space and distance may be superseded', that '"near" and "far" may lose their usual meaning'.[58] Past and future, or time itself seems to radiate through space in Fechner's view:

> The shortest moment of conscious life produces a similar circle of actions around it, just as the briefest tone that seems gone in a second, produces a similar circle, which carries the tone into endless space, far beyond the persons standing by to listen; for no action, or effect, is utterly destroyed, it goes on producing new effects of its kind for ever. (*LD*, 55)

On Life After Death distinguishes between the 'play of vibrations of a higher order, originating in our brain' and that which 'strikes our eyes and ears', protesting that the 'man of science knows and studies the play of waves of a lower order only, little caring for those of a higher order' (*LD*, 74). However, as the century wore on, an increasing amount of spiritual material was produced, concerning itself with the waves of the 'higher order'. The interest in radiation appears itself to have radiated through society. A further example of this, dealing with the 'Continuous Existence of the Soul' is a pamphlet by Hanson Hey, the secretary of the Spiritualists' National Union in Britain, which formed in 1886. The section on 'Vibratory Energy' begins with the observation that the same energy has different periodic frequencies:

> You have doubtless heard of the fact that vibratory energy produces different results when the rate of vibration changes. You have noted that the different tints of the prismatic ray differ not in essence, but in rapidity of rate of vibration. Thus, red, the first colour we perceive, is the colour produced by the lowest rate which the eye can register; the first we can grasp by mortal means. By leaps and bounds up through the scale we go, until in the millions of vibrations per second we see the violet rays, the highest rate of vibration registered by the retina. But there are rates of vibration both below and above our range of apprehension; colours below red, and colours above violet; lights that we have seen not.[59]

The thought waves by which spirits communicate are on a continuum, Hey goes on to explain, with sound, light, and so on.[60]

A lot has been written about the move from religious to scientific belief systems in the Victorian period, and historians have seen the spiritualist alliance with science in terms of a need to resolve this, conserving the transcendent or miraculous. Thomas Leahey, for instance, writes that 'many thoughtful people, including well-known scientists, turned to science itself for assurance that there was more to human life than the bodily machine'.[61] According to Gillian Beer, 'the arrival of thermo-dynamics and "the ether" gave a quite new "scientific" valency' to possibilities of materially evoking 'lost presences'.[62] As I have already noted, Fechner's attempts to give such valency to spiritualist ideas began earlier in the century. Throughout much of his life, as Hugo Wernekke observes in the preface to his translation of *On Life After Death* (in 1914), Fechner attempted 'to bring about a reconciliation, so much needed in our days, of science and religion, by looking not at one side of the universe only, but diligently examining it in its two aspects, the material and spiritual'.[63]

The quantification theory implicit in the idea of sensory thresholds thus suggests that all space is filled with inaudible and invisible spiritual vibra-tions. The idea of nervous energy suggests not only how quantity is converted into qualities, vibrations into sensations just as heat is transformed into light, but also that life continues after death. After death, Fechner proposed, man himself will become vibratory or wave-like, travelling harmoniously through sky and sea:

> Then he will feel the waves of light and sound not only as they strike his eyes and ears, but as they glide along in the oceans of air and of ether; he will feel not only the breathing of the wind and the heaving of the sea against his body bathing in them, but float along through air and sea himself. [...] The waves of that life [to come] shall move in harmony and union with the very waves of light and sound. (*LD*, 60–1)

The vibratory paradigm set out by physicists was developed by theorists of supernatural phenomena, as this section has shown, though this was not a one-way direction of influence from science to spiritualism; Fechner attempted to support his spiritual beliefs with his scientific experiments. However, the pleasurable ways in which boundaries seem to collapse for such spiritualists – between self and world, inner and outer space – in some situations seem to have become painful, or to be experienced as noise in contrast to the sense of 'harmony and union' with light and sound waves. The experience of hearing and feeling beyond the sensory thresholds, of transcending limits, may have been felt as exhilarating, as thrilling, and also threatening.

Sensitivity and suffering

Sensitive or over-stimulated nerves increasingly seemed to underpin pathological conditions around the turn of the nineteenth century, as my last chapter considered, although stimulation – within limits – could also apparently retain pleasurable and medicinal qualities. Later in the century emphasis began to shift away from excessive stimulation toward a heightened sensitivity to that which lies beyond the normal range of the senses, beyond the zero point: the extrasensory. Whereas scientific spiritualists tended to promote an optimistic view of spiritualism, certain literary authors provided critiques, focusing on the negative aspects of extrasensory vibration and the dangers of hypersensitivity. Responses to the idea of extrasensory sensitivity include George Eliot's 'The Lifted Veil' and Florence McLandburgh's 'The Automaton Ear', both narrated in the first person by unhealthy characters who believe themselves to be exceptionally sensitive to the extrasensory realm. With these short stories and with reference to other sensitive characters, including Mr Fairlie and Count Fosco in Wilkie Collins's novel *The Woman in White*, and Dorian Gray in Oscar Wilde's *The Picture of Dorian Gray*, I will next develop my investigation into the nineteenth-century concern with the growing dangers of vibration, which could be experienced as painful, sometimes even persecutory, as well as pleasurable. Spiritualist mediums and others in contact with otherworldly vibrations were typically female, and while these male figures accordingly cultivate a passive, receptive kind of feminine sensitivity, as I will go on to consider, vibration seems to pose a particular threat to the male body.

As Pamela Thurschwell has observed, telepathic and spiritualist reconceptualizations of the borders of individual consciousness were at times transgressive, redefining sexual ties between people in opposition to the norms of marriage, for instance. Séances became sites for contact between men and women, and while the goal of the Society for Psychical Research was to communicate without physical contact, to scientifically prove the workings of telepathy, seemingly making it 'safe from a distracting erotics' between men, in particular, 'the potential nature of the intimacy circumscribed by thought transference is not containable in these terms'.[64] Like Thurschwell, I will next map out how telepathic intimacy could signify 'dangerous proximity' and influence – as well as utopic pleasures of instantaneous communication (comparable to Coleridge's in the late eighteenth century) – through a range of literary texts, focusing specifically here on the vibratory quality of such relations. Later chapters will further explore the role of both male and female mediums, taking up the case of Daniel Paul Schreber in particular, and his documentation of his experiences of vibration as both intensely pleasurable and painful in *Memoirs of My*

Nervous Illness (in Chapter Three), and the exemplary feminine medium, Katie Fox (in Chapter Five).

In many ways Latimar, the first person narrator of Eliot's 'The Lifted Veil', is typical as a sensitive figure with an ability to detect spiritual frequencies of vibration. He is delicate and becomes unwell, he is poetic and he trembles, he is sensitive to everyday sounds as well as to otherworldly vibrations. Eliot engaged closely with the scientific and spiritualist ideas of her time, as the various studies of her wide-ranging interests have shown,[65] so her characterization of Latimar, with its emphasis on his pathological, effeminate suffering, can be understood as an informed critique of the semi-scientific spiritualist movement. Her partner, the science writer and philosopher George Henry Lewes, went on to borrow Fechner's metaphor of a curved line, used in *The Soul Life of Plants* and *Zend-Avesta* to explain that the objective and subjective, matter and mind are aspects of the same reality, as the same line can be viewed as convex or concave.[66] So we could speculate that Eliot probably knew of Fechner's work, but numerous scientists, spiritualists, psychologists and medical writers discussed ideas of waves and frequencies and nervous energy, of the thresholds of sensitivity, and sensitivity as a pathological condition; my purpose is less with tracing direct connections between writers such as Fechner and Eliot than in identifying corresponding themes in their work as part of the wider, radiating context of what Eliot referred to as a 'great wave of spiritualism'.[67]

George Levine has discussed how the 'ideal and the real were fused' for Eliot, as for scientists including Lewes and John Tyndall who preached that reality was 'inaccessible to mere common sense'.[68] Subjective experience or empirical observations were useful to poets and novelists as well as scientists in so far as they could provide a basis for intuitions and complex hypotheses, for a more unitary theory of an 'extra-sensible' world. Levine argues that *Middlemarch* and *Daniel Deronda* extend empiricism and literary realism 'by tentatively affirming an intuited but largely verifiable reality'.[69] The search for extra-sensible unity is itself described as unitary in *Middlemarch*, where a 'raw cocoon' is imaginable as a kind of energy with multiple qualities, various textures, for which the singular, 'European mind' is looking:

> This great seer [Bichat, a French physiologist] did not go beyond the consideration of the tissues as ultimate facts in the living organism, marking the limit of anatomical analysis; but it was open to another mind to say, have not these structures some common basis from which they have all started, as your sarsnet, gauze, net, satin and velvet from the raw cocoon? Here would be another light, as of oxy-hydrogen, showing the very grain of things, and revising all former explanations. Of this sequence to Bichat's work, already vibrating along many currents of the European mind, Lydgate was enamoured; he longed to demonstrate

the more intimate relations of living structure and help to define men's thought more accurately after the true order.[70]

Lydgate, a physician who is working on 'The Physical Basis of Mind' (the title of the third volume of Lewes's *Problems of Life and Mind*, featuring Fechner's metaphor), wants to reach beyond 'the limit of anatomical analysis', to identify the invisible, primary basis from which all else in the living organism (including the brain) is derived. Bichat's work is in turn a kind of primal energy, 'vibrating along many currents of the European mind'. It is as though the light, 'showing the very grain of things', would make the invisible present as a direct sensation, demonstrating the objective aspect of the subjective, the extra-sensible matter of mind, even the thought of 'men's thought' itself. In 'The Lifted Veil', however, the sensitivity needed for scientific vision becomes pathological.

Latimar narrates his childhood and upbringing, before describing the development of his spiritual sensitivities. He was 'a very sensitive child', especially to sound, a sensitivity that seems both painful and pleasurable:

> I remember still the mingled trepidation and delicious excitement with which I was affected by the tramping of the horses on the pavement in the echoing stables, by the loud resonance of the grooms' voices, by the booming bark of the dogs as my father's carriage thundered under the archway of the courtyard, by the din of the gong as it gave notice of luncheon and dinner. The measured tramp of soldiery which I sometimes heard – for my father's house lay near a county town where there were large barracks – made me sob and tremble; and yet when they were gone past, I longed for them to come back again. (*LV*, 5)

Latimar's sensitivity is located as a 'deficiency' and 'excess' in a phrenological examination of his brain by the tutor Mr Letherall, who then provides private tuition in scientific subjects in an attempt to remedy his defects. But at the age of 16, when Latimar is sent away to complete his education at Geneva, his poetic nature seems irrepressible. He spends his time in a 'sense of exultation, as if from a draught of delicious wine, at the presence of Nature in all her awful loveliness' (*LV*, 7). Latimar here resembles a poet like Coleridge, who as we saw in the last chapter was sensitive to nature, especially to its sounds and to the sublime wind. Latimar feels unable, however, to produce poetry. He says that despite his 'early sensibility to nature' he had no voice; his 'poet's sensibility [...] finds no vent but in silent tears on the sunny bank, where the noonday light sparkles on the water, or in an inward shudder at the sounds of harsh human tones' (7). This seems to echo the problem set out in the early stages of Coleridge's 'Dejection', with the 'unimpassioned grief / Which finds no natural outlet, no relief'.[71] Sensitivity becomes pathologically palpable rather than audible, the whole body vibrating when Latimar feels an 'inward shudder', when the noise of soldiers trampling made him 'sob and tremble', he was in 'a state of tremor' or 'tremulous exultation', 'cold and trembling'; a 'severe illness' results in being sent home. It is during his recovery that he experiences his first prophetic 'vision', of the city of Prague, which his father has told him they will visit in the future, when he is well enough to travel. He compares his newfound visionary ability to a vision such as Homer's of Troy or Dante's of hell, explaining it as a manifestation of his poetic sensibility now that illness could have 'given a firmer tension to my nerves', much as the painful sublime for Burke and other medical writers and poets in the eighteenth and early nineteenth century could stimulate the nerves. Again, such a stimulus is vibratory: 'I sent my thoughts ranging over my world of knowledge, in the hope that they would find some object which would send a reawakening vibration through my slumbering genius' (11).

Fiction and fact appear to meet where Latimar has read about the 'subtilising or exalting influence of some diseases on the mental powers' in 'genuine biographies'. His vision may also be a version of the scientific intuition of extra-sensible reality. Latimar sees himself as possessing enhanced mental powers, and might have found authority for such a judgement in the scientific literature itself; the science of sensitivity worked with the idea that some people are more sensitive than others. Fechner's *Elements of Psychophysics* points out that sensitivity is variable, for example that the discrimination between 1209 and 1210 vibrations per second demands a 'well-practiced ear', such as a violinist's (*EP*, 217). Through 'the method of average error' this is made compatible with statistical calculations based on very large amounts of data. *On Life After Death* explains that variabilities in sensitivity can also be found between a 'mind harmoniously developed' and 'certain abnormal conditions of the mind – in clairvoyance or mental disorder' (*LD*, 47). Variabilities are on the same scale or spectrum, differing quantitatively rather than absolutely. Observing that Eliot challenges any clear opposition between scientific rationality and poetic feeling, Jane Wood notes that absolute differences dissolve into a continuum:

> Latimer's diseased perception is made explicit in the text in language which draws attention to its slippage from, or its superfluity of, an implied norm. We are constantly reminded of an "excess" of sensitivity, passion, imagination, susceptibility, and of "superadded consciousness", and equally, of a "deficiency" of physique, of social skills, and of the power of self-regulation.[72]

For spiritualists, medical writers and psychologists throughout the later nineteenth century, abnormal conditions of mind in which a person could be especially sensitive included the trance states of mesmerism and hypnotism, hysteria and other kinds of mental and physical disorders usually involving the nervous system. Telepathic communication was frequently explained in terms of sympathetic resonance between nervous 'sensitives', as I have mentioned (in the section on 'Brain waves' above). The preoccupation with extra-sensitivity is also evident in the first volume of the *Proceedings of the Society for Psychical Research*, which set out as its third objective an inquiry into 'certain organisations called "sensitive,"' and whether they 'possess any power of perception beyond a highly exalted sensibility of the recognised sensory organs'.[73] According to *On Life After Death*, in sensitive or 'abnormal conditions of the mind' a person may be able to 'visit' the future which, like the past, appears to be somewhere:

> Even in this life it may happen, though very rarely, that the light of consciousness wanders from the narrow body into the larger body, and returning home gives information about things which are taking place far away in space, or things which, springing from present circumstances, will take place in some future time. [...] Sometimes [...] some part of our larger body is impressed with such uncommon intensity as to draw our consciousness, for a while, away from our narrower body, to rise above the threshold in an unusual place. Hence the wonders of clairvoyance, of presentiments, and dreams. [...] However, all these things are no signs of a healthy life. (*LD*, 100–1)

The place in 'The Lifted Veil' is Prague, which Latimar was to visit in the future, and which seems to be trapped in the past. The dead are nearly alive, the living dead, where the statues 'with their ancient garments and their saintly crowns, seemed to me the real inhabitants and owners of this place, while the busy, trivial men and women, hurrying to and fro, were a swarm of ephemeral visitants infesting it for a day' (*LV*, 9). Latimar seems able to transcend both space and time, to visit the 'far away' and 'future time', a future lost in the past. After a while there is another kind of collapsing of space, between people. The mental processes of people around him begin to intrude on his own telepathic consciousness,

> like an importunate, ill-played musical instrument, or the loud activity of an imprisoned insect. But this unpleasant sensibility was fitful, and left me moments of rest, when the souls of my companions were once more shut out from me, and I felt a relief such as silence brings to wearied nerves. (*LV*, 13)

All of time and space seems to swarm in on Latimar, who describes the increasingly persecutory sensations as noise. The noise of an 'ill-played musical instrument' is suggestive of the radiant, vibratory energy of nerves which speak as they hear. The 'loud activity of an imprisoned insect' suggests that Latimar's family and friends are the inhabitants of Prague, who 'were a swarm of ephemeral visitants infesting it for a day'. Latimar's wife-to-be, Bertha, is the only person whose 'soul' is still veiled for a while, whose presence 'possessed my senses and imagination like a returning syren melody which had been overpowered for an instant by the roar of threatening waves' (*LV*, 26). In this version of the myth of the syrens – the half women, half winged creatures whose singing lured unwary or non-paranoid sailors onto rocks (now more often spelled 'sirens') – the extra-sensible is an oceanic 'roar':

> Now it was my father, and now my brother, now Mrs Filmore or her husband, and now our German courier, whose stream of thought rushed upon me like a ringing in the ears not to be got rid of. [...] It was like a preternaturally heightened sense of hearing, making audible to one a roar of sound where others find perfect stillness. (*LV*, 18)

The acoustical instrument named after the winged women was invented in 1819 by Cagniard de la Tour, for measuring the vibrations in any tone. (The larger version was developed in the 1870s for use on steamships to give warning signals, acquiring the redoubled resonance with myth that it has today.) As we have seen, the siren was used to demonstrate how frequencies of sound and silence, like colours and heat, exist on the same scale of vibratory energy. The sense of sound depends on the physiological make-up of the ear and nerves, the sympathetic 'strings' which mechanically or unconsciously vibrate in response to certain frequencies, hear-speaking to the brain. In the case of Latimar, however, the sound of the siren is drowned out by noise. He appears to lack thresholds, to feel conscious of everything. Or from another perspective this could more precisely be described as a hallucinatory kind of speak-hearing, as the noise of the medium drowning out the message. As Kittler has put it, 'the very channels through which information must pass emit noise'.[74] Much of the story is ambiguous in this respect, as to whether the vibrations are a product of psychical ability or fantasy, as Wood points out: 'As narrator, he cannot be trusted to distinguish between external reality and internal impression'. Hence his autobiographical narrative slips 'imperceptibly' between a 'record of experience [...] and an absurd and fanciful fiction, whose origins lie in the creative impulse of the nervously susceptible mind'.[75]

Sensitivity to sounds was a cardinal feature of nervous conditions, as Bulstrode's symptom in *Middlemarch* of 'some little nervous shock' (the physician Lydgate's regular diagnosis) indicates where he would not allow his wife to be with him 'alleging nervous susceptibility to sounds and movements'.[76] The quantification of vibration in physics perhaps contributed to this apprehension. Acoustical studies referred to the 'shock' of a noise[77], but also to that of sound in general and of other phenomena including light and heat, as by John Tyndall: 'Millions of millions of shocks are received every second from the calorific waves'.[78] Latimar seems to feel himself suffering from every such shock as a result of his 'wearied nerves', his 'feeble nervous condition' (*LV*, 18). He hears 'all the intermediate frivolities, all the suppressed egoism, all the struggling chaos of puerilities, meanness, vague capricious memories, and indolent make-shift thoughts' (14), as though he hears all the thoughts of all the individuals who together form a swarm, or each of the millions of shocks which together constitute harmony or 'rainbow light' (9, 23). He hears a 'roar' where others find 'stillness' or 'silence', a noise which in *Middlemarch* is described in terms of a sensitivity to 'the very fact of frequency':

> Nor can I suppose that when Mrs. Casaubon is discovered in a fit of weeping six weeks after her wedding, the situation will be regarded as tragic. Some discouragement, some faintness of heart at the new real future which replaces the imaginary, is not unusual, and we do not expect people to be deeply moved by what is not unusual. That element of tragedy which lies in the very fact of frequency, has not yet wrought itself into the coarse emotion of mankind; and perhaps our frames could hardly bear much of it. If we had a keen vision and feeling of all ordinary human life, it would be like hearing the grass grow and the squirrel's heart beat, and we should die of that roar which lies on the other side of silence.[79]

George Eliot's concept of sympathy, of 'community of feeling', is often considered to have been the ethical and artistic foundation for all her major novels. Josephine McDonagh writes that Eliot's understanding of sympathy owed much to the work of the philosopher Ludwig Feuerbach, who argued that what distinguishes men from lower forms of life is their ability to recognize that they are part of a larger group or species that allows a man to 'put himself in the place of another'. McDonagh notes that 'Feuerbach writes at length about his notion of love as a strangely palpable, material thing'.[80] It is a material notion of physiological forms of sympathy that figures so much in eighteenth-century philosophy and poetry, as well as the scientific work of Eliot's contemporaries. Feuerbach wrote of 'a real love, a love which has flesh and blood, which vibrates as an almighty force through all living'.[81] In *Adam Bede*, the beautiful but unsympathetic Hetty is described as an instrument which does not vibrate so readily as others, where 'some of those cunningly-fashioned instruments called human souls have only a very limited range of music, and will not vibrate in the least under a touch that fills others with tremulous rapture or quivering agony'.[82] But as boundaries give way in 'The Lifted Veil' to the extent that distances collapse altogether, Latimar increasingly suffers from his sensitivity to other times, places, and people. This story is critical of the quality of sympathy, when taken to an imaginary extreme of telepathic insight that would be invasive if it were not delusional. It is not simply an inadequate basis for morality in this story, but takes on the horrendous shape of a different kind of objectionable character than the unsympathetic Hetty: the excessively vibrating Latimar. As the narrative wears on, a reader's increasingly alienated sympathy for the narrator is in inverse proportion to Latimar's imaginary insight into the minds of others, as a reader's insight into the mind of Latimar is imaginary. 'Are you unable to give me your sympathy – you who read this? Are you unable to imagine this double consciousness at work within me, flowing on like two parallel streams that never mingle their waters and blend into a common hue?' (*LV*, 21).

Feminine tremblings

By the end of the century numerous sensitive characters in fiction seem to have undergone the suffering involved in extrasensory perception, or in delusions of such perception, and to have become despicable or even evil, illustrating the growing sense that spiritualist practices could be dangerous. 'At the *fin de siècle*,' comments Pamela Thurschwell, 'hopeful cultural fantasies of the possibilities of telepathic contact were balanced by an anxious sense that someone or something might get inside one's mind and control one's actions'.[83] In particular, the threatening male figure with telepathic powers became a staple of popular fiction, such as Count Dracula in Bram Stoker's novel, or Svengali in George Du Maurier's *Trilby*, or Count Fosco, the key villain of Wilkie Collins's *The Woman in White*, who similarly uses his superior sensitivities to telepathically penetrate and control his victims. 'The Lifted Veil' gives us the first person perspective of the sensitive character who feels himself a suffering victim, whereas the villainous Fosco – whose powers of sensitivity are depicted as unambiguously real – is introduced to us by Marian, who is shortly to become one of his victims. He seems at first, however, to be curiously fragile and feminine, with a particular sensitivity to sounds:

> He is as noiseless in a room as any of us women, and more than that, with all his look of unmistakable mental firmness and power, he is as nervously sensitive as the weakest of us. He starts at chance noises as inveterately as Laura herself. He winced and shuddered yesterday, when Sir Percival beat one of the spaniels, so that I felt ashamed of my own want of tenderness and sensibility by comparison with the Count.[84]

In his sensitivity to sounds, Fosco resembles not only Laura but other characters in the novel, including the appalling Mr Fairlie who uses his self-professed illness to shirk all responsibility and to justify his relentlessly selfish demands. With his various feminine characteristics, including his 'effeminately small' feet, Mr Fairlie interrupts Mr Hartright's first attempt to communicate with him by asking him to speak more quietly: due to 'the wretched state of my nerves, loud sound of any kind is indescribable torture to me'.[85] But Count Fosco seems to exercise a far more complete power, over animals as well as humans, as the narrative soon begins to indicate. Though his 'nerves are so finely strung that he starts at chance noises', he is able to make a savage bloodhound crawl meekly back to his kennel by putting his hand on the dog's head, looking him 'straight in the eyes', and talking to him contemptuously.[86] We soon learn that with the assistance of his curious mesmeric powers he is able to exercise similar influence over his wife and Sir Percival, Laura and Marian herself, whose nerves he seems to palpably vibrate: 'His eyes seemed to reach my inmost soul through the thickening obscurity of the twilight. His voice trembled along every nerve in my body'.[87] Whereas the hideousness of characters like Latimar and Mr Fairlie lies in their delusion (or probable delusion, as Latimar's case remains slightly ambiguous) that they are somehow especially nervous and sensitive to sounds, possibly even sensitive enough to receive telepathic communications, it is Fosco's undoubted ability to overcome the boundaries between himself and others that is depicted in this novel as hideous and threatening. These sensitive figures are all depicted as abhorrent in their different ways, and they share certain characteristics, including sensitivity to sounds and a tendency towards a certain femininity. Latimar acknowledges a sense of his own unmanliness, which takes the form in his case of a 'half-womanish, half-ghostly beauty', which 'nothing but the belief that it was a condition of poetic genius would have reconciled me to' (LV, 14).

The description of Fosco's nerves as 'finely strung' is of course familiar, and it is a quality that is closely associated with femininity. In the previous century the sensitivity of the aeolian harp's strings to the wind made it especially appropriate as a model for the allegedly delicate nerves of a woman, in Coleridge's poetry and elsewhere. Though Coleridge was keen to use the strings of the harp as a model for his own poetically sensitive nerves, as we saw in the last chapter, and though he became increasingly careful to distinguish the poetic sensitivity of genius from 'effeminacy'[88], he had himself likened the harp to a 'maid' in his poem 'The Aeolian Harp'. The harp in this poem is 'by the desultory breeze caressed, / Like some coy maid half yielding to her lover'.[89] In Friedrich Schiller's 'Honor to Woman', the harp is similarly 'wooed' by a gentle wind; she quivers and trembles to the slightest touch:

> Alive, as the wind-harp, how lightly soever
> If wooed by the zephyr, to music will quiver,
> Is woman to hope and to fear;
> Ah, tender one! Still at the shadow of grieving,

How quiver the chords – how thy bosom is heaving –
How trembles they glance through the tear![90]

The scenes of seduction set out in these poems follow a long tradition in which the sympathetic vibration of strings – one string causes another, tuned to the same pitch, to tremble – has served as a metaphor for attraction between lovers.[91] In the case of the aeolian harp, the wind seems to symbolize the active male principle while the sensitive, receptive and responsive strings are female. If the breeze seduces the harp in 'The Aeolian Harp' and 'Honor to Woman' then the more violent vibratory motions of the wind in 'Dejection' could be seen to 'make love' with it in a less tender and more instrumental way. The painful pleasure undergone by the female instrument seems to turn it into a reproductive device – of poetry as a kind of life.

But we have also seen the shift from a valued feminine sensibility toward the pathologization of trembling women. Many feminine, 'finely strung' characters in nineteenth-century literature continue to tremble and quiver, to suffer from the vibratory movements that were increasingly associated with hysterical women (see above, p. 29). Even the heroic Mr Hartright in *The Woman in White*, in those less masculine, weaker moments belonging to his period of immaturity in the earlier stages of the novel, suffers nervous tremors. After he has left his beloved Laura, and before he sets off on his manly expedition to Central America, the unhealthy, overly sensitive condition of his nerves is indicated by his quivering movements: 'A momentary nervous contraction quivered about his lips and eyes [...] the same momentary spasm crossed his face again'.[92] Like Fosco, who resembles Laura when he 'starts at chance noises', Hartright's nervous quiver seems to sympathetically echo her own 'sensitive lips' which 'are subject to a slight nervous contraction'.[93] Marian, the other heroic and mainly non-feminine character, similarly has momentary sensitivities to sound, despite her usually unshaken nerves, as when she explores the grounds of Sir Percival Glyde's property and hears a whimpering dog: 'I listened intently for a moment, and heard a low, sobbing breath [...]. My nerves are not easily shaken by trifles, but on this occasion I started to my feet in a fright'.[94]

By the end of the nineteenth century, as we have seen, sensitivity was widely considered an unhealthy sign of a lack of manliness, rather than of poetic genius. Coleridge had already negotiated a period of transition through the shift from pleasure to pain, from harmonious seduction to violent convulsions in 'The Aeolian Harp' and 'Dejection', but at his point there was still room for ambivalence. For Coleridge, pain could be thera-peutic, a means of recovery for the sensitive genius, whereas the earlier signs of Latimar's fancied poetic nature seem lost to his overly feminine sensitivity. As Jane Wood comments:

Poetic sensibility [...] is everywhere construed as a pathological departure from a standard of male health. [...] Since the early decades of the nineteenth century there had been a change in real terms from a culture which had associated sensitivity and delicacy with civilised refinement to one in which economic, familial, and imperialist demands for a more robust manliness had come to view those same qualities with derision.[95]

In the nineteenth century male sensitivity was increasingly derided, while another variant of 'poetic sensibility' also emerged in that nervousness could now endow its victims with a heightened consciousness of extra-sensory reality. As female nerves were usually considered more delicate than those of men, women were considered more likely to be sensitive both to actual stimuli in the external world (especially sounds) and to supernatural vibrations – or to delusions of such. Spiritualists considered women to be especially apt for mediumship because they were innately passive, receptive vessels, weak in the masculine attribute of will-power, as historians of spiritualism have observed.[96] However, as Wood goes on to point out, nervous states could also render women and 'effeminate' men 'unable to distinguish between internal (impressionistic) and external (material) experience'[97], which the predominantly male medical profession had the power to determine, the view being that clairvoyance was more pathological than prophetic. Medical men denounced the trance state in which a person could be especially sensitive 'as a form of hysteria', as Judith Walkowitz similarly observes, 'to which women, given their inherently unstable reproductive physiology, were peculiarly liable'. Medical critics, alarmed by the growing popularity of spiritualism, 'caricatured spiritualists as crazy women and feminized men engaged in superstitious, popular, and fraudulant practices'.[98] Alex Owen notes that while some men culti-vated what they called 'mind passivity', undermining the strength of mind that differentiated them from women, critics were quick to point to the supposed 'effeminacy' of male mediums like Daniel Dunglas Home, which 'was enough to cast doubt on his moral integrity'.[99] It is in this context, then, that George Eliot and Wilkie Collins provide a critical view of the deluded, hysterical male (Latimar, Fairlie) as well as the sensitive male with actual extrasensory powers (Fosco) – both of whom are 'feminized'.

It is by now standard to observe that the late nineteenth century was a period of heightened anxieties about sexuality. *The Woman in White* with its sexually transgressive encounters (between the feminine male Fosco and the masculine Marian, for instance, as well as the more conventional sympa-thetic vibrations between the heterosexual, and finally married couple, Walter and Laura[100]) seems to pave the way. Pamela Thurschwell explores in depth the intersections between *fin de siècle* anxieties about sexuality and the kinds of communication promoted by psychical researchers, which new communication technologies helped to make conceivable (while I have mainly discussed musical instruments the role of auditory technologies such as wireless will feature briefly in the next section and much more fully in Chapter Three). Telepathy generated intense concerns, Thurschwell suggests, about the penetrability of the mind by the mental powers of others, about suggestibility and influence – which is notoriously central to Oscar Wilde's best known work. It is perhaps Dorian Gray who provides the most obvious illustration of a feminine, sensitive male, whose finely strung nerves are powerfully influenced – vibrated – by another male: the immoral aesthete Lord Henry. Again, of course, the influence of vibration is shown to be dangerous, and the sensitive Dorian becomes another villainous character with supernatural powers. When they first meet, the few words that Henry speaks begin to move Dorian: they 'touched some secret chord that had never been touched before, but that he felt was now vibrating and throbbing to curious impulses' (15). From Henry's perspective, Dorian is like a musical instrument: 'Talking to him was like playing upon an exquisite violin. He answered to every touch and thrill of the bow' (29). Again here we have the image of the feminine strings as sensitive and responsive, vibrating to 'every touch'. The mechanics of sympathetic vibration – the distant touch between musical strings – precedes the communication technologies that are the focus of Thurschwell's work, informed as it is by Kittler's. William Cohen proposes that the novel's aestheticism comes largely from its expansion of 'the field of sensory experience well beyond the verbal and visual to the senses classically ranked low'. Henry's initial vibratory infection of Dorian through the ear, the distant telepathic touch, is both verbal and palpable – an 'auditory corruption' that then 'expresses itself visually: cast out from his soul and incarnated in the painting, the sinfulness assumes visible form'.[101] Both beautiful and sinful, Dorian is of course far from the conventional masculine hero of the nineteenth-century novel. It is in the activity of one male vibrating another that a certain kind of sensuality seems most explicitly bodily.

The 'effeminate' male figures in these stories have been widely discussed in critical literature, not least in terms of anxieties about 'homosexuality' and scientific discourses which defined it as unnatural and pathological.[102] Alan Sinfield has argued that it was only in the nineteenth century that 'effeminacy' was associated with same-sex desire, an association that became established with Wilde. He observes the shift from the eighteenth-century perception of sensitivity as a valued characteristic of civilized cultivation to the new emphasis on manliness around the mid-nineteenth century, a shift accompanied by emerging anxieties that sensitivity – now seen as a sign of effeminacy – could also entail homosexuality. The association between effeminacy and homosexuality was of course not inevitable and was often resisted, but was also increasingly asserted by sexologists such as Karl Heinrich Ulrichs and Richard Krafft-Ebing who in the 1860s began to promote the theory that gay men were women trapped in male bodies.[103] The state went on to define and outlaw sexual acts between men as 'gross indecency' (in 1885), making judgements about its danger to the moral well-being of the nation.[104] In this context, then, it is likely that the pathologization of feminine, sensitive men – men who are vibrated – contributed to an increased anxiety that the male body should not be penetrated.

Eliot, Collins, and Wilde among other literary and scientific writers depict characters with vibratory powers as feminine, whether such characters are able to vibrate other male figures with their telepathic capacities (like Count Fosco, who vibrates the masculine Marian), are sensitive to such telepathic vibrations (like Dorian Gray), or may be suffering from pathological delusions of special sensitivity (like Latimar). All such figures seem to share certain characteristics: they are poetic or artistic (depicted in contrast to scientific men like Charles Meunier in 'The Lifted Veil' or Alan Campbell in *The Picture of Dorian Gray*), they are nervous or finely strung, and they are especially sensitive to sounds, not merely hearing but responsively vibrating. The use of stringed instruments as models for such sensitive figures as Dorian – 'an exquisite violin' – also ties in with their femininity; as mechanical objects with no (masculine) will or even life of their own they can only respond passively. I will next look at another kind of sensitive figure, whose sensitivity is enhanced not by his mechanical femininity so much as a prosthetic kind of technology, focusing on the short story 'The Automaton Ear'. This story intensifies the tension between opposing inter-pretations of extrasensory vibrations: Is this the universe, or my own ear? Is this a hallucination, or an otherworldly vibration?

'The Automaton Ear'

'The Automaton Ear', narrated by a professor who believes he can tune into vibrations of the past, is in some ways very similar to 'The Lifted Veil'. Both narrators are aware of scientific and spiritualist theories about sensi-tivity and vibration, and both believe themselves able to hear extrasensory frequencies, which become increasingly noisy and persecutory. The profes-sor's sensitivity, however, is more technological.

His invention of the automaton ear was inspired by the following paragraph, which he reads one day in the woods:

As a particle of the atmosphere is never lost, so sound is never lost. A strain of music or a simple tone will vibrate in the air forever and ever, decreasing according to a fixed ratio. The diffusion of the agitation extends in all directions, like the waves in a pool, but the ear is unable to detect it beyond a certain point. It is well known that some individuals can distinguish sounds which to others under precisely similar circumstances are wholly lost. Thus the fault is not in the sound itself, but in our organ of hearing, and a tone once in existence is always in existence. (*AE*, 8)

Sound is a form of energy, as where Fechner writes that every 'moment of conscious life produces a circle of actions around it, just as the briefest tone that seems gone in a second, produces a similar circle, which carries the tone into endless space' (*LD*, 55). The professor in McLandburgh's tale, though the information is familiar to him, is suddenly stricken with a desire to hear 'all the sounds ever uttered, ever born' which must be 'floating in the air *now*' (*AE*, 8), and so he begins work on the listening device. This is a prosthetic instrument, an ear-trumpet that is an improvement of 'My own ear' which is already 'exceedingly acute' (10). All it needs do is amplify those sounds that lie beyond the threshold of audibility. Fechner's suggestion of this possibility is in *Elements of Psychophysics*, which poses the question as to 'whether the limit of audibility of high tones has already been reached, or if still higher tones might not be audible with greater amplification' (*EP*, 216).

Like Latimar, the professor seems to engage with some of the scientific views of the time, as indicated by the 'careful study of acoustics' which he carries out in preparation for his work on the instrument. As though immersed in amplified sounds even at this stage, 'I buried myself among volumes on the philosophy of sound' (*AE*, 10). He eventually succeeds in improving the instrument 'so far as to be able to set it very accurately for any particular period, thus rendering it sensible only to sounds of that time, all heavier and fainter vibrations being excluded' (17). This 'particular period' is a period of time, a year, a day, or a second; a periodic frequency which the professor is able to set the automaton ear to hear. This ear hears and speaks, amplifies the sounds of the past, 'thus rendering it sensible'. Once perfected, he is able to hear all the sounds of joy and sorrow from human history, including the triumphant song of Miriam after the passage through the Red Sea.

In 'The Automaton Ear' the object, the sound of the past, becomes increasingly loud, while in 'The Lifted Veil' the subject, Latimar, becomes increasingly sensitive. Latimar's sensitivity is poetic, feminine and pathological; the professor's dependent on a 'device'. Spiritualists similarly used technological devices – from simple mechanical contraptions to specialist laboratory instruments – in their search for objective evidence of spiritual manifestations, devoid of 'interventions' from unreliable feminine mediums or deluded investigators, as Richard Noakes has shown.[105] While human mediums were themselves frequently compared to sensitive musical instruments (more to follow below in Chapter Three), there was some doubt that this kind of human device should be relied upon. William Carpenter, who attempted along with other physiologists and psychiatrists to pathologize spiritualism, warned in 1876 that the problem with most investigators of spiritualism was their 'ignorance of *the nature of their instruments of research*; putting as much faith in tricky girls or women, as they do in their thermometers or electroscopes'.[106] As well as combating the unreliability of the human medium, instruments far surpassed the limits of the sensory thresholds. The spiritualist investigator, William Crookes, argued that what qualified the 'scientific man' was his use of delicate 'instrumental aids' which surpassed the human senses and provided 'experimental proof' of spiritual phenomena.[107]

One of the best-known inventors to attempt to develop a device that could amplify the vibrations of spirits was Thomas Edison, inventor of the phonograph. In an interview in *Scientific American* in 1920 he claimed to have been building an apparatus to see if spiritual communications are possible, an apparatus that he suggested would be more sensible (in both senses) than human mediums: 'If this is ever accomplished it will be accomplished, not by any occult, mystifying, mysterious, or weird means, such as are employed by so-called "mediums", but by scientific methods'.[108] Edison hoped to design a delicate, sensitive 'valve', capable of amplifying spiritual vibrations, which followed the same logic as his earlier inventions, as Anthony Enns points out.[109] In his article 'The Perfected Phonograph' (1888), for example, Edison claimed that the phonograph is more sensitive than the human ear:

> [W]hile the deepest tone that our ears are capable of recognizing is one containing 16 vibrations a second, the phonograph will record 10 vibrations or less, and can then raise the pitch until we hear a repro-duction from them. Similarly, vibrations above the highest rate audible to the ear can be recorded on the phonograph and then reproduced by lowering the pitch, until we actually hear the record of those inaudible pulsations.[110]

Enns provides further examples of how sound technologies 'promised unlimited levels of sound amplification' which could 'be extended to the spirit world, as the voices of the dead were also understood as real, yet inaudible vibrations in the atmosphere'.[111] Edison's earlier experiments were also themselves depicted and elaborated on in the science-fictional tale by Villiers de L'Isle-Adam, *Tomorrow's Eve*, in 1886. The central invention dreamed up here is a perfect female android, with golden phonographs to serve as her lungs and voice, but the story begins with Edison's regret that he was not around at the beginning of humanity to record the sublime and beautiful and 'important speeches of men and gods, down through the ages'. He goes on to dream not merely of passively capturing sounds but of chasing them: 'I have this little spark ... which is to sound what the greyhound is to the tortoise. It could give the sounds a start of fifty centuries and yet chase them down in the gulfs of outer space'.[112]

The premiss of this story is anticipated in 'The Automaton Ear', as Steven Connor notes, which also works with the idea that sound continues to diminish for ever, becoming quieter and quieter and further away.[113] 'The Automaton Ear', however, casts doubt on the sensitivity of the listening device, which may be no more reliable than the human medium. The professor becomes increasingly uncertain as to whether his ear trumpet does indeed amplify the sounds of the external world, or just the sounds of himself. He overhears a child repeat the rumour that 'the professor ain't just right in his head', which keeps returning from the past, 'ringing in my ears until an idea flashed upon me even more terrifying than death itself. How did I know that I was *not* insane? How did I know that my great invention might be only a hallucination of my brain?' (28) Similarly, in 'The Lifted Veil', Latimar asks, 'But was it a power? Might it not rather be a disease – a sort of intermittent delirium concentrating my energy of brain into moments of unhealthy activity, and leaving my saner hours all the more barren?' (*LV*, 12)

Medical doctors and spiritualists alike often considered nervous illness a precondition of spiritualist experiences, as I have mentioned. Where medical men differed was in their view of these not as sensations of the external world but as hallucinations, illusions, and delusions. It is for this reason that psychical researchers such as Edmund Gurney, in *Phantasms of the Living*, attempted carefully to distinguish between sensations of spirits as opposed to the subject's 'own form or voice'.[114] Medical men similarly attempted to determine the origin of such experiences, the nervous patient being unable to distinguish between external fact and her own inventions, though they were far more likely to consider such experiences as pathological fantasies. Latimar and the professor are accordingly depicted as unwell in Eliot's and McLandburgh's tales, which are held together by a tension or suspension between these opposing interpretations of the extrasensory sensations (as psychical/spiritual, or as fantasy), both of which remain just about possible, and between which the stories waver, or vibrate, without quite collapsing into resolution. In another short story, Sheridan Le Fanu's 'The Familiar', Dr Hesselius attempts at the outset to classify between different cases of supernatural experiences on the basis of a 'primary distinction between the subjective and the objective', though this story similarly refrains from any clear resolution. He explains firstly that some cases of alleged 'supernatural impressions' are simply illusions caused by 'diseased brain or nerves', while others are indeed 'spiritual agencies, exterior to themselves', and then introduces a third category:

Others, again owe their sufferings to a mixed condition. The interior sense, it is true, is opened; but it has been and continues open by the action of disease. This form of disease may, in one sense, be compared to the loss of the scarf-skin, and a consequent exposure of surfaces for whose excessive sensitiveness nature has provided a muffling. [...] But in the case of the brain, and the nerves immediately connected with its functions and its sensuous impressions, the cerebral circulation undergoes periodically that vibratory disturbance, which, I believe, I have satisfactorily examined and demonstrated in my manuscript essay, A. 17.[115]

As we have seen, Latimar attempted to fit himself into this third category of a 'mixed condition', his illness serving to lift the veil between his consciousness and extrasensory reality. Illness operates similarly in many other stories, such as 'The Wireless' by Rudyard Kipling, in which tuberculosis allows Shaynor to tune in like a radio to the signals of the dead. In 'The Familiar', in contrast, the reality or otherwise of Barton's supernatural experiences is left an ambiguous mystery (fitting into that other category of Tzvetan Todorov's uncanny[116]). Similarly, for a while at least, in both 'The Lifted Veil' and 'The Automaton Ear' the narrators register the impossibility of telling the difference between a sensation and hallucination, the definition of which is a seemingly real perception of something not actually present. Latimar is unable to trust that his normal sensations are of reality, that he is not dreaming: 'I felt a dizzy sense of unreality in what my eye rested on; I grasped the bell convulsively, like one trying to free himself from nightmare, and rang it twice' (*LV*, 12). The possibility that the automaton ear is useless occurs to the professor, that the sounds he had heard were 'merely the creation of my diseased fancy, and the instrument I had handled useless metal (*AE*, 29). And so he tests it on an aged deaf woman, Mother Flinse. As she raises the trumpet to her ear she appears to him as 'some mummy that had been withering for a thousand years'.

> Suddenly it was convulsed as if by a galvanic shock, then the shriveled features seemed to dilate, and a great light flashed through them, transforming them almost into the radiance of youth; a strange light as of some seraph had taken possession of the wrinkled old frame and looked out at the gray eyes, making them shine with unnatural beauty. No wonder the dumb countenance reflected a brightness inexpressible, for the Spirit of Sound had just alighted with silvery wings upon a silence of seventy years. (*AE*, 35)

The life of the sounds of the past seems to give life to the life of the present, as though there is revitalising, electrical energy in the sound itself. Sound seems to give life to the inorganic, to the automaton ear, as the professor grows to love it 'not alone as a piece of mechanism for the transmission of sound, but like a living thing' (39–40).

The professor's and Latimar's sensitivity seem to pass similar tests, when in 'The Lifted Veil' the doctor, Meunier, brings Bertha's dead maid back to life with a blood transfusion. Latimar's suspicions of Bertha appear, finally, to be sensitive, not paranoid, when she gasps: 'You mean to poison your husband ... the poison is in the black cabinet ... I got it for you ... you laughed at me, and told lies about me behind my back, to make me disgusting ... because you were jealous ... ' (*LV*, 42). But Mother Flinse seems to the professor, after the 'Spirit of Sound' has transformed her 'shriveled features' to the 'radiance of youth', to transform again when she does not return the instrument to him, to degenerate this time, 'uttering a sound that was neither human or animal, that was not a wail or a scream, but it fell upon my ears like some palpable horror' (*AE*, 36–7). From this moment sound becomes noise, time and space and the other closing in on the professor. 'A savage fierceness' appears to infect him when he rushes to get his ear; as she flees 'the hideous cries of her wordless voice' echo around the tower, its acoustics immersing him from all directions (37). He brutally strangles, and tries to bury her, but having regained the instrument he is tormented by her death-cries, for these are all it will now transmit. The reverberation of her inhuman voice is redoubled, architecturally and technologically, echoing all around the tower and all through the forest before being amplified by his ear. Rather than decreasing in volume, 'the rasping sounds were louder than before'. Mother Flinse's soul, her 'invisible ghost', he realizes, has 'come from the spirit world to gain possession of the prize for which she had given up her life' (40).

Haunted to the point at which the beloved instrument becomes 'an absolute horror', the professor prepares to destroy it (41). A beetle crawls out. The death-cries were the amplified sounds of its wings. That sound becomes more and more persecutory through this story, time and space swarming in on the narrator, suggests that what he hears is indeed very close, intimate: himself. Finally, the professor realizes he had been insanely deluded from the beginning – the power of the ear was a fantasy; the sounds were imaginary.

In this story, then, it is the technological rather than the bodily medium that generates noise, interfering with perception of the external world. Earlier my focus was on the technology that provided a model for the bodily medium, on stringed instruments as an image for the nervous system and subjective perception, following out Kittler's and Crary's emphasis on sensations as originating in the mechanics of the body rather than purely in the external world, while here the noise is generated by the automaton ear itself. In my next chapter I will look further at the role of technologies, especially auditory technologies like the telephone and wireless, in mediating information – both as models or metaphors and as extensions of the human body and its sensory powers. In particular, the hallucinations and delusions of the sensitive Daniel Paul Schreber – nervous, poetic, feminine, and technological – illustrate the noise-making capacities of the machine. The spiritualist dream of capturing vibrations, of engineering a controlled kind of access to the realms of extrasensory frequencies in this as in many – but not all – cases goes horribly wrong. In this chapter, I want finally to look back, though, to emphasize the continuing role of older technologies, in contrast to much of the work of Crary and Kittler and other media theorists and historians who focus on the technologies of the nineteenth and twentieth centuries. A little-known poem by a hymn writer, Frances Ridley Havergal, takes the Romantic image of the aeolian harp into the nineteenth-century world of spiritualism, where it continues to figure as a sensitive instrument. Here, though, it operates no longer as a model for the nerves but as an extension, if only briefly, of limited human sensory powers; as a device, like the automaton ear, for detecting extrasensory vibrations. In 'The Message of the Aeolian Harp', written in 1869, spiritual vibrations are a source of pleasure or consolation, rather than pain. To hear the past, to escape the confines of time and space may be disturbing, even horrifying, and also, perhaps, pleasurable. Eleanor believes that though she is widowed the 'music of his life' continues, though 'our poor ears / No longer hear it'. Though his 'life is mute', she asks 'what if all my tuning fail!'[117] Eleanor's friend goes on to describe her harp. It seems a person's 'tuning' may fail, but that the harp is momentarily sensitive. It seems to hear and to speak for the dead, with its 'spirit tones' and 'soul messages'. A low note 'trembled out of silence':

> It seemed to die; but who could say
> Whether or when it passed the border-line
> 'Twixt sound and silence? for no ear so fine
> That it can trace the subtle shades away;
> Like prism-rays prolonged beyond our ken,
> Like memories that fade, we know not how or when.[118]

The sound of 'spirit tones' in this poem passes into silence, beyond the threshold or 'border-line' of the senses. Once again, sound seems to operate here as a kind of energy that fades away beyond one's limited powers of sensitivity, but may continue to exist. There is 'no ear so fine / That it can trace the subtle shades away'. Sound and light seem exchangeable, sound with its 'subtle shades', 'Like prism-rays', and in turn to figure in their vanishing as a kind of memory. It is to hear such vanishing tones that the professor invents his automaton ear in McLandburgh's tale, only to be haunted by the cries of the dead.

CHAPTER THREE

Wires, Rays and Radio Waves

My previous chapter looked at a series of fictional characters who imagine themselves to be especially sensitive to spiritual vibrations. Most of these fictions operate as critiques, ultimately exposing these characters as delusional. The spiritual messages turn out to be noise of the bodily or technological medium. I will next consider in contrast the case of Daniel Paul Schreber, who attempted in his *Memoirs of My Nervous Illness* to convince his readers that the noise is in fact the message.

Physicists used stringed instruments as an image for how the process of perception is subject to interference. Nerves, like strings, generate 'noise'. This chapter observes how physicists and psychiatrists developed this analogy, using wires as well as strings to explain the operation of the nerves, while engineers used nerves to explain the operation of wires. Schreber in turn took up the model of wires in his conception that his nervous system was linked up to a vast network, and indeed to God. By means of this network of nerve-wires, along with wireless communications, spatial and temporal distances – and the distinction between inner and outer reality – collapse entirely: voices from far distances seem intimately connected to oneself; voices originating in oneself seem to come from far distances.

My first section builds on Mark Roberts's observations that Schreber saw his own body and mind as mechanical to argue that his delusions were structured specifically around telecommunications. Roberts notes that Schreber grew up with quasi-mechanical devices, which gradually seemed to take over his very being. In several books his father, Moritz Schreber, a leading physician and pedagogue, described an all-encompassing childcare system involving devices such as the *Geradehalter*, consisting of boards and straps which force the body to sit up straight. Several commentators have discussed these contraptions in their discussions of how Moritz Schreber's dictatorial child-rearing may have contributed to his son's illness.[1] Roberts points out that as a medical scientist Moritz Schreber also engaged with the neuroscience of the time with its focus on the 'electromechanical aspects of brain physiology', which could have introduced to his son the idea that he was a mechanism among mechanisms. Schreber's own education in the late 1850s and the 1860s would have further exposed him to medical, biological and physical technologies and theories, including the work of Gustav Fechner and the Helmholtzian school of biophysics, which applied mathematical and physical mechanics 'to human perception, physiology, and, ultimately, to the entire life process', as we have seen (Chapter Two). Central to this was the theory of the conservation of energy which provided an explanation for the mystery of living things.[2]

Several readers of Schreber's *Memoirs* have observed the importance of modern communication technologies, especially the telephone, radio, and phonograph, in his delusions.[3] In particular, Anthony Enns has observed that spiritualists as well as psychotics like Schreber engaged with the noises produced by sound technologies: 'The strange, unearthly static produced by the telephone and radio, for instance', noises which 'seemed to be real acoustic events yet they did not refer to any original sounds in the outside world'.[4] Enns argues that spiritualist attempts to interpret such noises as messages from the dead reveals 'connections between sound technologies, psychic phenomena and schizophrenic hallucinations which pose a threat to the autonomy and integrity of the listening and speaking subject'.[5] I draw similar parallels between the noises experienced by spiritualists and by the hallucinating Schreber, along with sound engineers and inventors, while also taking a longer historical view. In some ways, then, I imagine Schreber – who judged himself suitably nervous, poetic, mechanical and feminine – to be a later version of Coleridge, who over a century earlier also modelled himself on an auditory mechanism, a stringed instrument characterized as feminine. My previous chapter considered a range of fictional characters who share such characteristics and who also considered themselves sensitive to the spiritual realm, but while such characters tend to operate as critical representations presented by authors who mark their distance from their deluded creations, both Coleridge and Schreber represent themselves in the first person, asking readers to believe in the value and reality of their vibratory sensitivities. Coleridge's sensations of pleasure and pain also seem to prefigure Schreber's, whose special sensitivity, he claimed, gave him access to a universe of vibratory movements that generate sensations of pleasure and sensual delight, or 'voluptuousness', but also made him vulnerable to persecutory noises, to invasion. Schreber experienced a kind of thrilling liberation from bodily and spatial boundaries, partaking in a utopic fantasy of direct and universal communication but also in fears of invasion such as could be imagined to take place during interplanetary war. These I compare with the fantasies and fears of other spiritualists and inventors, particularly those of Nikola Tesla and science fiction writers including H. G. Wells and Frederic Stimson.

Nerve-contact

The opening lines of *Memoirs of My Nervous Illness* are an account of the workings of the nervous system. Schreber's understanding here echoes eighteenth-century associationism – specifically the Hartleyan theory that vibration-sensations in the nerves are the basis for all mental life – and the more recent development of the theory of specific nerve energies, developed in the first half of the nineteenth century (see Chapters One and Two above):

> THE HUMAN SOUL is contained in the nerves of the body; about their physical structure I, as a layman, cannot say more than that they are extraordinarily delicate structures – comparable to the finest filaments – and that the total mental life of a human being rests on their excitability by external impressions. Vibrations are thereby caused in the nerves which produce the sensations of pleasure and pain [...] Part of the nerves is adapted solely for receiving sensory impressions (nerves of sight, hearing, taste and voluptuousness, etc. which are therefore only capable of the sensation of light, sound, heat and cold, of the feeling of hunger, voluptuousness and pain, etc.).[6]

Energy – vibrations in the nerves – is conserved and converted into sensations of light, sound, and so on. Strings, as we have seen, were a model for this activity of the nerves. I will next focus on wires, or what Schreber calls 'filaments', and electrical energy.

As well as pianoforte strings, Helmholtz in *Sensations of Tone* used telegraph wires to explain specific nerve energies, according to which quantity is converted into qualities:

> Nerves have been often and not unsuitably compared to telegraph wires. Such a wire conducts one kind of electric current and no other; it may be stronger, it may be weaker, it may move in either direction; it has no other qualitative differences. Nevertheless, according to the different kinds of apparatus with which we provide its terminations, we can send telegraphic despatches, ring bells, explode mines, decompose water, move magnets, magnetise iron, develop light, and so on. So with the nerves. The condition of excitement which can be produced in them, and is conducted by them, is, so far as it can be recognised in isolated fibres of a nerve, everywhere the same, but when it is brought to various parts

of the brain, or the body, it produces motion [...] and also sensations of light, of hearing, and so forth.[7]

Many scientific writers drew comparisons between nerves and wires in the nineteenth century, as many historical accounts point out. Elizabeth Musselman develops a longer perspective, tracing the links between David Hartley's *Observations on Man* and the development of a general interest in how the nervous system transmits information to the brain, arguing that attempts to construct efficient telegraphic systems built on the knowledge that in a physiological sense, human perception was imperfect. She writes that the 'operators who formed the first line of communication along telegraphic routes required careful supervision, just as the nervous system's sensory errors required supervision by the diligent mind'.[8] Hartley's own work, asserting that nerves are solid not tubular, features what could be considered an early kind of wire in the form of hempen strings. He proposed that electricity, as well as light and heat, is vibratory like sound; its 'motions along hempen strings resemble the motions along the nerves in sensation'.[9]

Comparisons between nerves and wires were drawn in both directions. Laura Otis shows that telegraphy was used to explain the body, arguing that for scientists including Helmholtz, 'the principles of telegraphy revealed the way that the body processed information: in both systems, indistinguishable impulses created by very different causes became meaningful only when received and interpreted'.[10] Scientists often claimed that electrical impulses in the nerves transmit information within the individual's body, just as electricity in wires transmits information between bodies.[11] Further, wires sometimes figured as an extension of the nervous system itself, apparently transcending great distances. Spiritualists took this idea furthest. 'Just as the electric telegraph annihilated spatial and temporal gulfs between continents, so the "celestial telegraph" was upheld as a bridge between this world and the next', writes Richard Noakes, 'and just as photographs, telephones, and phonographs embodied the voices of the distant living, so mediums were seen as instruments that embodied the appearances and utterances of the distant dead'.[12] Schreber saw himself as a kind of medium, his nerves as wires, which was how his psychiatrist and then God and various kinds of spirits formed 'nerve-contact' with him, speaking in 'nerve-language' (*NI*, 54). This is a telephonic development, as the language is audible: 'nerve-contact' and the 'talking of voices' are 'after all only different expressions for one and the same phenomenon' (82). Nerve-wires, also known as 'filaments' and 'threads', are alternatively inserted and withdrawn from his body:

I see these filaments, as it were, from one or more far distant spots beyond the horizon stretching sometimes towards my head, sometimes withdrawing from it. Every withdrawal is accompanied by a keenly felt, at times intense, pain in my head. The threads which are pulled into my head – they are also the carriers of the voices – perform a circular movement in it, best compared to my head being hollowed out from inside with a drill. (*NI*, 273–4)

Coming from 'far distant spots beyond the horizon', the wires drill their way into Schreber's head and turn it into a resonant cavity. From 'an apparently vast distance', the parts of God's nerves which become separated from the rest of God's nerves cry for help. As Roberts points out, Schreber further extends the analogy of signal reception in this Postscript section of his *Memoirs*, where he attributes his special ability to hear hardly audible 'cries of help' to a phenomenon like 'telephoning':

It is presumably a phenomenon like telephoning; the filaments of rays spun out towards my head act like telephone wires; the weak sound of the cries of help coming from an apparently vast distance is received *only by me* in the same way as telephonic communication can only be heard by a person who is on the telephone, but not by a third person who is somewhere between the giving and the receiving end. (277)

This account of telephoning is to explain how Schreber is sensitive to sounds which other people cannot hear at all. The sound of the cries for help, according to Schreber, 'which reaches my own ear – hundreds of times every day – is so definite that it cannot be a hallucination' (189). This line of defence is taken against the view that messages do not come to him from a vast distance, but that he instead 'received his own messages from somewhere else', as Peter Widmer puts it in his psychoanalytic account.[13] As Musselman and Otis have shown, wires were used to emphasize that nerves do not simply receive information: they 'processed' and 'interpreted', were prone to 'sensory errors'. 'Speculations and experiments on all manner of illusions and aches, phantasmagoria and pangs, appeared in the specialized and popular scientific literature', writes Musselman, arguing that by the mid-nineteenth century 'it had become clear that telegraphs and nervous systems faced the same managerial problems'.[14] With Schreber, this idea lengthens at the same time as he contradicts it, as the wires that represent the limits become an extension of his nervous system. Emil Kraepelin's *Textbook of Psychiatry* was lent to him while he was occupied with his manuscript, from which he learnt that 'the phenomenon of being in some supernatural communication with voices had frequently been observed before in human beings whose nerves were in a state of morbid excitation', and designated as 'hallucinations' (*NI*, 82, 83). It was because medical materialists considered such voices to be hallucinations that the psychical researcher Edmund Gurney distinguished between sensations of spirits

and the subject's 'own form or voice', as noted in my previous chapter.[15]
Schreber also believed that although 'in many of these cases we may only be
dealing with mere hallucinations', some are genuinely supernatural:

> Even so-called spiritualist mediums may be considered genuine seers
> of spirits of the inferior kind [...]. If psychiatry is not flatly to deny
> everything supernatural and thus tumble with both feet into the camp
> of naked materialism, it will have to recognize the possibility that
> occasionally the phenomena under discussion may be connected with
> real happenings, which simply cannot be brushed aside with the catch-
> word "hallucinations". (NI, 83–4)

The psychiatrist Kraepelin's descriptions of mental illness, however, particularly the *'hearing of voices'* characteristic of 'dementia praecox'[16], often
involve auditory technologies. He mentions a patient who 'says he has come
from the penal work-house, where he was "betelephoned"', for example.[17]

> The patient feels himself influenced by the telephone, is a "living
> telephone"; "it all came by telephone to the bed" [...] is "connected
> by telephone with M'Kinley", can "speak with the Kaiser", "tones
> constantly with God" [...]. Many patients feel themselves very much
> troubled by telephony.[18]

Cases such as these, of nervous conditions and psychoses involving the
telephone from this period are well-documented, being reported not only
by psychiatrists but also in specialist scientific literature and elsewhere.[19]

As well as spiritualists and mad people – many debated the difference[20]
– inventors employed technology for occult purposes. We have already
seen that Thomas Edison attempted to amplify the vibrations of spirits.
Alexander Graham Bell also sought spiritual applications for his work.
In his experiments with thought transference in 1891, Bell placed coils of
wire around his head and that of his assistant, linked by wires charged
with an electric current, in the hope of transmitting thoughts from one
brain to another.[21] Telephony was itself considered supernatural; time and
time again the newspaper reports of Bell's public lectures spoke of magic,
miracles, the powers of darkness.[22] Bell's partner Thomas Watson noted
that Bell's invention also attracted the attention of 'crazy' people, who,
as Anthony Enns puts it, 'immediately recognized the similarities between
telephonic voices and their own acoustic hallucinations'.[23] 'As in the case
of a séance peopled with nonbelievers,' writes Avital Ronell, 'Watson and
Bell had to prove that the telephone actually had spoken, that this was not
a rehearsed hallucination'.[24]

Not hallucinations, Schreber believed, though he received supernatural
messages without the use of his external sense organs. 'I receive light and

sound sensations which are projected direct on to my *inner* nervous system' (*NI*, 121). Ear and mouth are not necessary for communicating in nerve-language, as nerves 'vibrate in the way which corresponds to the use of the words concerned, but the real organs of speech (lips, tongue, teeth, etc.) are either not set in motion or only coincidentally' (54). Acoustical vibrations in the nerves, which since the eighteenth century began to replace the idea of animal spirits, were increasingly conceptualized as electrical in the nineteenth century. It was the oscillating current as opposed to the continuous current which made Bell's great invention possible, hence the numerous vague references in many kinds of commentary to vibrations along wire, and the 'popular impression', presumably received by Schreber, 'that the *sound* was in some way conveyed over the wire'.[25] Such an impression seems to have contributed to Schreber's sense of directly and immediately receiving sounds from far distances, communications which do not even need transforming or translating in order to be heard.

Historical commentators on the development of telephony soon picked up on the idea that telecommunications could 'magically' annihilate distances. In *The History of the Telephone*, published in 1910, Herbert Casson reflected on the mysterious nature of the various vibrations being transmitted along nerves and wires as well as through air, describing wires as 'voice-nerves', and nerves as 'nerve-wires', so that mechanical objects seem more human and nerves more mechanical, breaking down the distinction between object and subject. Again here wires seem to operate as an extension of the human nervous system (over 50 years before Marshall McLuhan's development of this idea):

> We have established in every large region of population a system of voice-nerves that puts every man at every other man's ear, and which so magically eliminates the factor of distance that the United States becomes three thousand miles of neighbours, side by side. [...]
>
> He [a future scientist] will deal with the various vibrations of nerves and wires and wireless air, that are necessary in conveying thought between two separated minds. He will make clear how a thought, originating in the brain, passes along the nerve-wires to the vocal cords, and then in wireless vibration of air to the disc of the transmitter. At the other end of the line the second disc re-creates these vibrations, which impinge upon the nerve-wires of an ear, and are thus carried to the consciousness of another brain.[26]

We have seen in my previous chapters how sympathetically vibrating strings provided an image of both nerves and vocal cords, as their process of reception was simultaneously one of transmission. The difference between nerves and cords is similarly blurred in Casson's account of wires as 'voice-nerves', which transmit as well as receive, or which 'hear-speak', as I have called it, much as the 'disc' at each end of the line is both sensitive and sonorous. This disc, also known as a diaphragm, acted like an eardrum. In his search for an instrument that would sensitively register sound, Bell experimented with a dead human ear. This experiment, as Steven Connor explains in his history of ventriloquism,

> focused the recognition that the ear does not merely receive auditory information, but also transmits it to the centres of perception and consciousness in the brain: that the ear, in short, speaks what it hears to the brain, which could be thought of as listening in on the output from its own ear.[27]

The telephone exteriorized this process, as Connor observes. It became possible to listen in not only on oneself but also other people. For Casson, as for Schreber, this seems to have made imaginable a kind of contact with others that is as intimate and instantaneous as contact with oneself, as the telephone 'magically eliminates the factor of distance'.

According to Carolyn Marvin's more recent history of electric communication, it was most admired for its ability to send messages 'effortlessly and instantaneously across time and space and to reproduce live sounds and images without any loss of content, at least by the standards of the day'.[28] But sounds were not always as effortlessly communicated as Marvin suggests, as the process of transmission produced noises which did not escape the attention of engineers, physicists, psychiatrists and journalists.[29] The noise of the medium could itself, however, be interpreted as the message. Casson claims that the noise of 'induction' was misinterpreted by Watson as a sign of aliens:

> Next after the transmitter came the problem of the *mysterious noises*. This was, perhaps, the most weird and mystifying of all the telephone problems. [...] Noises! Such a jangle of meaningless noises had never been heard by human ears. There were spluttering and bubbling, jerking and rasping, whistling and screaming [...] and at the ghostly hour of midnight, for what strange reason no one knows, the babel was at its height. Watson, who had a fanciful mind, suggested that perhaps these sounds were signals from the inhabitants of Mars or some other sociable planet.[30]

For psychiatrists the noise of nerve-wires produced hallucinations, for engineers it prevented communications. For Schreber, noise is the very substance of nerve-language. His technique resembles Watson's, as imagined by Casson, for listening to interplanetary signals, or to 'messages whose principal interest lay in the pure interference that noise conducts', as Ronell puts it.[31] His first experience of divine miracles came during a night when he heard 'a recurrent crackling noise in the wall', which he thought might be a mouse. 'But having heard similar noises innumerable times since then, and still hearing them around me every day in day-time and at night, I have come to recognize them as undoubted divine miracles – they are called "interferences" by the voices talking to me' (*NI*, 47). Interference, the technical language for non-information, for the noise of induction, the wires, the medium, *will not let him sleep.*

There are parallels, then, between the noise phenomena reported by psychotic patients, spiritualist mediums, and engineers or inventors and their assistants, as Enns has observed. But for engineers noise is usually the antithesis of messages, as represented by such characters as the spiritualist inventor of the automaton ear, the Professor whose messages turn out to be the meaningless noise of the bodily or technological medium (discussed in Chapter Two), whereas Schreber interprets the noise as itself the message. Schreber extends the psychophysical model of body as machine, of nerves as strings or wires, that was used to explain how the world is received and perceived by the individual subject. The extended nervous system suggests that distance is annihilated, that self and other are in intimate contact, virtually identical – between them, though, is interference on the line. For Schreber, this inhuman noise is itself the other, this alien noise of himself. He receives his own transmission, and re-transmits. He has to 'speak aloud or make some noise, in order to drown the senseless and shameless twaddle of the voices' (128).

Nerves of voluptuousness

Schreber has all the characteristics of sensitivity that I have identified in the eighteenth and nineteenth centuries: he is poetic or 'gifted', feminine, nervous or pathological, and mechanical. In the first chapter of his *Memoirs* he tells us that God forms nerve-contact 'with highly gifted people (poets, etc.), in order to bless them (particularly in dreams) with some fertilizing thoughts and ideas about the beyond' (23–4). Schreber here echoes the claim that genius is found in the male body but one prone to exhibit feminine reproductive traits of receptivity and the ability to produce 'intellectual children', a claim which can be traced through the work of Coleridge and through psychological ideas in the second half of the nineteenth century. The effeminate genius is also of course prone to illness, according to William James's findings, for example, that the genius is most likely to suffer nervous diseases.[32] The sensitive genius, or the later but related figure of the spiritualist medium, or 'that (usually female) individual with one foot in the world of the miraculous and the other in the back-waters of neuropathic degeneracy' named the 'gifted hysteric'[33], can all be considered precursors of the figure of Schreber. Spiritualists and neurological specialists not only shared a 'common intellectual heritage' with their use of a 'telegraphic model of the nervous system', but also of course shared the view that female nerves are uniquely sensitive.[34]

Twice Schreber felt the first signs of the life of a human embryo inside him, as 'by a divine miracle God's nerves corresponding to male seed had been thrown into my body' (18). He understood that his own pathological nervousness, or special sensitivity had made communication with such beings possible in the first place: the 'existence of a morbid state of nervous hyper-excitability [...] enabled and facilitated communication with supernatural powers' (83). This 'state of highly pathological excitement' becomes indistinguishable from the 'unmanning' that is repeatedly inflicted on Schreber, chosen by God to re-populate humanity after world calamity. His penis retracts, hairs are removed from his beard, and 'female nerves, or nerves of voluptuousness' – along with wires – penetrate his body. These are 'artificially set in vibration by rays on certain occasions so as to produce a sensation of timidity and to "represent" me as a human being trembling with feminine anxiety' (125). Schreber's nerves are not just spoken to, then, but shaken. Sound is palpable, the nerves themselves tangible: 'I can *feel* certain string or cord-like structures under my skin; these are particularly marked on my chest where the woman's bosom is, here they have the peculiarity that one can feel them ending in nodular thickenings' (246).

The voluptuous 'power of attraction', which Schreber has more of than any other being, causing parts of God's nerves to become separated from the rest and to cry for help (166), is presumably electromagnetic. Earlier in the century it was discovered that if wire, through which electricity is sent, was wound around soft iron it would become a magnet, after which many investigations were carried out as to how to produce more and more 'attractive power', which proved important to the workings of the telegraph and then telephone.[35] Patricia Fara has traced the development of long-standing associations between magnetic phenomena and sexual attraction in the eighteenth century, which continued to reverberate through the nineteenth century.[36] I have indicated that the emergence of telecommunications supported an interest in all kinds of telepathic and spiritual communications; for a further example the inventor Charles Wheatstone, whose better-known work was in the transmission of thought by telegraph, participated in experiments with thought transference between magnetizers and magnetized subjects.[37] It would seem that Schreber felt himself endowed with a kind of magnetic power which underpinned the authority that historians argue was possessed by the mesmerized patient, who, like the spiritualist medium, was thought to be especially sensitive to certain kinds of extrasensory communication. Alison Winter, in a history of mesmerism in the nineteenth century, notes that the authoritative and 'attractive subject' (whose attractiveness might be understood in two senses) was usually female:

> Men's superior physical strength and intellectual powers were often given as reasons why they were usually the mesmerists and women usually the subjects, though there were many important exceptions to the rule. But the mesmeric subject could also find authority in the trance state. The traditional role appropriate to this state was the oracular authority, the attractive subject whose body was freighted with information. This latter representation would supply the convention that would be taken over by spiritualist mediums later in the century. Women usually occupied this role, although several prominent mesmeric clairvoyants were men.[38]

Alex Owen's study of women and power in spiritualist circles in late Victorian England similarly notes that there were some male mediums, such as Daniel Dunglas Home, but they were usually portrayed as 'effeminate'.[39] The power of such mediums was somewhat fragile, however: 'Special female powers also rendered female mediums [or effeminate male mediums] vulnerable to special forms of female punishment: to medical labeling as hysterics and to lunacy confinement', notes Judith Walkowitz.[40]

Extrasensory or spiritual forms of communication were experienced in different ways, as we have seen, as thrilling or threatening, desirable or dangerous, or both. Winter describes how Harriet Martineau and Elizabeth Barrett, for example, held differing attitudes toward mesmerism. The invalid Martineau made a spectacular recovery after mesmeric treatment, which she found 'liberating' or 'empowering', whereas Barrett saw mesmerism's demonstration of the influence that seemed to operate between people as involving a nightmarish loss of boundaries and identity, fearing it as 'a form of personal obliteration'.[41] Barrett went on to view her developing feelings for her lover, Robert Browning, in terms of mesmeric intimacy, however. 'By the autumn of 1845 she had a completely different attitude to the erasure of boundaries between two people. Instead of obliterating her, as she had so feared before late 1844, it did the opposite: it "brought" her "back to life."'[42] Schreber experienced a similar sense of ambivalence about the transcendence of boundaries. His feelings seem to have swung precariously between the fear of invasion and elation, between sensations of pain and pleasure or 'voluptuousness', sensations which the opening lines of the *Memoirs* have told us are all caused by vibrations in the nerves. Though he experienced his unmanning as threatening, the theme of sensuousness pervades his *Memoirs*. Female nerves produced in his body a voluptuousness so intense that he could not but experience a feeling of sensual delight, as a woman who 'succumbs' to sexual intercourse.

In the last decades of the nineteenth century, ideas of mesmeric influence took on a more alarming character. Where the mesmerist had earlier

'played' upon the musical string-like nerves of his subject, later representations include Svengali's possession of the singer, Trilby – 'the ultimate
human instrument' – in George Du Maurier's novel of 1894, which became
hugely popular along with its various recyclings in verse and drama. Winter
comments that 'the sinister role of the conductor-mesmerist as a malevolent
demagogue in *Trilby* here involved a far more frightening image of mental
control and the destruction of individual identity than had ever appeared
earlier in the century'.[43] Schreber's mechanical passivity and fear of becoming
'spellbound' may be related to his 'sadistic' upbringing, as several analyses
of his case have proposed[44], but the scenarios enacted in séances and *Trilby*
and elsewhere were widespread (see also my discussion of *The Woman in
White* and *The Picture of Dorian Gray* in Chapter Two[45]), indicating that
personal and cultural histories are entangled, and that Schreber's experience
could have been shaped by ideas in general circulation.

The Helmholtzian school of biophysics viewed body and mind as
machine, but it was those subjects who could be mesmerized or fall
into trances who were portrayed as especially mechanical. The attempts
made by William Carpenter among other physiologists and psychiatrists
to pathologize mesmerism themselves acknowledged the extraordinary
powers of hypnotic 'suggestion', which causes 'Epidemic Delusions'.[46]
Carpenter believed that a hypnotized person's 'voluntary control over the
current of thought is entirely suspended, the individual being for the time
(so to speak) a mere *thinking automaton*, the whole course of whose ideas is
determinable by suggestions operating from without'.[47] On the other hand,
'so-called spiritual communications come from *within*, not from *without*,
the individuals who suppose themselves to be the recipients of them', which
is to say they are hallucinations.[48] On the other side, William Barrett, for a
report on mesmerism in the first volume of the *Proceedings of the Society for
Psychical Research* took the words of another spiritualist critic and alienist,
Henry Maudsley, to support the view that people are as sensitive to spiritual
influences as to suggestion: 'the mind of the patient becomes possessed with
the ideas that the operator suggests, so that his body becomes an automatic
machine set in motion by them'.[49] Barrett's account goes on to describe
a mesmerized girl who was so sensitive to the movement of the operator's fingers that 'the operation seemed very like playing on some musical
instrument'.[50] Actual instruments, ranging from simple mechanical contraptions to precision laboratory instruments, were developed in the search
for objective evidence of spiritualistic manifestations, devoid of 'interventions' from human mediums or deluded investigators, as I discussed in my
previous chapter.[51] In 'Science and Spiritualism', Barrett described the use in
physics of this kind of instrument:

> Physical science affords abundant analogies of the necessity of a medium,
> or intermediary, between the unseen and the seen. The waves of the

luminiferous ether require a material medium to absorb them before they can be perceived by our senses; the intermediary may be a photographic plate, the rods and cones of the retina, a blackened surface, or the so-called electromagnetic resonators, according to the respective lengths of those waves; but *some* medium, formed of ponderable matter, is absolutely necessary to render the chemical, luminous, thermal, or electrical effects of these waves perceptible to us.[52]

As Carpenter warned in 1876, the problem with most investigators of spiritualism was their 'ignorance of *the nature of their instruments of research*; putting as much faith in tricky girls or women, as they do in their thermometers or electroscopes'.[53] Spiritual mediums were increasingly deemed too unreliable for effective contact with the other world. A delegation of psychic researchers meeting in Paris in 1925 sought a machine that would 'eliminate mediums'.[54]

Since the eighteenth century, then, the pleasures and dangers of sensibility seem to have intensified, the role of a sensitive medium to have accrued both advantages and disadvantages. The case of Schreber is often seen as a precursor, as the origin of the psychoanalysis of paranoia, or the model for twentieth-century schizophrenia, or used to illustrate twentieth-century concerns with child abuse, or Nazism[55], but to extrapolate from this somewhat unusual case may be to obscure other historical resonances. Schreber may be viewed as a particular manifestation or paranoid culmination of something more continuous, at the end of a line as well as a beginning. Both sides of the debate as to whether mediums were especially gifted or deluded described them as mechanical, a characteristic attributed to feminine sensibility at least since the eighteenth-century image of the harp's vibrating nerve-strings. Schreber's special powers not only involved nerve-wires, however, but also rays, which seem to operate as an early formulation of the possibilities of radio communication, or what was often called 'wireless telegraphy', the fears and fantasies around which I shall next explore.

Rays, radio waves, and more automatons

Fears and fantasies, hopes and anxieties about technology in the public sphere are often vividly apparent in the delusions of the mad. In *Haunted Media*, Jeffrey Sconce observes that various paranormal theories and 'fantastic' tales of wireless communication began to emerge around 1900, tales which challenged the otherwise enthusiastic celebration of radio, presenting 'an increasingly uncertain world, one populated by citizens cut loose from previous social ties and now suffused with electromagnetic waves set free from tributaries of cable and wire'.[56] Among the enthusiasts was Guglielmo Marconi, whose study of Hertzian wave theory led to his first successful broadcast of a radio signal in 1895. He went on to pursue the possibility of radio contact with the dead, and attempted to create a device that would receive living voices from all human history. But liberation was at the same time felt as threatening, Sconce suggests: 'Boundaries of time, space, nation, and body no longer seemed to apply, and although this provided a giddy sense of liberation for some, it also threatened the security and stability of an older social order in which body and mind had been for the most part conterminus.[57]

Since Gustav Fechner had argued that psychophysical energy does not only travel along the nerves but radiates outwards, forever, after the discovery of high frequency X-rays by Röentgen in 1895 William Crookes and others believed this form of radiation could explain the phenomenon of telepathy (see Chapter Two above). Such influences are not necessarily confined to nerves or wires, then; Schreber seems to have combined the idea of telepathic communication along wires with a 'radio model of consciousness' whereby thought waves radiate beyond the confines of nerves and brain.[58] He wrote to his psychiatrist, Paul Flechsig (who, like Fechner, worked at Leipzig University), describing his experience of '*influences on my nervous system emanating from your nervous system*' (*NI*, 8). In an appeal against the judgement of 1900 concerning his confinement in the asylum, Schreber asked that an investigation of Röentgen rays be carried out in order to ascertain that his telepathic communications were not hallucinations (362).

Other sorts of rays were evident around 1900. By 1903 N-rays had been isolated to emanations from the nervous system. Roger Luckhurst writes that telepathy prospered in ether-physics, because of the 'rush of discoveries of forms of "invisible" phenomena' including X-rays, electromagnetic waves, black light, and radio waves.[59] But while spiritualists and others thought that rays may explain the wonders of telepathy, the psychiatrist Kraepelin observed that patients feel persecuted by 'Röentgen rays', along with other forms of 'wireless telegraphy' or 'Tesla currents'. Patients frequently complain of 'malevolent people' with whom they are connected by a machine, 'there is a "mechanical arrangement", "a sort of little conveyance", telepathy'.[60] Similar observations are reported in Thomas Watson's autobiography where 'several men whose form of insanity made them hear voices which they attributed to the machinations of enemies, called at the laboratory or wrote to us for help, attracted by Bell's supposedly occult invention'. One such 'crazy man' believed an apparatus had been implanted in his head enabling the enemies to make 'all sorts of fiendish suggestions', and asked Watson to take the top off his skull to find out 'how to telephone any distance without apparatus or wires'.[61]

Reactions to the phenomenon of rays, ranging from enthusiasm to suspicion, seem to reflect their use in medicine. As Steven Connor writes, 'Rays and radiations were both beneficient and menacing. The medical applications of X-rays were immediately apparent, but it did not take long for the dangers of exposure to them to reveal themselves'.[62] Nikola Tesla for example, inventor of the alternating current, among his various articles about Röentgen rays published in 1896 in the *Electrical Review*, described how 'the bones cast a shadow' while the flesh is transparent, writing in military terms that 'Röentgen gave us a gun to fire – a wonderful gun, indeed, projecting missiles of a thousandfold greater penetrative power than that of a cannon ball, and carrying them probably to distances of many miles [...] without any hurtful consequences'.[63] The case of Cornelius Mack, who had a bullet lodged in his chest during military service many years previously, is illustrative. Tesla managed to locate the bullet, which could then be extracted. By 1897, however, he was considering the harmful effects of X-rays and setting out precautionary measures. His concern was that the increasing number of reports of injuries 'impede the progress and create a prejudice against an already highly beneficial and still more promising discovery; but it cannot be denied that it is equally uncommendable to ignore dangers now when we know that, under certain circumstances, they actually exist'.[64] His assistant had been injured while experimenting with the rays, suffering the effects of severe burns. Along with the more obvious effects of light and heat, in his account of the sensation experienced when watching a powerful Röentgen bulb, Tesla suggests that it produces some kind of violent extrasensory sound:

> Exactly the same sensation is produced when working for some time with a noisy spark gap, or, in general, when exposing the ear to sharp noises or explosions. Since it seems impossible to imagine how the latter could cause such a sensation in any other way except by directly impressing the organs of hearing, I conclude that a Röentgen or Lenard tube, working in perfect silence as it may, nevertheless produces violent explosions or reports and concussions, which, though they are inaudible, take some material effect upon the bony structure of the head.[65]

Schreber seems similarly to feel not only injured or persecuted by rays but also that they are a great source of good. 'The nerves of God', he reports, 'have the faculty of transforming themselves into all things of the created world; in this capacity they are called rays; and herein lies the essence of divine creation' (*NI*, 21). The beneficient creativity of God's nerve-rays is the other side of destruction. Rays have destroyed the world and its inhabitants. Among these rays are the sun's and stars', which are not exactly part of God himself, but very close relations 'through which God's miraculous creative power travels to our earth'. The sun speaks with Schreber in human language, as though light and heat are also sound, combining the ancient belief in the 'light and warmth-giving power of the sun, which makes her the origin of all organic life on earth', with newer possibilities of wireless transmission (21). As Carolyn Marvin writes: 'The power of electricity was sometimes compared to the power of the sun, whose limitless capacity to sustain life was an old and potent motif. Solar energy and the wireless trans-mission of electric power were both utopian dreams of the late nineteenth century'.[66] Among the best-known attempts to carry out such dreams were those of Tesla, who, along with his ambition to develop the medical uses of X-rays, planned to harness the power of the sun for the benefit of all humankind, and transmit energy and messages across space.

Tesla was convinced that all space was filled with the rays of the sun. His biographer Margaret Cheney notes that this theory (let alone Schreber's) was not accepted by scientists at the time, though subsequent investigations proved elements of it correct.[67] In June 1900, Tesla published 'The Problem of Increasing Human Energy, with Special References to the Harnessing of the Sun's Energy' in the *Century* magazine, hoping that this would attract new money for a projected 'World System' of wireless power and message transmission, which it did. Tesla considered the harnessing of the sun's energy to be most important by far of the possible solutions to the problem of energy, because 'all this movement, from the surging of the mighty ocean to that subtle movement concerned in our thought, has but one common cause. All this energy emanates from one single center, one single source – the sun'.[68] In the process of experimenting on methods for the utilization and transmission of this energy, he produced a system of 'wireless teleg-raphy'. Like David Hartley and others in the eighteenth century, and many scientific writers in the nineteenth who used sound to explain the behaviour of nerve impulses, light, heat and electricity, Tesla also used sound to explain the behaviour of electricity, in this case as a kind of echo: 'Exactly as the sound, so an electrical wave is reflected [...]. Instead of sending sound-vibrations toward a distant wall, I have sent electrical vibrations toward the remote boundaries of the earth, and instead of the wall the earth has replied'.[69] The transmission of both electrical and sound vibrations was very much a part of Tesla's idea of the World System, which would provide an infinite supply of energy and allow all people to be in contact, bringing about world harmony. As he commented in his autobiography:

> The greatest good will come from technical improvements tending to unification and harmony, and my wireless transmitter is preeminently such. By its means, the human voice and likeness will be reproduced everywhere, and factories driven from thousands of miles away by waterfalls furnishing power. Aerial machines will be propelled around the earth without a stop and the sun's energy controlled to create lakes and rivers for motive purposes and transformation of arid deserts into

fertile land. [...] Only through annihilation of distance in every respect, as the conveyance of intelligence, transport of passengers and supplies and transmission of energy will conditions be brought about some day, insuring permanency of friendly relations.[70]

In contrast to Tesla's, Schreber's version of a World System does not bring about world harmony, but rather the most personal, intimate noise. Reaching deep inside from way out there, all the vibrations, the rays and radiations seem to invade his core being. His communication system resembles Tesla's in some respects, however, including in its 'annihilation of distance' not only on earth but between planets. According to Schreber, human souls are 'called to a new *human* life on other planets' from which he receives messages (27); Tesla's System also involves communication with other planets, such as Mars. 'That we can send a message to a planet is certain, that we can get an answer is probable: man is not the only being in the Infinite gifted with a mind'. The idea of harnessing the sun's energy to transform arid deserts into fertile land may long ago have been realized by 'intelligent beings on Mars [...] which would explain the changes on its surface noted by astronomers'.[71]

Energy, according to physicists, is the life force. That this vibrant power is life itself, and is key to such a utopian vision as Tesla's, makes it all the more devastating. The dangers of electricity were at least as widely publicized as its enormous potential. Much of the testimony that alternating current – which Tesla invented as an alternative to direct current – was the best means of killing people by electrocution was allegedly orchestrated by Thomas Edison and his associates, whose investments were in direct current. According to Cheney, this relentless publicity campaign involved electrocuting family pets in crude experiments with alternating currents.[72] The imagination of persecutory rays may also have been shaped by the host of rumours, following the detection of X-rays and so on, about rays of destruction. For years it was rumoured that Tesla had invented a death ray. Cheney notes that in 1924,

> a flurry of news reports from Europe claimed that a death ray had been invented there – first by an Englishman, then by a German, and then a Russian. [...] Then a newspaper in Colorado proudly reported that Tesla had invented the first invisible death ray capable of stopping aircraft in flight while he had been experimenting there in 1899.[73]

Besides the rumours of rays, Tesla had believed that wars could be stopped by making them more destructive. In 'The Problem of Increasing Human Energy' he proposed that 'greatest possible speed and maximum rate of energy-delivery by the war apparatus will be the main object', reducing the number of soldiers involved. Finally, instead of wars between man and

man: 'machine must fight machine'. Peace will be assured, as the battle
will become 'a mere spectacle, a play, a contest without loss of blood'.
Each fighting machine will 'perform its duties as though it had intelligence,
experience, judgement, a mind!'[74] This idea of dangerous rays or 'energy'
delivered by fighting machines also features in H. G. Wells's *The War of the
Worlds*, which merged his 'serious [scientific] speculations' with his role as a
'story-teller', helping to popularize the imagination of harmful rays wielded
by machines, in this case from Mars.[75] The rays are terrifying in part
because, like X-rays, they cannot themselves be seen, but are only visible
in their effects: 'It was sweeping round swiftly and steadily, this invisible,
inevitable sword of heat. I perceived it coming towards me by the flashing
bushes it touched'.[76] Tesla's utopic imagination of peaceful world-wide and
interplanetary communication, of 'friendly relations', in Wells's fiction turns
into an apocalyptic scenario of invasion by alien machines.[77]

Tesla considered man an automaton. Energy, as taught by physicists, is
the life force for man as for machine. 'I conceived the idea of constructing
an automaton which would mechanically represent me'. This machine
would respond to signals from a distance, its movements controlled much
as Schreber's seem to be. Tesla found that satisfactory control of the
automaton could not be effected by those rays that 'pass in straight lines
through space'.[78] The life or death rays aimed at Schreber's head 'do *not*
come towards me in a straight line but in a kind of circle or parabola' (*NI*,
275). Tesla goes on to explain that

> the sensitive device of the machine should correspond to the ear rather
> than the eye of a human being, for in this case its actions could be
> controlled irrespective of intervening obstacles, regardless of its position
> relative to the distant controlling apparatus, and, last, but not least, it
> would remain deaf and unresponsive, like a faithful servant, to all calls
> but that of its master. These requirements made it imperative to use [...]
> waves or disturbances which propagate in all directions through space,
> like sound.[79]

Like Schreber, and before him Coleridge, and indeed like his own imagined
machine, Tesla himself had been exceptionally sensitive to sound. According
to his autobiography, this sensitivity intensified in 1881 when he suffered
a 'breakdown of the nerves'. He could hear the ticking of a watch from
three rooms away. A carriage passing a few miles away seemed to shake his
whole body. A train whistle 20 miles distant made the chair on which he sat
vibrate so strongly that the pain became unbearable.[80] Schreber, too, experienced the whistle of a train as palpable and painful, due apparently to the
sensitivity brought about by his nervous illness: 'I feel a blow on my head
simultaneously with every word spoken around me, with every approaching
footstep, with every railway whistle, with every shot fired by a pleasure

steamer, etc.; this causes a variable degree of pain' (*NI*, 89). Sensitivity to everyday sounds is the condition for receiving telephonic and radio signals from spirits and God.

Schreber's and Tesla's conceptions of man as a sensitive machine are of course not unusual at this time when scientific thinkers from physicists to psychiatrists emphasized the material mechanics of the human body and mind. In previous chapters I have already discussed how poets and fictional characters from Coleridge to the Professor in 'The Automaton Ear' modelled their sensory capacities on instruments such as the aeolian harp and the automaton ear. Schreber and Tesla take this idea a step further with their understanding that the human *is* a machine; the machine is human. Such a concept is of course explored in various fictions, often featuring mad or at least rather fanatical inventors, such as the fictionalized character of Edison in Villiers de l'Isle-Adam's novel *Tomorrow's Eve*, who, like Tesla, harnesses the power of the sun's vibrations, only in this case for the purpose of energizing the nerve-wires of the mechanical fantasy woman-object, Hadaly.[81] Like Tesla's machine, Hadaly is to be controlled from a distance, telepathically. Lord Ewald struggles to understand the leap from wires to the wireless transmission of thought:

> I'm sure it's already a remarkable thing that electric current can now transmit energy to great heights and over enormous, almost limitless distances [...]. This trick is perfectly comprehensible, given the use of tangible conductors – magic highways – through which the powerful currents flow. But this INSUBSTANTIAL transmission of my living thought, how can I imagine it taking place, at a distance, *without conductors or wires, even the very thinnest?*[82]

As Pamela Thurschwell has commented, Ewald's anxious doubts here indicate 'that one limit of conceiving of transmission at that particular moment in the historical development of electrical technology was materiality itself'. When wires – however thin – are no longer necessary for transmission, 'then, for Ewald, we have crossed a line which divides science from the occult [...] we come face to face with the unknown'.[83] The exchangeability of Tesla's and Schreber's ideas similarly indicates a sense of difficulty at the time with maintaining a secure boundary between scientific and occult or fictional ideas, or between those of the mad-inventor-genius and the demented nervous patient.

In *Tomorrow's Eve* the machine is described as human (even as an improved, enhanced version of humanity); in other stories the human is described as mechanical, similarly controlled entirely by external forces. In Frederic Stimson's 'Dr. Materialismus', for instance, human emotions and behaviour are entirely responsive or even equivalent to frequencies of vibration, so that power over such frequencies allows the scientist to control humans like puppets. In this short story the professor Dr. Materialismus invents a mechanism that can produce extremely high frequencies of vibration. In a lecture to his students, Materialismus explains the scale of vibrations from the lowest to the highest, much like a spiritualist materialist such as the well-known William Crookes (see above, p. 52):

> Materialismus began with a brief sketch of the theory of sound; how it consisted in vibrations of the air, the coarsest medium of space, but could not dwell in ether; and how slow beats – blows of a hammer, for instance – had no more complex intellectual effect, but were mere consecutive noises; how the human organism ceased to detect these consecutive noises at about eight per second, until they reappeared at sixteen per second, the lowest tone which can be heard; and how, at something like thirty-two thousand per second these vibrations ceased to be heard.[84]

The professor then claims that as mind as well as matter are merely innumerable points of motion, emotion is simply the subjective result of merely material motion. Light, then, is apparently a 'subtler emotion' than sound,

> dwelling in ether, but still nothing but a regular continuity of motion or molecular impact; to speak more plainly, successive beats or vibrations reappear intelligible to humanity as light, at something like 483,000,000,000 beats per second in the red ray [...] until they disappear again, through the violet ray, at something like 727,000,000,000 beats per second in the so-called chemical rays.[85]

Beyond violet, the professor goes on to explain, '*these higher, almost infinitely rapid vibrations may be what are called the higher emotions or passions – like religion, love and hate*'. The range of frequencies produced by his mechanism, which by revolving with great rapidity can produce 'any number of beats per second'[86], thus produces corresponding emotions in his victim, Tetherby. Tetherby himself figures as a kind of mechanism, his nerves strained like a 'violin-string' as he hears the vibrations move up through and beyond the musical scale into emotions of murderous anger, suicidal despair, envy, greed, lust, and, at 'many sextillions' of vibrations per second, 'love of God'.[87]

Tetherby's experience is in a sense comparable to Coleridge's, as the vibrations of his nerve-strings triggered thoughts, fancies and the poetic imagination: 'Millions of thoughts, fancies, inspirations, flashed through my brain as he [the professor] left me to the slow beating of the Power on the Murder pulse'.[88] Schreber similarly feels himself controlled through his nerve-wires and by various forms of waves and rays, while Tesla (and the fictional Edison) has the fantasy of himself controlling his automaton from a distance. In another short story, 'The New Accelerator', by H. G. Wells, the fantasy is not of controlling vibrations but the receptive powers of the human: the professor has invented a 'nervous stimulant' that speeds up perception so that sound vibration breaks apart into a 'sort of faint pat, patter [...] the slow, muffled ticking of some monstrous clock'.[89] Because vibration, with all its potential benefits and dangers, can apparently trigger such a vast range of mental experiences and behaviours, intensities of pain and pleasure, such fantasies of control are not unusual in the increasingly technological world of the late nineteenth and early twentieth centuries. My next two chapters will continue to document a wide range of attempts to count and to manage vibrations, including those produced by railway trains and street musicians, and to produce very specific frequencies with such mechanisms as the percuteur, the vibratode and manipulator. I thus turn now to focus further on the impact of vibrating machines – from the railway train to the vibrator – on the body that is itself conceived of as mechanical, to consider its place within a world of machines.

CHAPTER FOUR

Pathological Motions: Railway Shock, Street Noises, Earthquakes

In the 1860s physicians started to theorize extensively about conditions like 'railway spine', often said to be caused by the excessive vibrations experienced on trains and in collisions. In this literature we find further instances of how the human body was conceptualized as a sensitive mechanism, influenced by vibrating machines. This chapter, though, is about the endeavour to understand how vibration physically impacts on people, rather than the more 'spiritual' effects discussed in preceding chapters.

I will focus here on a modern kind of shock, particularly the shock produced by the motion of trains. Trains seem to have been the source of a renewed interest in or concern about shock, although the concept itself was not new. Earlier versions include the shock of the wind. As early as the fifteenth century, the word 'blow' in English took on the meaning of a violent stroke, in addition to its existing use to describe the movement of wind or fresh air. This is precisely the doubled sense which is at play in the early nineteenth century when the harmonious breeze becomes a stormy wind which makes the nerves of the harp scream and shudder in Coleridge's 'Dejection' (see Chapter One), and, as I will show, it is this vibratory reaction that corresponds with the development of 'shock'. By the seventeenth century, the term 'shock' had come to refer to: 'A sudden and violent blow, impact, or collision, tending to overthrow or to produce internal oscillation in a body subjected to it'.[1]

I have argued in earlier chapters that the idea of the wind as a violent force in the eighteenth and early nineteenth centuries was part of a wider paradigm, in which the nerves were thought to respond to vibratory stimuli in the external world (especially sound) by vibrating themselves. As one of the first propositions for *Observations on Man*, Hartley set out to demonstrate that 'External Objects impressed upon the Senses occasion, first in the Nerves on which they are impressed, and then in the Brain, Vibrations of the small, and, as one may say, infinitesimal, medullary Particles'.[2] Hartley's principal investigations were into how vibrations such as sound, light and the nerves generate sensations, but he also proposed that other kinds of vibration impact on the body and mind. He speculated as to how 'irregular and dissonant vibrations' can cause giddiness and confusion, as they propagate through the nerves to the spinal marrow and brain. 'Some effects of concussions of the brain', he continues, 'and perhaps of the spinal marrow, also of being tossed in a ship, of riding backwards in a coach, and of other violent and unusual agitations of the body, seem to bear a relation to the present subject'.[3] Although Hartley goes no further on the subject here, saying that 'it would be too minute to pursue these things', the progressively more violent and far reaching vibrations of transport and technology in the nineteenth century were increasingly thought to be detrimental to the health of society, and a growing body of professional experts formed around these concerns. These 'nerve doctors' had formed a speciality among medical practitioners since the eighteenth century, as G. S. Rousseau observes, and with the further development of industrialization and urbanization they continued to flourish in the nineteenth century, as 'modern nerves found themselves increasingly frayed'.[4]

In previous chapters I have examined the work of Hartley, and then Helmholtz and others who aimed to develop a materialist account of mind, tracing some of the links between these investigations and spiritualist theories and delusions such as Schreber's. I now return to the 1860s to focus on the development of a scientific approach to the study of 'shock'. Helmholtzian psychophysics grew up in the more established and well-funded German universities, whereas railway shock emerged earlier in Britain as it was the most advanced industrial nation, in so far as rail development is concerned[5], but there is no sharp dividing line between these modes of investigation into the effects of vibration, which might be imagined to run along individual but parallel tracks through the 1860s and 1870s. The work on psychophysics and psychopathology, along with the interests in technology and spiritualism, came together to some extent in the late nineteenth century, in the work of Joseph Mortimer Granville, George Henry Taylor and other practitioners of 'vibratory therapy'. After an account of the work on railway shock, then, which will be the focus of the present chapter, I move on in Chapter Five to the theories behind this medical practice and its related inventions like Granville's percuteur, which was initially used to treat conditions including railway spine but is now more widely known as an early version of the vibrator. As the nerves were considered vibratory, they seemed especially sensitive both to the dangerous vibrations on the railway and to medical vibrations, both of which could be painful but also pleasurable, even sexually stimulating. Furthermore, medical vibrations could be used to treat the nervousness suffered by sensitive, spiritual mediums, according to Taylor, whose patients included the internationally renowned medium Katie Fox. Taylor theorized that the principle of conservation of energy, which for spiritualists supported the possibility of life after death, meant that vibrations had unlimited healing potential. So in these next two chapters again we see how vibrations were both feared and desired, being potentially both dangerous – in their capacity in this case to 'shock' – and beneficial. It is not only in the spiritual realm that vibration could be both threatening and liberating, in its capacity for example to disturb sexual norms and the boundaries of the human body, as we have seen, but also in the material world of evidently palpable sensations.

The development of medical, therapeutic vibrations was one way of attempting to control, even to counteract the increasingly powerful vibrations of the modern world and their effects on the body and mind, including sexual over-excitement. This chapter looks at another kind of attempt to manage the new forms and quantities of vibration, by registering and measuring it, raising awareness of its presence. We have already seen how physicists attempted to produce scientifically measureable frequencies of vibratory stimuli with the use of instruments like the siren, while inventions such as the automaton ear, Materialismus's revolving mechanism, and the 'new accelerator', further illustrate the dream of detecting and producing vibrations beyond the sensory thresholds. Such forms of detection and measurement seem part of a wider struggle against the increasing speeds that characterize modernity, at which things move too fast to be consciously registered, like ultrasound. The sense of motion on a train, in particular, differs from pre-industrial experiences of travel such as by horse and coach, as the velocity causes each jolt or 'shock' to follow in such rapid succession that they are no longer sensed as individual shocks but as continuous vibration, as Wolfgang Schivelbusch suggests. Schivelbusch argues that the railway gave the middle classes their most direct experience of industrialization, which the working classes encountered in the factory. Anxieties about railway vibration derive from a new relation between humans and machines, from the passenger's parcel-like passivity in contrast to the pre-industrial subject's more participative relation with the 'organic' motion of horse and coach. He describes how the shift from coach travel to the railway journey produced new experiences – of self, of landscape, of space and time – above all because of the increase in speed:

On the one hand, the train proceeded so very smoothly – which is why early travellers felt that they were 'flying' – but, on the other, wheel and rail produced a new kind of vibration that was quite different from the jolts experienced on a coach journey on the highway. This vibration resulted from the exact interaction between steel rail and steel wheel, from the speed and, particularly, from the distance between the rails. What differentiated it from pre-industrial forms of mechanical shock was the train's velocity, which caused the jolts to be so brief and to follow in such rapid succession that they were no longer felt as individual jolts but as a condition of continuous vibration.[6]

This is a feeling of what is 'no longer felt', of the blurring together of 'individual jolts' into 'continuous vibration'. The jolts are more numerous, yet less palpable, than those undergone on a coach journey. The sense that any single jolt has become indistinguishable from the continuous vibration suggests that travellers are not precisely aware of what their bodies are subjected to. This chapter explores the various attempts to counteract such unconsciousness, to maintain awareness of each single vibration – which medical writers claimed could damage the nervous system – through the activity of counting them.

Nicholas Daly has developed an account of the concern with rail vibration in relation to sensation novels. Like rail travel, sensation novels were thought to assault the reader's nervous system. While 'nerves are everywhere aquiver' in *The Woman in White* (as we saw in Chapter Two), 'the effect of the novel seems to be to set the reader's nerves jangling in sympathetic vibration'. Both the reader and the railway traveller, writes Daly, seem 'to be reduced to a position of passive reception, but also to be over-stimulated by this experience, to be rendered uneasy, even fearful'.[7] Following Walter Benjamin, Daly suggests that the shock of modernity consists in such 'hyperstimulation', an excess of sensation, and that 'heightened consciousness [...] is the subject's *defence mechanism* against shock'.[8] This heightened consciousness is of time, which is generated in readers of the briskly paced, suspenseful sensation novels, in which victory goes to those who master the new speeds of transportation and communication, armed with timetables and watches, arriving punctually at necessary scenarios in accordance with the new, standardized time imposed by the railways. This argument can also be applied to the direct experience of rail travel, the vibrations of which are themselves envisaged as a form of hyperstimulation. The rapid succession of vibrations seems to produce a new excess of sensation, which at the same time threatens to become extrasensory, to escape consciousness, as I have said. The effort to count, to keep up with each vibration, to draw attention to the danger, may serve to maintain 'heightened consciousness' and thereby hold at bay the threat of numbness.

By focusing on vibration as a phenomenon to which travellers felt in/sensitive, I identify a specific sense of 'shock' – a term used in physics as well as medicine to refer to large quantities of vibration – that is lost to contemporary academic discourse. The connection between railway accidents and the psychology of trauma, which is to be distinguished from railway vibration and shock, is well established. From the early 1990s, in response to the rise of post-traumatic stress disorder and related conditions, anthropologists and historians of science, medicine, literature and culture found a role for themselves in viewing trauma as a discursive construction. Critics routinely argue that 'trauma' originally referred to a physical wound, and only as a result of nineteenth-century discussions about railway accidents gained the meanings associated with psychological damage.[9] Along these lines Allan Young claims that the study of railway accident victims contributed to a new 'traumatic memory' which was culturally constructed or 'invented' by different forms of scientific inquiry.[10] The invention of trains, however, does not appear as a possible contributory factor. With the current emphasis on trauma as psychological, the origins of which are found in nineteenth-century medical discourse, the physical impact of railways on the body tends to feature only as a point of departure. Bodily or sensory experience of rail travel is overlooked where disorders like 'railway spine' (characterized by a variety of symptoms in accident victims who apparently suffered no significant bodily injury) are drawn into the context of late-twentieth-century patterns of diagnosis. In contrast, sensory experience in modernity has been studied in some depth by Benjamin and others who work with the idea that from about 1850 subjectivity is characterized by experiences of shock. Where trauma has its origins in the wound, shock is said to have its origins in a modernity characterized by speed, chaos, and sensory overload, due to urbanization, crowds, new modes of transportation and communication, film and other technologies. Considering the extensive use in these strands of theory of the terms 'shock' and 'trauma', further investigation of their origins and meaning in the period under discussion is in order. According to Tim Armstrong, the distinction between them has become somewhat vague as accounts of modernity have increasingly concurred in its characterization as an age of traumatic shock. Armstrong observes that 'recent accounts of modernity tend to use the terms 'shock' and 'trauma' interchangeably', which provides the context for his investigation into a Freudian distinction between them, contrasting 'the *economic* model of shock, in which experience is conceived as a succession of stimuli which must be processed in time', with 'the timelessness of the unconscious wound'.[11] Shock is understood in terms of processing speeds, rather than the wound. It is part of the everyday modern life of industrial, technological and urban physicality. At the speeds at which vibration exists beyond the threshold of the senses, shock may have an unconscious presence, as opposed to the unconscious memory of trauma.

My earlier chapters observed that knowledge of sound was extended to explain other forms of vibration, and further than this, to explain that which cannot be experienced at all, such as X-rays and spiritual waves. As Gillian Beer has put it, 'Wave theory, acoustics, radiation, all seemed to indicate that our senses are contracted and that we are battered by continuous events beyond their registration'.[12] This chapter maps out of some of the ways in which the abstract theory of wave motions was lived out in embodied forms, as a kind of ultrasound. Although beyond consciousness, it seemed each 'shock' could be harmful, as we will see. By calculating the amount of vibration undergone on the railway medical writers could attempt to maintain awareness of this extrasensory threat to society. I will go on to explore Charles Dickens's ambivalence toward the railway as representative of far more widespread fears and hopes about its power to harm on the one hand, and to bring about economic and social improvements and even health benefits on the other (rail travel was itself occasionally prescribed as a medical treatment). While the railway was one of the leading symbols of progress, Dickens in *Dombey and Son* described the laying of tracks as a massive, disastrous shaking up of things, like an earthquake, before the trains even begin to move.

Periodical times of shock

In the 1860s physicists were analysing vibration in terms of frequencies or 'periodic times', which is to say the number of motions in a second, or some other period. I considered how musical tones, colours and other phenomena were defined in this way as different quantities, on a single scale (Chapter Two). These frequencies of vibration extend beyond the sensory thresholds, though spiritualists thought that nervously sensitive people might perceive such things. One of my examples of the mathematical approach was Helmholtz's study 'On The Physiological Causes of Harmony in Music', which used the siren to measure the number of vibrations in a second, that is the speed it takes to produce a musical tone. I will quote another part of this here, which, in its comparison between the siren's sound and a train, indicates shared interests in sound and railway vibrations that were taken up in medical circles:

> On beginning to blow the instrument, we first hear separate impulses of the air, escaping as puffs, as often as the holes of the disc pass in front of those of the box. These puffs of air follow one another more and more quickly, as the velocity of the revolving discs increases, just like the puffs of steam of a locomotive on beginning to move with the train. They next produce a whirring and whizzing, which constantly becomes more rapid. At last we hear a dull drone, which, as the velocity further increases, gradually gains in pitch and strength.[13]

As the sound gets louder we lose consciousness, in a sense, of repetition.

Multiple 'impulses' give way to a single 'dull drone'. While the vibrations that constitute sound cannot themselves be experienced, the siren is used to calculate their number or quantity, the audible range of which extends 'from about 20 to about 32,000 in a second'.

This chapter, as I have mentioned, focuses on another sort of inaudible sound, at the other end of the scale to that of high frequency spiritual communications. The vibration of trains is lower, and louder. Hearing gives way to a sense of being shaken, sensed through the body, rather than by the ear. As Schivelbusch suggests, the movement of trains differed from pre-industrial forms of mechanical shock as the train's velocity caused the jolts to follow in such rapid succession that they were no longer felt as individual jolts but as continuous vibration, like the progression from 'separate impulses' to the 'dull drone' produced by the siren.

As well as physicists, in the 1860s physicians were trying to calculate how quantities of vibration affect people. Helmholtz's study was into the physiological causes of the sensation of harmony, whereas physicians were observing how vibrations might damage the nervous system. The surgeon John Erichsen was one of the first among many to address the particular character of injuries resulting from railway accidents, including the 'emotional or hysterical state' in which victims found themselves, for which he attempted to identify the cause: 'Is this due to the frantic terror which often seizes upon the sufferers from railway collisions, or is it due to some peculiarity in the accident, some vibratory thrill transmitted through the nervous system by the peculiarity of the accident?'[14] This account goes on to suggest that the psychological feeling of terror is the better explanation, rather than the physical impact of vibration. Historians of the concept of trauma tend to portray the definition of 'railway spine' as arising from attempts like Erichsen's in the 1860s and 1870s to extend compensation for psychological as well as physical injuries[15], although railway directors attempted to limit the circumstances in which they had to pay compensation earlier than this, for physically and severely injured people. Newspapers such as *The Times* presented sceptical arguments during the 1870s, 1880s and 1890s regarding the simulation of conditions like 'railway shock' and 'nervous shock', and the 'growing evil' of false claims for compensation[16], while medical periodicals including the *Lancet* were more sympathetic to the medical profession than to railway companies. The first mention I have found of a court case – 'Cox v. The Midland Railway Company' – is from 1849, followed by increasingly critical portrayals of companies who refused to pay doctors attending to life-threatening conditions of accident victims unable to pay for themselves.[17] By 1862, however, according to the *Lancet*'s eight-part report entitled 'The Influence of Railway Travelling on Public Health':

It is no longer the fear of accidents so much as a vague dread of certain undefined consequences to health resulting from influences peculiarly produced by this mode of travelling. [...] It is especially important that the causes and the character of the motion experienced in all railway travelling to be clearly understood.[18]

This is the kind of vibratory motion in which I am presently interested, rather than accidents. W. Bridges Adams, a railway engineer, provided an account of this subject for the *Lancet*, explaining that among the effects on health caused by railway travelling, 'the majority are attributable to the peculiar motion which characterizes travelling on railways'. He goes on to explain the causes and to elaborate further on the nature of this 'peculiar motion':

Ordinary carriages on common roads have flexible springs, and an irregular rough surface to roll over. Railway carriages have very rigid springs, and a regular rough surface to roll over. The large irregular concussions of the highway are converted on the railway into a series of smaller regular concussions. [...] The rough motion is changed into a mild but constant vibratory motion.[19]

Adams goes on to suggest that although travelling by coach is felt to be much rougher, it is not so harmful as the 'mild but constant vibratory motion' of rail travel. Though the motions of the highway are 'large', the 'smaller regular concussions' are more numerous. The reason for this, Adams claims, is 'friction', which is 'greater in amount on the rail than it is on the road'. Like many physicists, who used sound as a model for other kinds of vibration, Adams uses sound as a model for this more palpable kind of vibratory phenomenon:

The sounds produced from a violin are a result of friction; i.e., a succession of minute blows produced by the leaping from particle to particle of the powdered rosin which adheres to the horsehair of the bow. This is easily proved by applying grease to the horsehair, when all sound ceases. Sound is vibration; vibration is minute concussion – mischievous in proportion to its regularity and continuance.[20]

The vibration or concussion undergone on the railway is dangerous, then, in its very regularity or smoothness; it is the lack of 'large irregular concussions', the smoothness of railway travel which, like music, is perceived as 'mischievous'. To return to the example of the siren, an increased number of impulses is eventually converted into the singular 'dull drone'. Or to take a more vivid extreme, the X-rays in which physicists and spiritualists became interested cannot be perceived at all, yet exist at a speed of millions of vibrations per second, or '2,305763,009213,693952 per second or even higher', according to the spiritualist William Crookes.[21] The fear of railway travel appears to be that it might damage the body in ways that cannot be sensed or understood, that harm is being done without our noticing. Adams seems to share with physicists and with other medical writers a distrust or a fear that we are losing our capacity to sense what is actually happening, to attend to the thresholds of attention, though of a different kind from those investigated by the physicists and spiritualists. Fechner established the zero point beyond which vibration cannot be sensed at all, whereas physicians were concerned with vibration that is harmful despite an absence of discomfort or attention. 'The traveller's mind takes little note of the thousands of successive jolts which he experiences, but every one of them tells upon his body', according to the *Lancet*.[22] Regarding the pros and cons of different modes of travel, an article contributed by J. Reynolds to *The Book of Health*, for another example, explains that the nerves receive 'impressions' from the motions of the railway, 'which are none the less real because they are unconsciously inflicted'.[23]

In an effort to gain credibility perhaps, the *Lancet* report brought together the opinions and measurements of various scientific writers, including engineers, chemists, but mostly doctors. It was edited by a 'commission' of doctors, the members of which wrote many of the passages. The surgeon and M.P. for Finsbury, Thomas Wakley, was perhaps the leading contributor, as he was the editor of the journal as a whole. Because the report on railway travelling includes the various contributions that make up any periodical, I find it more representative of the concern with continuous vibration than a book such as Erichsen's, dealing with railway accidents and collisions. As a periodical, an object that is published at the rate of once a week, it seems to resonate with the kind of temporality or speed that is its subject. Mark Turner, in an article for the journal *Media History*, proposes that in order to understand the nature of nineteenth-century periodicals, it is necessary to ask questions about time. As time sped up, as the telegraph and railway 'radically accelerated communications across time and space', the need was emphasized for a standard global system of measuring time. The asynchrony between newly linked communities, Turner suggests, is echoed by the periodical press which provides 'no single rhythm', which 'moves to a number of different beats': quarterly, monthly, daily.[24] Contributing to the cacophony of periodical time described by Turner, then, are the more physical rhythms of such phenomena and technologies as sound, light, X-rays, and railways, which were discussed at length (often in the periodicals themselves) in the nineteenth century, as we have seen.

In the *Lancet* report the number of movements experienced per hour are counted and compared to the 'violent shocks' of a collision. After listing some of the symptoms caused by shocks to the nervous system, it is claimed that 'each of those short, sharp vibrations felt in a railway carriage (and of which the number in every hour amounts to upwards of 20,000) resembles, on a small scale, the jerk and violent motion produced by a collision, from which it differs only in degree'.[25] This identification of a scale or continuum of vibration suggests that all such motion is a form of shock. If there are upwards of 20,000 vibrations or shocks every hour they are delivered at the rate of about six or more every second. Possibly the figure of 20,000 was based on the number counted by a chemist (not identified, but possibly R. Angus Smith, whose measurements of air quality begin two paragraphs later), included in another part of the report:

> The actual number of movements in a given time varies according to many circumstances. An eminent scientific chemist thus writes to us on this subject: – "I once counted 90,000 movements in a first-class carriage from Manchester to London, but how many more there were I did not further examine. There was a considerable variety in the kind of movement. I never attempted to count the number in a carriage without cushions".[26]

This is a remarkable claim, not only because the chemist apparently counted as many as 90,000 in the first place, but because he did this quite a while ago ('I once counted') and continues to find it significant enough to report to the *Lancet*, and because the editors found this significant and perhaps scientific enough to publish. The fastest journey from Manchester to London took five hours in 1860[27], which would mean there were nearly 20,000 movements per hour. Probably with the aim to present this area of medicine as properly scientific, these quantities sound factual, like the experimental results of physicists, as opposed to a more subjective 'loads' or even 'thousands'. Many historians have viewed the history of physics, physiology, psychology and other areas of enquiry, in terms of a quest for legitimacy, as these disciplines were in formation in the nineteenth century.[28] Fechner intended that his equation, according to which quantities of vibration produce corresponding qualities of sensation, would confer scientific validity onto the study of the introspective and spiritual realm of human experience. In a parallel way, the *Lancet*'s contributors attempted to demonstrate that quantities of railway vibration have certain pathological effects on the body.

The interest exhibited by the chemist and medical writers in counting the vibrations and presenting the findings is thus typical of the time: counting had become a favoured means of presenting facts in physics, evolutionary theory and many other branches of scientific inquiry following a growth in numeracy from the seventeenth to the nineteenth centuries.[29] The counting of railway vibrations can accordingly be seen as an instance of a general preoccupation with numbers at this time, while I am arguing that it can also be seen as a response to a new kind of sensory experience: a sense of the extrasensory. Railway travellers felt themselves shaken by a large number of shocks, each of which was barely distinguishable from the rest, and which seemed to be occurring with increasing rapidity. The concern with vibration could thus be viewed in relation to Jonathan Crary's analyses of the measurement of sensation, subjectivity and the limits of attention in the later nineteenth century.[30] Medical attempts to calculate vibrations per hour developed alongside enterprises such as psychophysics, which attempted to calculate and control subjective experience and the limited powers of human attention – deploying technological means of measuring vibrations with such instruments as the siren, or, in the case of rail vibrations, with an invention by Charles Babbage to record and to count each individual shock, as we shall see.

The *Lancet* also claimed that the sounds of railway travel – along with the more palpable vibratory movements – could be harmful, operating beyond consciousness. The author of a report published in 1872, 'The Narcotic Influence of Railway Travelling', attempted to identify what it is about travelling that sends many people to sleep, again suggesting that vibration is harmful to the extent that it is unnoticeable, not only existing beyond the limits of our conscious awareness but contributing to our loss of it:

> In these days of railway catastrophes, the timid traveller, possessing a strong imagination, – an essential element in great timidity – might weave a curious fancy of a syren lulling to sleep the victims whom she lures to destruction, or of grimy-handed Art imitating the redder touch of Nature in the unconsciousness to pain into which, as Livingstone has taught us, the victims of the carnivora pass before their death. But to the physiologist the phenomena has a scientific interest as another illustration of the strange effect of reiterated sound upon the brain-cells; gently loosening, by its vibrations, the links which bind together the centres of consciousness and sensation.[31]

The name of the siren (also spelt 'syren', as in this report) was derived from the mythology of monsters – part woman, part bird – who were supposed to lure sailors to destruction with their enchanting singing, as I mentioned in Chapter Two. De la Tour chose the name for his instrument for measuring the vibrations in any tone (the instrument used by many physicists in the nineteenth century to demonstrate the frequency thresholds of audibility), as the instrument was capable of making sound in water. It was only when a larger version of this instrument was developed in the 1870s for use on steamships to give warning signals that the name acquired the redoubled resonance with myth that it has today. Here, the desire to avoid being lulled to sleep is another instance of how vibration was perceived as a threat. The dangers of near-unconsciousness are linked to the mythical properties of sound vibration, to imaginary beasts whose powers exist beyond the reach of reason, which the physiologist aims to understand and thereby defeat with scientific knowledge.

The eight-part *Lancet* report of 1862 also describes the repetitive sounds of travelling as harmful, due to their vibratory impact on the body, as where 'the rattle and noise which accompany the progress of the train create an incessant vibration on the tympanum, and thus influence the brain through the nerves of hearing'. Noises causes headaches and fatigue.[32] Palpable and audible vibrations are frequently coupled suggesting that noise is experienced as a kind of high-pitched shaking, or shaking as infrasonic noise. Among the various contributors, Dr C. J. B. Williams observes that 'the shaking and noise' is worst in second- and third-class carriages, and on certain lines. 'For noisiness', writes Williams, 'the Brighton line certainly carries off the palm, perhaps from the number and length of its tunnels and deep cuttings; but for *shakiness*, the South-Eastern express trains have the pre-eminence'.[33]

The Lancet emphasizes that noise has physical effects, observing that the ear is vibrated by 'noisiness', while the whole body is vibrated by '*shakiness*'. It seems that noise is on a continuum with the palpable vibrations, differing in quantity more than quality, where both have harmful effects. The physics of acoustics supports this idea, that to hear is to be shaken, as where John Tyndall in his lectures on sound explained that hearing involves sympathetic vibration not only of the membrane, but the bones of the ear:

When the tympanic membrane receives a shock, that shock is transmitted through the series of bones above referred to [between the drum and the brain], and is concentrated on the membrane against which the base of the stirrup bone is planted. That membrane transfers the shock to the water of the labyrinth, which, in its turn, transfers it to the nerves.[34]

The quantification of vibration in physics may have contributed to the apprehension of a scale of shock, ranging from the everyday motion and noise of trains to collisions. Acoustical studies referred to the 'shock' of a noise[35], but also to shocks of sound in general (as shown in the quotation above from Tyndall's *Sound*) and other phenomena including light and heat. In his lecture on radiation, for example, in which Tyndall used the model of sound to describe the scale or spectrum of light waves, which differ only in 'periods of recurrence' from heat, he observed that 'millions of shocks are received every second from the calorific waves'.[36] This sense of multiplicity resonates with the original, pre-military meaning of shock, the first entry for which in the *Oxford English Dictionary* is 1325, denoting 'some definite number of sheaves', often 60, or an indefinite 'heap, crowd, multitude'[37], as in the surviving expression of a 'shock of hair'. The later encounter with an enemy at war is with a large number of opponents which make up an army, as the 'seven thousand' traitors which 'our battalia trebles' in Shakespeare's *King Richard III* might suggest, which become united in a 'doubtful shock of arms'[38], or the reference in *The Annual Register* of 1758, to 'the Prussian infantry, which had often stood, and often given, so many terrible shocks'. Filling up space and repeated in time, what these very different kinds of shock have in common – a shock of sheaves, of an army, sound and heat – is the sense in which they are each a singular multiplicity. Schivelbusch develops his analysis through consideration of developments in military organization. He describes the fusion of energies, those of horseman and steed into a powerful force, followed by the mass unit of the army which emerged in the sixteenth century:

> The basic principle of this new tactical organization was that the warriors no longer did battle individually but as parts of the new combat machine. [...] The new military organization concretized the entirely specific sense of the word [shock]: the clash of two bodies of troops, each of which represented a new unified concentration of energy by means of the consolidation of a number of warriors into one deindividualized and mechanized unit.[39]

Schivelbusch compares this shift from horse and rider to the army with the shift from horse and coach travel to the railway, in which passengers, like warriors, no longer travel (or battle) as individuals but as a unit, which becomes a condition of modernity more generally: 'In the modern army individuals are for the first time mechanized, or even subsumed, into an organizational scheme that is completely abstract and exterior to them. In the further history of the modern age, this condition becomes increasingly common in all spheres of life'.[40] The sense of a 'consolidation of a number' is also, and more directly, applicable to the shocks experienced on the railway. In the nineteenth century the meaning of shock has an increasingly temporal orientation, as when a large number of vibrations is experienced in a limited period of time. There is a point at which the perception of each individual motion gives way to an experience that is something else, as when 'separate impulses' are lost to the 'dull drone' of the siren. In the first of his eight lectures on sound, Tyndall describes the perception of shocks as a continuous sound:

> Imagine the first of a series of pulses which follow each other at regular intervals, impinging upon the tympanic membrane. It is shaken by the shock; and a body once shaken cannot come instantaneously to rest. The human ear, indeed, is so constructed that the sonorous motion vanishes with extreme rapidity, but its disappearance is not instantaneous; and if the motion imparted to the auditory nerve by each individual pulse of our series continue until the arrival of its successor, the sound will not

cease at all. The effect of every shock will be renewed before it vanishes, and the recurrent impulses will link themselves together to form one continuous musical sound.[41]

The motion of trains is louder and lower, or slower, though, than musical sound. The individual shocks are just about, almost discernable. Whereas the dull drone consists of many impulses felt as a whole, continuous sound, the motion of trains is sensed simultaneously as many and one, an infinitely large yet small number, a discontinuous sort of continuity. Consciousness of the multiple, however, threatens to give way to an illusion of safety.

It is perhaps Max Nordau who most alarmingly generalized an unconsciousness of numerous kinds of shocks, in his *Degeneration*:

Even the little shocks of railway travelling, not perceived by consciousness, the perpetual noises, and the various sights in the streets of a large town, our suspense pending the sequel of progressing events, the constant expectation of the newspaper, of the postman, of visitors, cost our brains wear and tear. [...] The many affections of the nervous system already bear a name which implies that they are a direct consequence of certain influences of modern civilization. The terms 'railway-spine' and 'railway-brain' which the English and American pathologists have given to certain states of these organs, show that they recognise them as due partly to the effects of railway accidents, partly to the constant vibrations undergone in railway travelling.[42]

Counting as counter-strategy

The effort to calculate the number of shocks and so on, in the *Lancet* and elsewhere, may serve to bring the speed of that which exists beyond the sensory thresholds into awareness. It is perhaps a way of registering, assessing, remembering and regurgitating that which would otherwise pass by unnoticed. Referring to the rapid spread of railway travel, Nordau reports that: 'In 1840 there were in Europe 3,000 kilometres of railway; in 1891 there were 218,000 kilometres. The number of travellers in 1840, in Germany, France, and England, amounted to 2½ millions; in 1891 it was 614 millions'.[43] He continues by reporting the increase in the number of letters received per year, the number of newspapers and books published per year, the yearly increase in the value of exports and imports, and the number of tons contained by the ships which entered the ports of Great Britain. Part 1 of the *Lancet* report includes a typical account of the yearly rise in rail travel, too: 'The number of individual journeys undertaken in the United Kingdom have increased, during the last ten years, at the rate of nearly ten millions per annum'.[44] Part 2, in which further calculations are contained, opens with numbers:

> THE existing railway stock in this country is now represented by upwards of a quarter of a million of vehicles. If joined into one long train, with their 5800 engines, (consuming 260 tons of coal per hour,) they would form a continuous line of about 600 miles [...].[45]

The interest in counting vibrations, journeys, vehicles and so on, forms part of that attempt to maintain awareness in an attempt to counteract unconsciousness, while medical writers seem also to be persistently reaching for a way to present the subject of railway shock scientifically, using factual sounding figures such as 20,000, like the experimental results of physicists. Like physicists, medical professionals describe a world in which certain frequencies of vibration occur, which often threaten to escape the sensory capacities, or at least the capacity to sense what is actually happening. Senses through which the unfavourable conditions of railway travel are experienced, along with sound and hearing, while hearing is itself is to be touched or shaken, include sight and smell. The eyes apparently suffer from the 'dazzling' rapidity of passing sights, and from an illusion of vibration or wavering. 'Dr. Budd, F. R. S., has directed our attention to the peculiarly dazzling effect of passing in rapid succession the white telegraph posts, from which the wires seem to fall and rise, appearing to the eye to undulate'.[46] Responding to the claim in 1875 that sound vibrations send travellers to sleep like the syren's lullaby, Dr Stewart wrote a letter protesting that it is the 'vibrations of light' itself, and the 'rapidity with which objects travel into and out of sight' that fatigues the eyes.[47] Dr R. Angus Smith wrote to the *Lancet*, regarding the poor quality of air in the carriages, for which, perhaps because of the unreliability of subjective perception, incapable as it is of sensing just how harmful railway conditions are, he employed a method of objective measurement. He explains that permanganate solution is decomposed by different volumes of air, according to its state of purity. Smith provides a table of numbers, which represent the volume of air required to decompose a given amount of the solution, that is: 'the proportionate purity of the air'. The purest of air is measured inside his laboratory at All Saints, figuring at 72,000 cubic inches, in contrast to a packed railway carriage which is represented by 8,000 cubic inches, as is a time when the smell of a sewer entered the laboratory.[48] Cushions and carpets soften the vibrations but, it is suggested, need be 'disinfected occasionally'.[49]

The most scientific method of measuring railway shocks, as it does not rely on limited human perception, or ability to count, may be provided by Charles Babbage, inventor of the 'Difference Engine' and 'Analytical Engine' for performing mathematical calculations (often seen as the earliest versions of the computer). An ongoing debate as to whether the Great

Western Railway should use broad or narrow gauge lines led the directors to ask Babbage for his opinion, for which he devised a method for tracing on paper the number of 'shakes' of a train travelling on different lines. To do this, Babbage firstly removed all the internal parts of the carriage, as his autobiographical *Passages in the Life of a Philosopher* explains. 'Through its bottom firm supports, fixed upon the framework below, passed up into the body of the carriage, and supported a long table', on which 'slowly rolled sheets of paper, each a thousand feet long. Several inking pens traced curves on this paper, which expressed the following measures'.[50] These measures are of the vertical and lateral shakes of the carriage at its middle and end, while a chronometer marked half seconds on the paper. This made it possible to count the number of shakes which occurred every second. After covering over two miles of paper in this way, Babbage was convinced that the broad gauge was 'safest and most convenient' for the public. Had it not been for his speech at the London Tavern, he claimed, upon the walls of which some of the paper was displayed, Brunel's broad gauge system would no longer exist in England.[51] (It was finally replaced with narrow gauge.)

For physicists, medical and other kinds of writers, as we have seen, counting served as a scientific way of registering the multiplicity of shocks experienced as a singular sensation, or not sensed at all. Railway shocks seem to have become increasingly uncountable, incomprehensible, extra-sensory – which can be taken to refer to both an excess, and loss of sensation – against which medical writers struggled in the later nineteenth century. The sexual effects of railway vibration (among other kinds of transport and technologies, including bicycles and sewing machines, as I will discuss in Chapter Five), which were somewhat notorious, and reported in the *Lancet* and elsewhere, may also have contributed to the interest in attempting to calculate exactly what this mode of travel was doing to the body and mind. To counteract the lapse into degenerate unconsciousness, with its potentially disastrous social consequences, counting is an attempt to maintain rational, conscious control.

Street noises

The various attempts to manage railway shocks formed part of a wider reaction against industrial and urban vibrations. Babbage protested at length against noise, including that of steam engines, music machines, harpsichords, hurdy-gurdies, organ-grinding, and psalm-singing. He published the pamphlet *Observations of Street Nuisances* in 1864, which he then incorporated as a chapter, 'Street Nuisances', in his autobiography. Babbage's enthusiasm for recording the vibrations of trains seems to extend to his detailed lists of noises. The performers include English fiddle players,

German brass bands, Indians with tom-toms, and Italian organ-grinders, of whom there are 'above a thousand' in London, 'employed in tormenting the natives'.[52] Among the encouragers of street music are tavern-keepers, servants and children. Babbage calculated that over the previous 12 years, 25 per cent of his working power was destroyed by street nuisances.[53] He compared the interruption of his calculations with that of the rest needed by the '4.72 persons per cent. [who are] constantly ill'.[54] The sensitivity of ill people may explain why the *Lancet*'s editor found it appropriate to comment on 'Vexatious Noises'. 'Everything that screams is a nuisance', as is cock-crowing, children playing, howling dogs and other animals, and the music of 'the poor organ-grinder'. It is requested that people regard their neighbours.[55] Sick people suffer in cities from the sound of church bells, claims a later report.[56]

In 1864 the first Bill passed through Westminster for the control of street noise. Many of those who contributed to the publicity campaign leading up to this appealed to the impact of noise on bodily and mental health, especially the nerves. Michael Bass, M.P. for Derby, first attempted to bring into Parliament his 'Act for the Better Regulation of Street Music in the Metropolis' in 1863, supporting his side of the debate by gathering together a collection of letters, press reports and official documents to be published under the title *Street Music in the Metropolis* in the following year. The letters focus mainly on the suffering of noise by people with nervous illness, and by intellectuals who require quiet to concentrate on their work, such as the 28 professors and practitioners of arts or sciences who added their signatures to a letter from Charles Dickens.[57] Among the letters is Babbage's most extensive register of the number of interruptions, included as a 'P.S.':

1860				Brass Bands		Organs		Monkeys
July 3	...	...	...	3	...	—	...	—
4	Stone hit me	...		—	...	2	...	—
5	...	...	...	—	...	1	...	1
6	...	...	...	—	...	1	...	—

This register continues through the rest of July and August, and is resumed in 1861 until May 1st, although from August onwards the 'Monkeys' category changes to 'Others'. (Organists were often accompanied by ring-tailed monkeys, for added entertainment value. The monkeys were trained to perform various tricks, to come when called for example, to collect pennies, and to fire guns.[58]) The final total, though this is 'partial', as Babbage was not able to record all the noises, is: 165 interruptions in 90 days.

The noisy vibrations of rail travel were only one source among many of shocks to the nervous system. Many historians have painted the picture of fearful middle and upper class Victorians, subject to 'shattered nerves'[59], for which vibration, in its various forms, might be identified as a most dominant force (as for degeneration and all kinds of disorders and classes, often in contradictory ways). This way of describing the nerves of sensitive people evokes the fragility of glass, material most easily shattered by vibration. In *Victorian Soundscapes* John Picker suggests that such sensitivities were suffered mainly by particular classes, arguing that the professional status of writers including Babbage, Dickens and Thomas Carlyle, was threatened by urban noise. Throughout much of Bass's *Street Music in the Metropolis* and elsewhere, the intellectual is presented as a frail professional, linking the bedridden and home-ridden during this period. In Picker's account, the 'sound-proof study' built for Carlyle is representative of the desire to establish a space, territorially, upholding divisions between the lower classes and middle-class professionals, and protecting English national identity from foreign infiltration. Picker argues that 'many professionals who felt threatened by street organs considered it vitally important to maintain the semantic distinction between "music" as intended for those of refined tastes indoors and grinding noise as meant for the exterior masses'.[60] Within this general category of 'grinding noise', many of the writers about street music attempted to order the chaotic collection of performers into further categories, the number of which counted by Charles Manby Smith was nine. These include 'hand-organists', 'monkey-organists', 'blind bird-organists', 'flageolet-organists', and 'horse-and-cart organists'. Under this last heading, Smith describes a cacophony of sounds which range from the high frequencies of 'piercing notes' to the booming of gongs and the bass, as though produced by a wilderness of animal species, which 'squall', 'bray', 'snort', and especially 'roar' – so loud and low, that each of the separate vibrations are audible:

> The piercing notes of a score of shrill fifes, the squall of as many clarions, the hoarse bray of a legion of tin trumpets, the angry and fitful snort of a brigade of rugged bassoons, the unintermitting rattle of a dozen or more deafening drums, the clang of bells firing in peals, the boom of gongs, with the sepulchral roar of some unknown contrivance for bass, so deep that you might almost count the vibrations of each note – these are a few of the components of the horse-and-cart organ, the sum total of which it is impossible to add up.[61]

If the sharpness of 'piercing notes' is a stabbing motion, while the bells are 'firing', the roar of the bass is more like the shocks experienced on the railway. Just as the categories of different musicians are almost too numerous to calculate, Smith suggests, 'you might almost count the vibrations of each note', while the 'sum total' of the components of the horse-and-cart organ 'is impossible to add up'.

The periodic analysis of railway vibration, as we have seen, reflects a more general approach to the establishment of scientific facts. The calculations of categories and frequencies of street noises also parallel Babbage's proposal for the establishment of the 'Constants of Nature and Art'. These 'constants' include the velocity of light, the distances of the planets and their period of revolution. Babbage intended that the Royal Society of London, the Institute of France and the Academy of Berlin would undertake to compile constants, and update them every two years. His list identified 19 categories, which progressed from the constants of optics and the solar system to 'the numbers of known species of mammalia, moluscs, insects', for instance. He proposed 142 numbers measuring different parts of the bodies of mammals.[62] This dedication to categories and counting can be viewed in the perspective of the Enlightenment that extends through the eighteenth and nineteenth centuries, through which the classification of the natural world emerged as one of the ideal achievements of modern science, and became part of what can be seen as an imperialistic mission to reduce exotic territories to intellectual order by collecting and cataloguing their productions. Harriet Ritvo argues that the colonialism of zoological nomenclatures was only the edge of a more comprehensive project of domination, 'encompassing both foreign colleagues and less elite fellow citizens'.[63] Both 'foreign' and 'native' street musicians appear in this way to have been categorized as degenerate species, identified with the animals by which they were often accompanied.

Much, much quieter sounds than those of trains and cities seemed also to pervade the atmosphere. In Chapter Nine of *The Ninth Bridgewater Treatise* (1837), 'On the Permanent Impression of Our Words and Actions on the Globe We Inhabit', Babbage claimed that the human voice continues to vibrate forever through the atmosphere, though passing beyond the realm of the sensory thresholds. This belief, of which I wrote a great deal in Chapter Two, was shared by Fechner, Crookes and other scientists and spiritualists. Fechner's *On Life After Death* explained that 'vibrations only *seem* to die out, in so far as they spread indefinitely in all directions; or, if dying out for a time, transformed into energy or tension, they are able to begin afresh, in some form or other, in accordance with the law of the conservation of energy'.[64] Like Fechner's work, Babbage's *Treatise* was an attempt to reconcile spiritual phenomena with scientific reasoning. He argued that miracles such as the appearance of new species could be explained rationally, within the limits of probability, if changes in organic life over time were seen as an equation series designed by God. This theory has tended to overshadow Chapter Nine of the *Treatise*, which explains that after sounds become inaudible the motions they impress on the particles of the atmosphere continue to be communicated to further particles. Setting out a distinction between harmony and noise, 'good' and 'ill', as though already anticipating the 'worthless and base' street noises, Babbage continues:

Every atom, impressed with good and with ill, retains at once the motions which philosophers and sages have imparted to it, mixed and combined in ten thousand ways with all that is worthless and base. The air itself is one vast library, on whose pages are for ever written all that man has ever said or woman whispered.[65]

This idea that every atmospheric atom is 'impressed' or written on, might be suggestive of the attempt to gather together a historical sense of what the past sounded like, by reading. For Babbage, according to Picker, 'the air acts as a giant scroll or phonograph, permanently recording voices that, he concedes, only God possesses the knowledge to play'.[66] Babbage's instrument for recording the 'shakes' of the railway is further imaginable as pre-phonographic, with its inking pens tracing curves on slowly rolling sheets of paper, 'each a thousand feet long'.[67] Or rather this is an early version of the phonautograph, invented by M. E. Léon Scott in 1857. This consisted of a horn as an ear and a membrane as an eardrum. When the horn was spoken into it vibrated the membrane, attached to the centre of which was a bristle, which drew a trace over a turning soot-covered cylinder. It converted sound into a wavy line, a lasting visible trace. (In 1878 Edison patented the device for converting a wavy line back into sound.) The shakes of the railway recorded by Babbage are no longer audible or palpable, but made visible, and controllable. The shakes are transformed, into stillness and silence, 'curves on this paper'.[68] Here again we see the technological dream of capturing vibrations that operate beyond the limited range of the human senses, from the rapid vibrations of rail travel and street noises to the spiritual vibrations of ancient history.

Picker examines the role of hearing in Victorian culture as a metaphor, and a challenge, as in the case of street noise, to the communication of meaning in literature. He shows that this was a period of 'unprecedented amplification', which I have taken further with the more intense sound that is shaking. Or rumbling, in the case of Mr Morfin's deaf landlady in Dickens's *Dombey and Son*, who, when her tenant plays his violoncello, 'had no other consciousness of these performances than a sensation of something rumbling in her bones'.[69] The *Lancet* also reported observations of sound as a potentially palpable, rather than audible vibration, as experienced on the railway, as we have seen, and also in other circumstances. 'For Mrs. S—, who has been deaf for over thirty years, it is not that she can hear sound '*but that she can feel it*', reported W. Bolton Tomson.[70] Picker argues that the noise of the railway in *Dombey and Son*, its immediacy and dynamism, was a means of expression for Dickens's own authorial voice, and something against which he felt a struggle, 'of being heard, of *getting through*'.[71] As both an expressive ideal and a sort of rival, there is an ambivalence which I want to develop, with shaking as an amplified, palpable kind of sound in *Dombey and Son* – first published in 18 monthly parts between October 1846 and April 1848 – and other reports about the railway, published in Dickens's weekly journal *Household Words*. My next section will ask how noise and shaking – through their opposition to stasis and silence – are not always conceived as in some way bad, painful or detrimental to health, but as both a destructive and progressive, even creative force.

The quaking of Stagg's Gardens

The first mention of the railway in *Dombey and Son*, apart from Mr Toodle's employment as a 'Steaminjin' stoker, misheard by Miss Tox as 'choker'[72], is the violent scene at Stagg's Gardens:

> The first shock of a great earthquake had, just at that period, rent the whole neighbourhood to its centre. Traces of its course were visible on every side. Houses were knocked down; streets broken through and stopped; deep pits and trenches dug in the ground; enormous heaps of earth and clay thrown up; buildings that were undermined and shaking, propped by great beams of wood. [...]
> In short, the yet unfinished and unopened Railroad was in progress; and, from the very core of all this dire disorder, trailed smoothly away, upon its mighty course of civilisation and improvement. (*DS*, 68)

This scene confuses any straightforward notion of the railway as the embodiment of progress, the very tracks of progress. As a metaphor for the 'course of civilisation and improvement', Dickens chose the most naturally destructive, shattering noise possible: the quaking of the earth, the foundation of everything. In contrast to the preoccupations of the *Lancet*, the construction of the railway in the first place is described as a violent shock, while the tracks trail 'smoothly away'. This is an account of the impact of 'shock' and 'shaking' not on the human body or mind, directly, but on the places in which people collectively live: the neighbourhood, the home.

Dickens among many other Victorian authors read Charles Lyell's influential *Principles of Geology*, which most likely provided one of the sources for his account of earthquake activity[73], while he also shows a more general awareness of geological formations and processes. Railway historians have pointed out that the cuttings made for the London to Birmingham line – the building of which is being described in *Dombey and Son* – revealed strata in the rocks that seemed to demonstrate Lyell's understanding of geological formation. Later in *Dombey and Son*, the breathless descriptions of the now working train speeding through the countryside seem to refer to such layers, as critic Humphrey House has observed, as the train moves rapidly 'through the fields, through the woods, through the corn, through the hay, through the chalk, through the mould, through the clay, through the rock' (DS, 298).[74] But in the scene in Stagg's Gardens the railway does not expose geological history so much as it is itself a powerful geological force. Along with earthquakes and the destruction of cities, Lyell's accounts of volcanic activity (he theorized that both earthquakes and volcanoes were caused by pressure erupting from the intense subterranean heat of the earth) could form part of the context for Dickens's narrative where 'Hot springs and fiery eruptions, the usual attendants upon earthquakes, lent their contributions of confusion to the scene'.[75] But Dickens's conception of geological science was not just based on scientific narratives. Adelene Buckland demonstrates that while critics have discussed the links between Dickens's novels and science at length, such discussions have ignored the importance of material culture. She points out that Dickens frequented London's shows which often involved dramatic simulations of earthquakes and volcanic eruptions. Such popular entertainments sometimes incorporated vibratory effects: 'The cyclorama in London', notes Buckland, 'opened with a recreation of the Lisbon earthquake of 1755, including rumbling floors, violent light, and sound effects'.[76]

One way of responding to the powerful impact of a vibratory world was to attempt to manage it through the activity of counting and categorizing, as we have seen. Lyell can provide evidence here of how such attempts extended not only to medicine and physics but also to geology, and while I am entirely convinced that London's shows influenced Dickens this does not of course exclude the possibility that scientific texts also play a role in his novels. Lyell exhibits an interest in counting which could be compared to the quantification of railway shocks and so on, where he mentions 'a register of the shocks [...] in the year 1783, the number was nine hundred and forty-nine, of which five hundred and one were shocks of the first degree of force; and in the following year there were one hundred and fifty-one, of which ninety-eight were of the first magnitude'.[77] Dickens seems to mimic such a scientific method in his comparable attempt to count not the vibrations themselves but to list their effects on the environment, as if to manage or take some control of their impact. The sense of shock as a 'heap, crowd, multitude', an indefinite number or frequency which threatens to escape all such attempts to document, resonates in the scene at Stagg's Gardens, as in the counting of vibrations or the cataloguing of street musicians. The list of damaged or deficient items receives endless additions, including 'carcasses of ragged tenements, and fragments of unfinished walls and arches, and piles of scaffolding, and wildernesses of bricks, and giant forms of cranes, and tripods straddling above nothing. There were a hundred thousand shapes and substances of incompleteness' (DS, 68). The very building of the railway tracks, Dickens suggests, like the vibratory shocks of the journeys that they will eventually make possible, has an affect that we can only attempt to quantify, that threatens to escape our capacity to count, or to list.

Critics have debated whether the railway in *Dombey and Son* symbolizes destruction or progress, death or birth, or both.[78] Buckland argues that London's scientific shows introduced Dickens to nineteenth-century theories of 'catastrophism', and that catastrophe is essential to this novel's (and *Bleak House*'s) conception of progress. Theories of catastrophism accounted for the fragmentary geological record and the fossilized presence of now extinct creatures in terms of a series of catastrophes, in a world that had apparently once been more catastrophic than it presently was. Such theories were opposed by the 'uniformitarian' history put forward most famously by Lyell, a relatively gradual history of the earth in which catastrophes had always been of the same scale. As Buckland points out, far more attention is given to Lyell's theory as his uniformitarianism became so important to Darwin's theory of evolution, but 'popular entertainments maintained the popularity of geological catastrophes long into the nineteenth century'.[79] In this context of interest in fossils and evolution critics have also paid little attention to Lyell's own interest in earthquakes. But while uniformitarian geologists such as Lyell as well as popular shows could have informed Dickens's account of the earthquake in *Dombey and Son*, I agree that the catastrophism of the latter was best placed to shape the novel's narrative of progress and change. Dickens considered the chaos of catastrophe as necessary for progress, and further, presented the alternative as a less preferable, sterile condition of silence and stasis. He was interested in producing effects, often comic, through the contrast or conflict between such extremes, and thus presented the construction of the railway and its ensuing panic in sharp opposition to its negative of silence.[80] Before we are introduced to the 'dire disorder' of Stagg's Gardens, the 'dark, dreadfully genteel street' is described, in which Mr Dombey's house is situated. Even the street nuisances retreat:

> The summer sun was never on the street, but in the morning about breakfast time [...]. It was soon gone again to return no more that day; and the bands of music and the straggling Punch's shows going after it, left it a prey to the most dismal of organs, and white mice; with now and then a porcupine, to vary the entertainments; until the butlers whose families were dining out, began to stand at the house doors in the twilight, and the lamp-lighter made his nightly failure in attempting to brighten up the street with gas. (*DS*, 23–4)

The 'bands of music' in this region do not so much annoy as brighten or cheer up the street, all too fleetingly. Instead of monkeys, the quietest of animals accompany the organists: mice. Darkness, coldness and quietness are presented as absences, after the light and heat of the sun and the sound of the bands are gone. The exterior bleakness matches the interior, where the lights seem hushed: 'Every chandelier or lustre, muffled in holland, looked like a monstrous tear depending from the ceiling's eye' (DS, 24). It is a house of loss, in which furnishings take on the form of grief, 'a monstrous tear', for Mrs Dombey. The straw from outside the house, used to quieten the noise of wheels on the street, blows in: 'Every gust of wind that rose, brought eddying round the corner from the neighbouring mews, some fragments of the straw that had been strewn before the house when she was ill' (24). After the death of her son, Paul:

> Noise ceased to be, within the shadow of the roof. The brass band that came into the street once a week, in the morning, never brayed a note in at those windows; but all such company, down to a poor little piping organ of weak intellect, with an imbecile party of automaton dancers, waltzing in and out at folding doors, fell off from it with one accord, and shunned it as a hopeless place. (DS, 337)

Again and again, the temperature of the house and Mr Dombey shifts from cold toward freezing, which is not a shivering or shaking, but silence as of stone. Shortly before the visit to Stagg's Gardens, the scene of Paul's christening party takes place, at which

> Mr. Dombey alone remained unmoved. He might have been hung up for sale at a Russian fair as a specimen of a frozen gentleman. [...] Mr. Chick was twice heard to hum a tune at the bottom of the table, but on both occasions it was a fragment of the Dead March in Saul. The party seemed to get colder and colder, and to be gradually resolving itself into a congealed and gelid state, like the collation round which it was assembled. (DS, 63, 66)

Where Stagg's Gardens is shaken to the core, the patriarchal figure of Mr Dombey expects obedience and order, and is central to everything in this household. The order that is his very stiffness seems to radiate, to infect the atmosphere and each member of the party, including the child named after his father: "He will be christened Paul", his mother is told at the beginning, '"His father's name, Mrs. Dombey, and his grandfather's! I wish his grandfather were alive this day!" And again he said "Domb-bey and Son" in exactly the same tone as before' (DS, 2). Like a phonographic recording, instead of change or movement through time or through space, things remain stationary. Years later, the coldness of Mr Dombey is offered as an explanation for the numerous diseases from which his son suffers: 'The chill of Paul's christening had struck home, perhaps, to some sensitive part of his nature, which could not recover itself in the cold shade of his father' (96).

Where Mr Dombey believes that the formula of tradition and convention must be conserved through the generations, the inhabitants of Stagg's Gardens undergo a process of massive change, in which all previous roads and modes of conveyance seem defeated, even buried in the wake of the earthquake:

> Here, a chaos of carts, overthrown and jumbled together, lay topsy-turvy at the bottom of a steep unnatural hill; there, confused treasures of iron soaked and rusted in something that had accidentally become a pond. Everywhere were bridges that led nowhere; thoroughfares that were wholly impassable [...] and mounds of ashes blocked up rights of way, and wholly changed the law and custom of the neighbourhood. (DS, 68)

'WHERE IS IT?' is the coachman's exasperated response to Susan Nipper, some time later, following Paul's request during his last illness for his nurse in infancy, Mrs Toodle from Stagg's Gardens. 'There was no such place as Stagg's Gardens. It had vanished from the earth' (DS, 232–3). But this vanishing is not the same kind of loss from which the Dombey household suffers, as the 'old' is transformed into an abundance of new places and pathways. The 'old rotten summer-houses' are transformed into 'palaces', the 'miserable waste ground' into 'tiers of warehouses, crammed with rich goods and costly merchandise', and the 'old by-streets now swarmed with passengers and vehicles of every kind'. Where the bridges had led previously to 'nothing', they now lead 'to villas, gardens, churches, healthy public walks', and the 'beginnings of new thoroughfares, had started off upon the line at steam's own speed, and shot away into the country in a monster train' (233). Stagg's Gardens becomes wealthier and healthier. The violent quaking of the earth is transformed into the smoother vibration of rail travel. Only the 'monster train' seems to anticipate the horrendous rhythm of Dombey's journey, beating out an endless reminder of mortality amidst the progress of modernity, the repetition of 'the triumphant monster, Death', 'the remorseless monster, Death!', 'the indomitable monster, Death' (298–9). As nearly every critic notes, Dickens's 'prose poem' or even 'music' is here controlled by the motion of the carriage wheels[81], which also seem to contribute to his disturbed state of mind. The short-tempered and extremely uneasy Dombey seems to suffer from symptoms thought to be caused by the repetitive vibration of rail travel, with its capacity to shake the nerves, including 'anxiety', 'irritability', and 'restlessness', as noted in the Lancet report.[82] Between destruction versus progress, regret versus hope, the railway in Dombey and Son, to which I will return shortly, seems itself to oscillate, vibrate even.

Regarding the vibration of a completed, functioning railway, by the end of the century the Lancet observed that its motion and noise have a destructive impact not only on the human body but also on the places in which people live. 'The chorus of approval' gives way to the noise of 'complaints', more decisively than in Dickens's narrative. It is recommended that companies should be made liable for the structural damage caused to houses near to new railway lines.

> The chorus of approval which greeted the opening of the Central London Railway having subsided the voice of those residing near it is making itself heard in complaints to the effect that the constantly recurring noise and vibration due to the passing of trains will compel them to leave their houses unless means are taken to abate the nuisance. They have good cause of complaint, for many of them live in comparatively tranquil streets off the main road under which the "twopenny tube" runs, and even at a considerable distance from it they have to put up with daily discomfort and with the knowledge that should any member of their households become seriously ill quiet would be unattainable. The usual laying-down of straw that deadens the rattle of the passing cab or cart will not avail against the far-reaching vibration of the electric trains smashing along in the narrow space allotted to them.[83]

The problem of trains below as well as above ground continued into the first decade of the twentieth century. An expert in vibration who served on a government commission to inquire into damage caused to houses by tubes and underground railways, A. Mallock, invented a machine for measuring vibrations, much as Babbage had done. In 'The Study of Vibration', published in *Pearson's Magazine* in 1907, he noted the many complaints about the vibrations caused by underground and over-ground trains. 'We are told', he continued, 'that steel axles break, that houses crack, and bridges are rendered dangerous, all by vibration'.[84] Mallock included a series of diagrams showing the vibratory movements of various structures, such as the rocking of the Albert Suspension Bridge; the vibrations of a house caused by the passing of a 'subterranean tube' train; and the vibrations of the floor of a third-class railway carriage on 'a badly-laid line' in contrast to those of a better constructed third-class carriage on a 'more carefully laid line'.[85] Once again, it is those rapid semi-perceptible vibrations which are the cause of most concern: 'The sort of vibration which has caused most complaint from householders – such as the vibration from trains – is of a kind which is too quick to be counted, but not quick enough to be heard; that is to say, from ten to thirty vibrations a second'.[86] Although these vibrations can cause discomfort, however, Mallock considered the notion that these small vibrations, in cumulative fashion, do structural damage to houses, to be 'quite groundless'.[87]

Railway trains, Schivelbusch has claimed, produced a new kind of vibration, and this impacted on the environment as well as on human bodies. For historians more generally, in prefaces and introductions most usually, this mode of movement – through variations of shaking, quaking, tremors, and convulsions – frequently provides a metaphor for emphasizing the dramatic, earthquake-like shattering of old conventions through the changes brought about by industrial, technological, and other aspects of modernity. Julie Wosk for example, in *Women and the Machine*, looks at images of 'women living in a world being transformed by the tremors of technological change'.[88] In a biography of Ada Lovelace, a friend of Babbage (and Byron's daughter), Benjamin Wooley writes that 'the effects of industrialization and mechanization were felt across all levels of society, each new development feeding another in a chain reaction that shook the world, and shakes it still'. Ada Lovelace herself is said to have 'felt every tremor'.[89] This kind of history might be traced back into the nineteenth century, through Nordau's *Degeneration* for instance, which describes the changes taking place as a kind of earthquake, in this case to emphasize the destructiveness of such dramatic transformation: 'There is a sound of rending in every tradition, and it is as though the morrow would not link itself with to-day. Things as they are totter and plunge, and they are suffered to reel and fall'.[90] The classic work of Karl Marx and Friedrich Engels also uses the rhetoric of earthquakes to convey how change is not simply progressive. The preface to *The Communist Manifesto* (for the Russian edition of 1882 and the German edition of 1890) describes how the competition generated by mass production is 'shaking the very foundations of landed property – large and small'.[91] While theorists of degeneration can be seen to have feared a return to some animal state, and Marx and Engels were concerned with mechanical dehumanization and alienation, they also deployed the idea of degeneration in some ways, as Daniel Pick points out.[92] The motion of 'shaking' is used in their work along with the 'retrogressions and circular movements' that occur in spite of the ideal of progress.[93] Recalling the images of vibration in the prefaces, the condition of absolute and relentless change as opposed to 'fixed, fast-frozen relations', is also conveyed through the metaphor of melting – probably the most well-known image of how stability and solidity gave way to change and uncertainty:

> All fixed, fast-frozen relations, with their train of ancient and venerable prejudices and opinions are swept away, all new-formed ones become antiquated before they can ossify. All that is solid melts into air, all that is holy is profaned, and man is at last compelled to face with sober senses, his real conditions of life, and his relations with his kind.[94]

Vibratory movements are of course not simply metaphors for the condition of modernity, however; the rhetoric of shock corresponds with a persistent concern in the nineteenth century with what vibration is actually doing to things, including the human body and the buildings in which people live. Dickens's account of the transformation of Stagg's Gardens, and his own neighbourhood, from a quiet and sluggish suburb to a hectic business centre, in 'An Unsettled Neighbourhood' (1855), describes a more literal sense of being shaken. He asks:

> What changed our neighbourhood altogether and for ever? I don't mean what knocked down rows of houses, took the whole of little Twig Street into one immense hotel, substituted endless cab ranks for Fly the garter, and shook us all day long to our foundations with waggons of heavy goods; but, what put the neighbourhood off its head, and wrought it to that feverish pitch that it has ever since been unable to settle down to any one thing, and will never settle down again? THE RAILROAD has done it all.[95]

Previously, Dickens claims, his neighbourhood was 'rarely shaken by any conveyance', and there were no visitors except Stabber's Band, which used to come once a week and play for three quarters of an hour. The band was popular in this rather lonely sounding neighbourhood, and Dickens used to drop halfpence into the hat, but the transformation of the area into the high-speed of a 'feverish pitch' seems to take things to another, unwelcome extreme. Dickens's catalogue of railway goods, in both 'An Unsettled Neighbourhood' and *Dombey and Son*, might even be compared to the account of the 'absurdity' of the crises of overproduction in *The Communist Manifesto*, which by their 'periodical return' threaten the existence of bourgeois society.[96] In 'An Unsettled Neighbourhood' Dickens mentions 'Railway Dining Rooms', 'The Railway Larder', 'The Railway Ham, Beef, and German Sausage Warehouse', 'The Railway Pie Shop', and the list goes on through to 'Railway Double Stout at a gigantic threepence in your own jugs'.[97] Dickens is less concerned with the 'overproduction' though, the benefits of which he has tasted, than with a sort of over-excitation, with the 'unsettled, dissipated, wandering' state of his neighbours, who seem highly disturbed, as they 'go off their heads', are 'fired out of their wits', or in the case of J. Wigzell as a representative for those who are compelled to travel nowhere particularly at five minutes' notice, 'rendered perfectly insane'.[98] This is perhaps the kind of 'craze' mentioned by the *Lancet*. It is reported in 1897, with some determination, it seems, not to let anyone forget that rapid vibration has injurious effects, that 'speed is the craze, but there is no reason why speed should not be attained without the discomfort due to noise and rapid vibration, not to mention the, perhaps, permanently ill-effects which a constant series of joltings may have upon the nervous passenger and invalid'. The good news is that some lines, by now, including the Great Western Railway, are 'smooth and free from vibration', 'free from shock and noise'.[99]

In *Dombey and Son*:

> There were railway patterns in its drapers' shops, and railway journals in the windows of its newsmen. There were railway hotels,

coffee-houses, lodging-houses, boarding-houses; railway plans, maps, views, wrappers, bottles, sandwich-boxes, and time tables; railway hackney-coach and cab-stands; railway omnibuses, railway streets and buildings, railway hangers-on and parasites, and flatterers out of all calculation. There was even railway time observed in clocks, as if the sun itself had given in. (*DS*, 233)

These scenes of overproduction, in contrast to Marx and Engels's analysis, do not appear to convey a sense of impending cycles of crises. It seems the crisis has already happened. Though unsettled, this is another kind of activity to the violent earthquake-like shattering of everything. The new speeds which led to the chaos of asynchronic times, intensified in Mark Turner's account of 'periodical time'[100], become organized through the production of 'railway plans', 'time tables' and a standard 'railway time observed in clocks, as if the sun itself had given in'. Now the construction of the railway is complete, the vibrations are no longer those of the earth in the process of demolishing the past and transforming the course of history – they become smoother, tamer, and full of promise:

Night and day the conquering engines rumbled at their distant work, or, advancing smoothly to their journey's end, and gliding like tame dragons into the allotted corners grooved out to the inch for their reception, stood bubbling and trembling there, making the walls quake, as if they were dilating with the secret knowledge of great powers yet unsuspected in them, and strong purposes not yet achieved.

(*DS*, 234)

Tremor here is the magic of the organic, of vitality. The crowds pulsate in rhythm – 'To and from', 'day and night', 'rushed and returned', 'departing and arriving' – like a heart-beat:

To and from the heart of this great change, all day and night, throbbing currents rushed and returned incessantly like its life blood. Crowds of people and mountains of goods, departing and arriving scores upon scores of times in every four-and-twenty hours, produced a fermentation in the place that was always in action. (234)

Rather than tremors or shaking, Andrew Sanders chooses the sense of vibrancy to describe how Dickens articulated the spirit of his age, that is, 'its essentially rootless dynamism and its receptivity to innovation'. Sanders describes the 'peculiarly vibrant identity' of the British in the 1830s, and Dickens's 'equally vibrant responses'.[101] Dickens, like Engels and Marx, was concerned with making sense of the disconcerting phenomena of urban life, and with class division, misuse of economic privilege and economic deprivation. He was critical, for example, as were many others including the contributors to the *Lancet* and Dickens's journals, of railway companies who were seen to overwork drivers, guards and signal-men, and to neglect further safety measures, due to a profit-oriented economy and lack of government control.[102] But as a novelist, Sanders suggests, Dickens was more interested in individuality and regeneration than the fragmentation of human society.[103] The sense of vibrancy, however, seems most incompatible with the mood of millenarianists, for whom the troublesome signs of the times suggested a 'convulsive end to all things'.[104] The apocalyptic end predicted in *Dombey and Son* by Reverend Melchisedek Howler, who produced a violently 'rapturous performance of a sacred jig' in his congregation of Ranters (often confused with Quakers, known for their capacity to shake[105]), features as little more than a joke (*DS*, 221). The rigid frozenness of Dombey seems a more sinister force than that of the industrial, economic and social developments at Stagg's Gardens. The changes discussed by Sanders include the passing of the Reform Act in 1832, the Act for the abolition of slavery throughout the British colonies in 1833, and a Poor Law Amendment Act in 1834. He suggests that for Dickens, change was not always benevolent and painless, but continuous and inevitable, and potentially if not practically useful, as for example he saw the overall development of the railway. As Carker's long and nightmarish coach journey toward the end of *Dombey and Son* might suggest, or the driver's struggle in the early stages of *A Tale of Two Cities* to get the horses to move at all, rail travel was known to have great advantages over the notoriously uncomfortable mode of transport by horse and coach, including speed and a gentler kind of vibratory movement. With a somewhat Dickensian sort of comic irony, where pain is prescribed as a medical cure, Joseph Conrad's *The Secret Agent* describes how the shaking of the horse-driven cab in which Winnie Verloc travels to her husband seems to neutralize any sense of progression:

> The cab rattled, jingled, jolted; in fact, the last was quite extraordinary. By its disproportionate violence and magnitude it obliterated every sensation of onward movement; and the effect was of being shaken in a stationary apparatus like a medieval device for the punishment of crime, or some very new-fangled invention for the cure of a sluggish liver. It was extremely distressing; and the raising of Mrs Verloc's mother's voice sounded like a wail of pain.[106]

The drops of blood, after Winnie has stabbed her husband, might provide a metaphor for the smoother vibration of trains, the speed of which causes the individual jolts to join up into a musical tone. An acoustical background is set up for the scene, where the sound of Mr Verloc's voice 'filled the small room with its moderate volume, well adapted to the modest nature of the wish. The waves of air of the proper length, propagated in accordance with correct mathematical formulas'.[107] As though echoing and anticipating the change from the jolts of the cab in which Winnie arrived, to the vibration of the train in which she will leave, *ticking* becomes *trickling*:

> [Mrs Verloc] had become aware of a ticking sound in the room. It grew upon her ear, while she remembered clearly that the clock on the wall was silent, had no audible tick. What did it mean by beginning to tick so loudly all of a sudden? [...] Tic, tic, tic. [...] It was the handle of the domestic carving knife with nothing strange about it but its position at right angles to Mr Verloc's waistcoat and the fact that something dripped from it. Dark drops fell on the floorcloth one after another, with a sound of ticking growing fast and furious like the pulse of an insane clock. At its highest speed this ticking changed into a continuous sound of trickling. Mrs Verloc watched that transformation with shadows of anxiety coming and going on her face. It was a trickle, dark, swift, thin ... Blood![108]

Like the ticking of the bomb, an exterior heart-beat, the change into trickling signals the moment of death. Winnie brings about her own by jumping from the train, which Ossipon had felt 'roll quicker, rumbling heavily to the sound of the woman's loud sobs'.[109] Once again, the smoothness of railway travel seems to involve a loss of consciousness that is here final.

Vibration is considerable as more than a metaphor for the dramatic, 'earth-shattering' changes which took place during the nineteenth century, or what is often described as the coming of modernity. This movement might be taken more literally, as new kinds of vibration ranging from infra-red and X-rays and spiritual frequencies to much lower and louder forms of shaking were investigated and invented. While extrasensory forms of vibration tended to be associated with the conservation of energy, or even eternal life, the more violent and vibrant kinds of vibration were associated with change, though not always in a linear, progressive direction. While vibration itself is a returning, repetitive movement, it can shake things to pieces, destroying conventions, collapsing traditions. The transformations brought about by industrial and other developments were often experienced as extremely destructive, as well as progressive. The shaking of an earthquake is a destructive force of nature, however, in Dickens's work, while the construction of rail tracks results in a smoother, speedier, more continuous kind of technological vibration. As Sanders mentions that 'familiar perceptions of time and space' were transformed by the new speeds, vibration might be included among the 'physical excitements of the age of steam', with its 'invigorating new potential'.[110] Dickens observes that out of all the chaos and destruction there emerges a new kind of vibrancy, with all its energy, and yet he seems to blend an exhilarated optimism and celebration with nervous disquiet, to remain uneasy, even fearful of the modern machine.

Toward the end of *Dombey and Son*, Carker's death – he is run over by a train – recalls the earthquake-like shaking and the rhythmic repetition of Dombey's journey earlier in the novel. We have observed concerns that the too-rapid vibrations or shocks of continuous travel tended to escape consciousness, while more recent commentators have argued that railway accidents occur too suddenly to be processed in the present time.[111] Railway occurrences, then, which cannot easily be experienced in the present, may only be fully perceived retrospectively, or even, when one's own death makes that impossible, in advance, with the 'heightened consciousness' of foresight. Carker's death is anticipated by events earlier in the novel, while he seems to sense the future in the days leading up to it: 'Some other terror came upon him [...] suddenly, like an electric shock, as he was creeping through the streets. Some visionary horror, unintelligible and inexplicable, associated with a trembling of the ground' (*DS*, 810). A few days later, he hears the trains go by in reality, which shake him up with a further foreboding sense of his own disaster: 'The ground shook, the house rattled [...] It made him shrink and shudder even now [...] A trembling of the ground, and quick vibration in his ears; a distant shriek' (820–1). And finally, the event happens in reality: '[He] felt the earth tremble – knew in a moment that the rush was come – uttered a shriek', and is killed by the end of the paragraph (823). Beyond this fictional incident, and that of the railway worker in Dickens's short story 'The Signal-Man' who similarly anticipates his death, it seems that Dickens's own involvement in an accident at Staplehurst – by which he was seriously and literally 'shaken' – later helped to confirm his fears.[112]

In an age when the railway was one of the leading symbols of progress, Dickens, like so many other Victorian and later writers and artists, including Conrad, maintained a certain ambivalence about that technology that was also so often associated with death.[113] Railway accidents and suicides, frequently reported in newspapers and sensationalized in fiction, were of course among the main reasons for this association, but we have also considered the medical concerns about ongoing vibrations, the rapidity of which caused them to seem both imperceptible and dangerous. Chapter Five, then, will continue to consider the question of whether mechanical vibrations were progressive or destructive, harmful or healing, 'noise' or 'music' even, as in the case of street musicians.

Sexual Health: Sewing Machines, Bicycle Spine, the Vibrator

From railway compartments to horseback riding

Railways, sewing machines, bicycles, and the noises of city life were among the factors which appeared in nineteenth-century medical literature as having a damaging impact on the nervous system. Historians of medicine, neurology and psychology, literature and culture have unearthed from this literature a host of conditions, ranging from 'railway spine' and 'neurasthenia' to 'nervous shock' and 'traumatic hysteria', which register modernity as a distinctly shocking, even traumatic age.[1] As Chapter Four considered the general problem of railway vibration in some depth, this chapter will focus on a wider variety of kinds of mechanical vibration with specific attention to its capacity to cause sexual excitation. Some doctors argued that mechanical vibration could lead to unhealthy habits of masturbation, while others proposed that it might also have certain medical benefits. As the unhealthy impact of modernity has been discussed at some length, and considering that much of the shock of the nineteenth century took a distinctly vibratory form, this chapter will go on to concentrate on the mechanics of vibration as a therapeutic method, as a way of attempting to counteract or recover from the damage done to the nervous system.

From the 1860s through to the twentieth century, railway vibrations feature quite frequently in the *Lancet* and the *British Medical Journal* as a source of injury, along with other vibratory motions such as those produced by bicycles and sewing machines. These technologies were widely considered beneficial and progressive, but some medical writers were concerned with their harmful 'side-effects', particularly that of sexual excitation. This sense of vibratory stimuli is another reason for the attempts to control railway shocks. We have already seen some of the dangers associated with telepathic vibrations, whereby sexual contacts could become transgressive (in Chapter Two). Railway vibrations, as well as communication technologies such as telephony, could also encourage transgressive sexual encounters, not least because the railway compartment brought strangers of both sexes together in a new, relatively private, vibratory space. As Nicholas Daly notes, 'The train, as harbinger of modernity, appeared to threaten not just to shake up the individual body, but to erode the social barriers between the sexes in a way that was both tantalizing and frightening'.[2] The concern with the amount of vibration experienced on trains as illustrated in the *Lancet* report of 1862, 'The Influence of Railway Travelling on Public Health', may thus be related to an unspoken concern about uncontrolled sexual pleasure, while the quantitative approach is an established method of scientific analysis that could be employed in an attempt to manage it. The sexual effects of trains feature in a variety of Victorian documents. Their aphrodisiac power seems so assumed in *The Odd Woman* (1893), for example, that little further explanation is needed for Everard Barfoot's impregnation of Amy Drake, for which he apparently bears no responsibility whatsoever. His explanation seems to involve changing gender roles, whereby women can talk more freely to men and can travel alone, and his suspicion that certain women, like the apparently manipulative Amy Drake, take advantage of such changes:

> We had to change at Oxford, and there, as I walked about the platform, Amy put herself in my way, so that I was obliged to begin talking with her. This behaviour rather surprised me; I wondered what Mrs Goodall would think of it. But perhaps it was a sign of innocent freedom in the intercourse of men and women. At all events, Amy managed to get me into the same carriage with herself, and on the way to London we were alone. You foresee the end of it. At Paddington Station the girl and I went off together, and she didn't get to her sister's till the evening.[3]

Amy apparently engineers the whole affair, duly finds herself pregnant and passes the blame on to Everard who has to foot the bill. Rail travel could thus, it seemed, be dangerous to men as well as women. The threat to the increasing number of single women travellers from unwanted male attention and even sexual attack was paralleled by male fears of predatory females and from false accusations. Everard's predicament has certain similarities to other cases, such as that of Colonel Valentine Baker, accused of indecent assault on a young woman in 1875, insofar as he was perceived to have suffered from 'a mere escapade', and to be paying for the increased equality in social intercourse between the sexes. As Peter Bailey comments, when men and women came together in the confined space of the carriages, distrust tended to operate 'in both directions'.[4] Changing social relations permitted women to have a more active role in erotic adventures and fantasies, as feminist critics have also increasingly observed. Sally Ledger points out that significant journeys are made by railway by a number of lone women in *The Odd Woman*, including also the shopgirl Monica, who meets her husband-to-be Widdowson on her unchaperoned travels, walking about London.[5] Widdowson soon comes to disapprove of Monica's freedom and knowledge of London transport, and while he is the obvious traditional male despot, his disapproval is echoed by Everard's disapproval of Amy, another shopgirl. Everard's adventure seems equally to end in disaster (at least for him, according to his version of events) and to serve as a warning against the danger of the travelling female. Much as this novel applauds certain aspects of 'The New Woman', then, the ideal of female equality and freedom is contained and restricted, as many critics have noted, not least to the middle and upper classes, excluding such characters as the predatory working class Amy, whose status is closer to the prostitute than the 'New Woman'. The travelling shopgirl, Ledger comments, is thus 'a sexually suspect and socially disruptive figure', disrupting gender codes by 'occupying the public spaces of the city'.[6]

Much as *The Odd Woman* cautions against indiscriminate moral approval of women entering the public sphere, medical writers warned against the dangers of women travelling. As numerous historians and critics have observed, medical professionals often claimed that social morals were a legitimate concern of medicine, or even that medicine should be their cornerstone. Many feminist critics in particular have demonstrated that the professionalization of medicine had a major impact on perceptions of women and their proper domestic roles.[7] So while more and more women were beginning to embark on railway journeys we can also of course find medical literature that warns against excessive travelling in terms of the health problems it could cause the reproductive body. Doctors claimed that both collisions and prolonged rail travel could influence women in particular ways. In a letter to the *Lancet*'s editor in response to the report of 1862, for instance, Robert Ellis considers that as the state of the nervous system in women is 'more impressionable' than in men, women are influenced to a 'higher degree' by railway travel.[8] He goes on to mention the anatomical area most directly 'shaken' when sitting on trains: to a woman suffering from diseases of the cervix, 'the effect of travelling by railway for any considerable distance is undoubtedly injurious, in consequence of the direct application of a series of little concussions to the parts already in an inflamed and tender state'. As it is unusual for women to travel frequently by train, whereas men commute to their businesses in the city, Ellis claims that many further complaints are avoided. He thus seems to promote the domestic ideal whereby women should be protected from the masculine worlds of travel and industry, city life and work. As though to ensure that these roles are established at the outset of married life, he goes on to advise that newly-married women should not go on the long wedding journeys by rail on the Continent, as the 'perpetual locomotion' is conducive to the abortions which often occur among newly-married persons.[9] When subjected to railway vibrations, then, the problems caused both by and to the female body apparently range from the conception of unwanted children to accidental abortions and premature deliveries, a view that is mocked by Charles Dickens in *Martin Chuzzlewit* when Mrs. Gamp insists that new and noisy technology – 'hammering, and roaring, and hissing' steam engines – upsets her midwifery by inducing premature births.[10]

Domestic ideologies also came up against resistance; they were contested as well as asserted across a range of Victorian writing.[11] As we might expect, Elizabeth Barrett Browning presents a particularly striking alternative to the prohibitive view of women on public transport, for instance. In *Aurora Leigh* she endorses the possibility of the professional woman writer who refuses marriage and travels without male company and with her working class companion Marian Erle. In opposition to literary and artistic traditions which tended to present the silent, sexualized female body for consumption, this poem presents the female as autobiographical subject, with her own sexual experiences.[12] In Book Seven, Aurora travels with Marian through Italy on a train whose rhythmic vibrations seem to be experienced as sexual and male:

> So we passed
> The liberal open country and the close,
> And shot through tunnels, like a lightning-wedge
> By great Thor-Hammers driven through the rock,
> Which, quivering through the intestine blackness, splits,
> And lets it in at once: the train swept in
> A-throb with effort, trembling with resolve,
> The fierce denouncing whistle wailing on
> And dying off smothered in the shuddering dark [...].[13]

As in Dickens's 'prose poem' discussed in Chapter Four, the rhythm of the poetry here echoes that of the train: its 'quivering', throbbing, 'trembling' in the 'shuddering dark'. But where in Dickens's narrative the rhythm consists of harmful vibrations which shake the sensitive nervous system, in Browning's the narrator seems to partake in the momentary vibratory thrill, to take part in the penetrative movement. Several critics have observed Barrett Browning's enthusiasm for the materiality of poetry, for its communication of the pulse of bodily experience through metrical, sonorous rhythms, which is evident here as it is in her more spiritual communications.[14]

Women's sensual experience of travel was not necessarily new, just increasingly mechanized in the nineteenth century. And the vibratory pleasures of travelling were not always deplored by male or medical figures. One of the most influential founders of sexology, Havelock Ellis, observed that horseback riding, as well as railway journeys, could produce sexual excitement and even orgasm. 'Several writers', Ellis observes, 'have pointed out that riding, especially in women, may produce sexual excitement and orgasm. It is well known, also, that both in men and women the vibratory motion of a railway-train frequently produces a certain degree of sexual excitement, especially when sitting forward'.[15] He claims that this quality of rail travel has never to his knowledge been considered a 'sexual perversion' (although more attention was paid to the more problematic nature of the sewing machine, which we will come to shortly). Rather, far from being disapproved of as a harmful influence on female health, many physicians prescribed horse riding – and later railway journeys – as a beneficial treatment for hysterics, along with other unwell people (which led Coleridge to try 'horse-exercise', as noted above in Chapter One), as Rachel Maines observes in her history of hysteria and technologies of orgasm. 'The movement of a railway car', comments Maines, 'clearly provided a similar but perhaps more intense experience of the same kind' as the movement of a horse. It was the increased frequency of vibration on the railway, Maines goes on to propose, that 'was applauded by some physicians and deplored by others as a kind of overdose of physical therapy, which was thought to produce arousal or orgasm in woman travellers'.[16]

The question as to whether a woman on horseback should ride side-saddle or could choose to ride with her legs either side of the horse, and later the bicycle, was presumably related to the theme of sexual excitation, as well as to the appearance of feminine elegance and propriety. As horseback riding became an increasingly popular and widespread pursuit beyond the male world of work, as a leisure activity, it became 'customary for women to ride for display or pleasure', but, as with rail travel, there remained certain anxieties about appropriate dress and behaviour.[17] Bathsheba, in Thomas Hardy's *Far from the Madding Crowd*, seems conscious of the impropriety of riding in an alternative position to the customary side-saddle, when she 'looked around for a moment, as if to assure herself that all humanity was out of view, then dexterously dropped backwards flat upon the pony's back, her head over its tail, her feet against its shoulders, and her eyes to the sky'. This position is one among a number of possibilities, it appears:

> The performer seemed quite at home anywhere between a horse's head and its tail, and the necessity for this abnormal attitude having ceased with the passage of the plantation, she began to adopt another, even

more obviously convenient than the first. She had no side-saddle, and it was very apparent that a firm seat upon the smooth leather beneath her was unattainable sideways. Springing to her accustomed perpendicular like a bowed sapling, and satisfying herself that nobody was in sight, she seated herself in the manner demanded by the saddle, though hardly expected of the woman, and trotted off in the direction of Tewnell Mill.[18]

The speed of the horse – usually categorized as walking, trotting, cantering or galloping – seems most conducive to a vibratory effect. Although more ground is covered in less time by cantering, this involves longer and thus slower strides than a trot. (Galloping involves the probability of falling off.) Bathsheba's discovery that Gabriel Oak had seen the 'strange antics she had indulged in when passing through the trees' leads to palpitations and much blushing.[19] The need which some physicians seem to have felt to eradicate female sensual pleasure – of which we shall see more shortly with respect to sewing machines – contrasts with Gabriel's amused and slightly surprised enjoyment of Bathsheba's techniques, and that of the men in George Eliot's *Middlemarch* who found Dorothea 'bewitching when she was on horseback'. Bathsheba's pleasure resembles Dorothea's, except the latter seems to find further pleasure in the intention to renounce it:

> She loved the fresh air and the various aspects of the country, and when her eyes and cheeks glowed with mingled pleasure she looked very little like a devotee. Riding was an indulgence which she allowed herself in spite of conscientious qualms; she felt that she enjoyed it in a pagan sensuous way, and always looked forward to renouncing it.[20]

Like Barrett Browning or the later figure of 'The New Woman', both Dorothea and Bathsheba take up traditionally masculine modes of travel, but the latter pair seem more hesitant, more ambivalent about their potential freedom and sexuality. Although opinions differed as to the beneficial or harmful nature of 'auto-erotic' stimulation[21], and although her audience seem far from troubled by her enjoyment, Dorothea in particular seems to share the widespread sense of moral disapproval of such sensual experience, to the extent that she intends to give it up, a move that she decisively makes with her tragic marriage to Mr Casaubon.[22] Medical views as to the dangers of vibratory activities – views which helped to endorse such morals – seem to have been most concerned, however, with mechanical vibrations, including those involved with the use of sewing machines, and bicycles, along with railway travel. Such concerns usually revolved in particular around the assumption that such activities could cause masturbation, which seemed to pose particular dangers to the health of both women and men, as my next section will consider.

Masturbation, sewing machines and bicycles

A physician to the Earlswood Asylum and London Hospital, J. Langdon Down, published his article 'On the Influence of the Sewing machine on Female Health' in the *British Medical Journal* in 1867, arguing that sewing machine work leads to unhealthy habits of masturbation. This article begins by suggesting that the progressive benefits of new technologies like trains produce new problems: 'The rapidity of transit which steam has introduced, while it has multiplied our means of enjoyment, and enabled men to expand their minds by visiting distant and varied scenes, has produced, in many, evils to the nervous system, which have rendered it a not unmixed good'.[23] Down claims that although sewing machines have improved the miserable conditions in which many women work, the symptoms of 'a large and rapidly increasing number of patients' at his hospital coincide with the use of these machines, such as 'heart palpitation when horizontal at night, pain in back extending down thighs, dilated pupils [...] and a sensation of cobwebs floating before their eyes'.[24] His observations at Earlswood Asylum had taught him to connect this series of symptoms with masturbation, from which he concluded that it was 'not due to machine labour *per se*, but to the immoral habits, which had been induced by the erethism which the movement of the legs evoked' (sewing machines were operated by foot pedals).[25] Several woman admitted to these habits, and some found other employment as domestic servants, feeling unable to break the addiction.

Langdon Down was not the only doctor to express concerns about sewing machines. Later in the century Havelock Ellis observed that while the sexual excitement caused by railway travelling is not considered a sexual perversion the sewing machine has seemed more problematic: 'the sewing-machine has attracted considerable attention on account of its influence in exciting auto-erotic manifestations'.[26] This machine can not only lead to masturbation and 'involuntary sexual orgasm during sleep'; it can apparently be a direct cause of orgasm. Into his account of sewing machines Ellis incorporates a lengthy description by the French doctor, Thésée Pouillet in *L'Onanisme chez la Femme*, of the scene on a factory floor where individual women seem to frequently reach orgasm, a state that is apparently preceded by various signs including movement of the machine with increased rapidity, an opened mouth and dilated nostrils. It is not long before these signs give way to the climax: 'Soon I saw a convulsive look in her eyes, her eyelids were lowered, her face turned pale and was thrown backward; hands and legs stopped and became extended; a suffocated cry, followed by a long sigh, was lost in the noise of the workroom'.[27] As with the railway, the concern with the sexual effects of sewing machines could also reflect an anxiety about women in the public sphere, an anxiety that is intensified when it concerns women at work beyond the domestic realm.

Sewing machines are on the one hand associated with female work within the home, but on the other are also employed in the mass production of the traditionally male industrial workplace. Companies seeking to sell their machines to individual consumers thus tended to emphasize the domestic uses to which they could be put, and to evoke their more industrial uses with more caution. Judith Coffin points out that in order to enhance the apparent femininity of the machine, to distance it from its masculine uses in the workplace, manufacturers around the mid-nineteenth century offered models with elaborate ornamentations, while many advertisements brought these two realms together, juxtaposing modern industrial images including 'portraits of sewing machine factories' with those of 'the world of women' – of home. 'In so doing', observes Coffin, the advertisements 'acclaimed the excitement of progress, industry, and technology and strove to wed that excitement to the reassuring imagery of separate spheres'.[28] But, as the century wore on, images of virtuous domestic labour which dominated advertisements from the 1850s–1880s began to be associated with drudgery and to be replaced by images of a more modern femininity, of the self-confidence and freedom of 'The New Woman'. Coffin comments that in this shift in advertising in the 1890s from images of domestic toil 'to images of freedom and self-expression […] the infusion of erotic fantasies and dreams of liberation loosened the literalness of older conventions'.[29] Such fantasies, however, were of course accompanied by fears that the female body and sexuality was careering out of control, escaping domesticity. While advertisers promoted it, Coffin points out that medical discourse pathologized the erotic stimulation caused by the sewing machine, firstly associating it with the dangers of women's work, and later with the dangers of modern female sexuality.[30]

Measures to prevent sexual excitation were sometimes extreme, though not always popular. In his article for the *British Medical Journal* published earlier in the century, Langdon Down mentions the practice of 'interfering surgically with the integrity of the female organs', by which he presumably means removal of the clitoris, but the results of one case which had come under his observation did not convince him that this led to much physical or moral improvement.[31] Clitoridectomy had been recommended for many female patients by Isaac Baker Brown, indicating how necessary it seemed to some doctors to prevent masturbation, considered the cause of various forms of nervous illness in women, and of sterility. Brown's *On the Curability of Certain Forms of Insanity, Epilepsy, Catalepsy, and Hysteria, in Females* (1866) was generally viewed with scepticism, but debate as to whether women could be cured by clitoridectomy continued through letters between those who opposed the operation and those who recommended it (mainly limited to Brown himself), published in the pages of the *British Medical Journal* and the *Lancet* over the next year or two.[32] Similarly, in both journals, debate also continued as to whether sewing machines were in general good or bad for women. Those who did not object to continued use of the machines sometimes proposed methods of avoiding 'excitation'.[33]

Some feminist critics have viewed clitoridectomy as part of a widespread male denial of female sexual pleasure[34], but there were of course conflicting views about the sexual effects of vibration, which were not necessarily deemed problematic, as we have seen. Masturbation – in men as well as women – was often treated with suspicion, largely because it posed a threat to the nineteenth-century construction of the social norms of heterosexual marriage and procreation, although the link between masturbation and nervous illness in women was denied by some doctors.[35] Ornella Moscucci has argued that 'the capacity of the clitoris for homo- and autoeroticism was increasingly perceived as a threat to the social order': to the heterosexual coupling seemingly made natural by the notion of two opposite sexes. But female sexual pleasure was usually only deemed pathological or problematic if it was the result of masturbation, homosexual or promiscuous activities; it was far more likely to be construed as 'healthy and socially constructive if it was pursued within the context of the marital relationship'. Hence some people objected to clitoridectomy as it seemed to render wives 'frigid'. The seat of female sexual pleasure was also increasingly located in the vagina, however, rather than the clitoris. It was not necessarily, then, that Brown wanted to suppress female sexual pleasure, but to redirect 'it toward an acceptable social end: heterosexual, vaginal intercourse'.[36]

Medical writers similarly expressed concern over the ill effects of male masturbation which could apparently have a range of serious – sometimes devastating – effects on health. The loss of semen as a result of masturbation was widely considered to result in a wastage of bodily energy that could result in impotence and effeminacy, general debility, nervous diseases, deterioration of eyesight and a whole host of other symptoms.[37] Further, as Diane Mason observes, masturbation could apparently impact not only on male virility, 'not only on a man's sexual performance but also on the vitality of his offspring and, ultimately, his race'.[38] In this respect bicycles seemed to pose a particular problem for the boys who most often rode them, for their future and for their children's future, as bicycle riding could cause sexual excitation leading to damage which might never be wholly reversed, even, it was feared, if the perpetrator managed to give it up. Much as Down observed in his account of the sewing machine that new technologies like the railway could bring about improvements but also 'evils', a report on bicycle accidents and surgery in the *Lancet* begins: 'Human sorrows, it is seen on all hands, keep pace with human progress, – the new mode of transit being no exception to this universal law'.[39] The immediate concern with bicycles, as with railway travel, was to do with accidents, but continuous vibration was soon explicated as a problem, particularly for boys. Despite the protestations of Dr Richardson, Dr Allbutt and others, that cycling is both pleasant and healthy, 'an attractive therapeutic means of combating directly some of the most prominent evils incidental to town life', a 'wholly beneficial' form of exercise[40], many became concerned with bicycle vibration and sexual excitation. In his article for the *Lancet*, 'Bicycle Riding and Perineal Pressure, Their Effect on the Young', S. A. K. Strahan argued that the pressure on the perineum tends to 'lead to a great increase in masturbation in the timid, to early sexual indulgence in the more venturous, and ultimately to early impotence in both'. This aspect of transport was not unheard of, only worsened by new technologies. Horseback riding seems to have had devastating effects on humanity in the past, but the bicycle apparently intensified this problem, perhaps tenfold:

> We all know that among the Tartars horse-riding causes complete impotence in many of their strongest and most daring men, with wasting of the testes, dropping of the beard, and change in the pitch of the voice; and we also know that the introduction of the horse into the western world had quite as much or more to do with the extermination of the red man than had the almost simultaneous introduction of the European. [...] If, then, these sad results are the outcome of immoderate equitation where there are an extensive seat and a stable foot rest, and where the adductor muscles of the thighs are used, what are we to look for, where our boys of ten and upwards spend the greater part of their own time riding bicycles, and get over thousands of miles in the year, perched upon a saddle no bigger than the hand which conveys every jolt of the machine to the body; where the jolts are ten times more numerous than those experienced by the equestrian and, occurring without any approach to rhythm, are conveyed unexpectedly to the person?[41]

As with railway travel, the vibration or large number of jolts – 'ten times more numerous than those experienced by the equestrian' – was identified as a very serious problem, one which appears no less than to threaten the future health and even survival of the British race. Such concerns about national destiny accompanied the imperial project, as a strong national character was considered necessary to carry it forward. Alan Hunt observes that anti-masturbation panic was directed primarily at adolescent boys as the perceived danger was that auto-erotic behaviour could lead to habits of sexual indulgence which erode self-control, control being crucial to the idea of character. So it was not just that masturbation posed a threat to the individual body but to national well-being. Hunt comments that a characteristic of the persistent anxiety about Britain's capacity to sustain its imperial mission, an anxiety that emerged in the late 1850s, was 'an obsessive concern with the fate of great empires that is embodied in the preoccupation with the "decline and fall" of great civilizations and the thesis that empires fall because of the moral degeneration of their people or their leaders'[42] – a preoccupation that seems evident here in Strahan's claims about the decline of the Tartars. Strahan seems to anticipate the *fin de siècle* concerns of theorists of degeneration that modern technologies – from railway trains to radio – would in fact help to put evolutionary progress in reverse, concerns that intensified at this time of imperial decline.[43]

In a letter published about a month later George Herschell supported Strahan's observation that the succession of shocks conveyed to the spinal column in bicycle riding is harmful, by pointing out that this is a recognized cause of 'railway spine':

> It is already a fact well established and known to those who have much experience in the treatment of nerve-troubles that continued longitudinal vibrations communicated to the spinal cord are very injurious, and frequently set up a peculiar condition termed neurasthenia. In fact, so well is this a recognised fact that a special name has been coined, and these cases are commonly called 'railway spine'.[44]

Herschell proposes that these cases will have to be renamed 'cyclist's spine'. Due to the wheels becoming smaller and made to revolve faster by the method of chain gearing, the frequency of vibration seems to become more and more 'high-pitched', as the increasing amount of space covered in a decreasing amount of time involves an increasing number of shocks, which are of course harmful. In conclusion, Herschell writes that 'when we come to the universal use of the small-wheeled "safety," doing one hundred miles in a little over seven hours, over rough roads, with its enormously quicker rate of vibrations, we may expect to see soon some tangible results'.[45] By 1897 the new 'anatomical bicycle saddle' was invented in order to avoid perineal pressure, so cycling could be seen as a 'healthful' rather than a 'harmful exercise'.[46]

During the 1890s 'The New Woman' joined in the bicycle-riding craze, contradictory views of which soon followed, often regarding the issue of women's especially impressionable nerves. Havelock Ellis reports that 'irritation of the genital organs' may be produced in both men and women while cycling, but focuses mostly on women, reflecting a growing concern about their increased use of the bicycle. Ellis argues that while several studies claim that when cycling leads to sexual excitement the fault lies with the woman rather than the machine, he has found instead that 'with the old-fashioned saddle, with an elevated peak rising toward the pubes, a certain degree of sexual excitement, not usually producing the orgasm (but, as one lady expressed it, making one feel quite ready for it), is fairly common among women'.[47] As with railway travel and the sewing machine, attitudes to female use of the bicycle seem highly ambivalent. While Ellis proposes that the new 'improved flat saddles' reduce irritation to a minimum, and thus seems relatively unconcerned about women's future use of bicycles, others seem more preoccupied with its dangerous capacity to lead to masturbation.[48] The female condition could be improved by the healthiness of exercise and air on the one hand, but bicycling could lead to further nervous disorders on the other. The 'tremors of technological change', which Julie Wosk observes were transforming the world in which women lived, seem to have contradictory effects. Wosk notes, for example, that 'straddling bicycle saddles was often seen as leading to masturbation and excitation, posing a great threat to women's sexual innocence and purity'[49], and yet, on the other hand, 'electromechanical vibrators were used to help women achieve sexual orgasm as a cure for neurasthenia and hysteria'.[50] The opposing views of mechanical excitation as being both dangerous and beneficial is symptomatic of the deeply divided attitudes to women taking on new roles and using the new machines, echoing and intensifying the earlier conflicted views about men's subjection to bicycle vibration.

Male masturbation was of no less concern than the female variety, but with the exception of bicycle riding fewer doctors seem to have associated this specifically with mechanical vibrations. The greater concern about the female body's subjection to this kind of vibration may be explained in part by the fact that women were most likely to be expected to remain at home, safely protected from the industrial world of machines. As more and more women began to partake in railway travel and bicycle riding and entered the industrial workplace, all of which involved subjecting the female body to ever-increasing speeds or frequencies of vibration, doctors endorsed the idea that female sexuality was becoming uncontrollable. Judith Coffin observes that as advertisers drew upon medical images of the female body, it is not surprising 'that images of automated femininity (like women on bicycles or at sewing machines) carried strong sexual associations and that female sexuality seemed so utterly unpredictable and out of control'.[51] Doctors tended to regard masturbation in both women and men as a problem of control, often urging the importance of self-control in patients and emphasizing the harmful consequences of unmanaged sexuality, but when it came to mechanical vibrations the dangers seemed greater to women whose idealized roles as caretakers would not normally subject them to the excitements of travel and industry. Working class women already seemed sexually suspect (like the shopgirls in *The Odd Women* or the sewing machinists as depicted in medical literature), but toward the end of the century the middle class 'New Women' also seemed to pose one of the greatest threats to the domestic, passive ideal of pure femininity, being depicted not only as having dangerous sexual appetites, as Sally Ledger points out, but also as straying from their imperial duty of healthy motherhood; 'as the mothers of a degenerate "race", as the breeders of "monsters".'[52] Ledger shows how despite their different agendas, decadent, effeminate men were frequently associated with masculine, modern women in the popular press, both of whom seemed to threaten gender definitions and evolutionary, racial progress, threats that were linked with the perceived crisis in the British Empire at the *fin de siècle*, with the need for a strong, pure British race.

The harnessing of vibrations in medicine, then, with the use of vibrating therapeutic instruments such as the percuteur and the electromechanical vibrator, might be considered a way of attempting to regain much needed control within the relatively managed setting of a hospital or doctor's surgery. Such instruments are now best known for their capacity to generate pleasurable sexual sensations, but they were not necessarily intended for such purposes. Indeed, at least one doctor considered such sensations an unfortunate, potentially even catastrophic result of misuse of his tools, when they escaped his attempts to control their application.

The percuteur

Rachel Maines observes that genital massage of female patients was a staple of medical practice among some – certainly not all – Western physicians from the time of Hippocrates until the 1920s. Maines argues that the vibrator, which emerged as an electromechanical medical instrument at the end of the nineteenth century, had evolved from previous techniques and technologies in response to demand from physicians for more rapid and efficient physical therapies, particularly for hysteria.

As we have seen, many physicians before the nineteenth century thought that horseback riding benefited hysterics, while the movement of railway travel later provided a similar, though perhaps more intense kind of treatment. The development of various forms of therapeutic vibration provides the background in Maines's account of mechanical vibrators, while I wish to look more closely here at the wider context of vibration as I have outlined it in previous chapters, and in particular, to begin with, at the vibrating nervous system. Natural philosophers, physicists, spiritualists, physicians and psychiatrists in the eighteenth and nineteenth centuries wrote a great deal about both internal and external vibrations, as we have seen, which provides further background for the development of mechanical vibrations in medicine. The vibrating nerves of the human body seemed especially sensitive to vibrations in the external world, ranging from physical and spiritual energies to new technologies – from railway trains and bicycles to auditory technologies such as telephony and radio. The rhythms of neurological vibrations could, it seemed, be easily upset by mechanical vibrations – by the shocks of the railway, for example (as we saw in Chapter Four) – or indeed be stabilized or even improved by the same. Hence the importance of attempting to control the world of vibration, to manage its frequencies and amplitudes. Mechanical vibrations, then, were not necessarily prescribed solely for sexual purposes but could also be employed in attempts to intervene in the body's precarious vibratory rhythms, to re-establish where possible some kind of rhythmic harmony.[53]

Medical publications increasingly featured vibration as a form of treatment for pain and various disorders and diseases. In contrast to its usual production of sensations, including painful and pleasurable sensations, the anaesthetic role of vibration seems to eliminate sensation altogether, as reported in Joseph Mortimer Granville's article entitled 'Treatment of Pain by Mechanical Vibrations', published in the *Lancet* in 1881. Granville had developed this form of treatment as a result of observing women in child-birth, beginning in the 1860s, whose sensations of pain, he claimed – pain being caused by disorderly vibrations in the nerves – 'might be *interrupted* by appropriate mental and physical methods and appliances'.[54] Since the mid-nineteenth century anaesthesia had increasingly been used to alleviate the pain of childbirth, but the use of chloroform, in particular, was contro-versial as it seemed to trigger sexual excitation. Self-control and propriety were judged more important than insensibility to pain. The search for alter-native methods of relief from pain in childbirth, methods which did not suggest that woman was essentially a sexual rather than a moral creature[55], perhaps helped motivate Granville's experiments. For the purpose of inter-rupting pain, then, Granville designed the 'percuteur', which could deliver a certain quantity of vibration, 'a known number of blows per second', to various parts of the body.[56] The first version of this was driven by a spring which operated a lever, which in turn caused an ivory hammer to vibrate. It needed to be wound up. Granville eventually came to prefer the percuteur driven by electricity, largely because the speed of delivery could be sustained and controlled, as he explains in his fullest account of nerve-vibration, *Nerve-Vibration and Excitation as Agents in the Treatment of Functional Disorder and Organic Disease.*[57]

Following his investigations with women in childbirth, as Granville explained in a letter to the *Lancet*'s editor later in 1881, he came to see that other conditions may also be treated with mechanical vibrations, including 'railway spine' among a variety of nervous disorders – the causes of exhaustion 'ranging from mechanical shock to sexual excess'. In the case of railway spine, Granville suggests that travelling causes vibrations to propagate up the spinal column, or vertically, the damaging effects of which are neutralized if vibrations are sent in the opposite, horizontal direction:

> I believe the *modus operandi* of the treatment is to counteract the tendency to a lax and flaccid condition of the cord by exciting it to vibrate in a direction *at right angles* to its axis; most of the vibrations which act injuriously on the cord being propagated *in the line* of its axis.[58]

Underlying this practice of nerve-vibration was the theory of nerve function as inherently vibratory, as developed through eighteenth-century Hartleyan theory, which held that vibrations in the nerves transmit sensations to the brain. Like Hartley and Coleridge in the eighteenth century, and Fechner among many other scientists and spiritualists in the nineteenth century, Granville of course considered that the action of the nerves, which underlies physical and mental life, is vibratory. The vibration of nervous elements is a mechanical process, subject to the same laws that govern the 'vibratile movement of other bodies, whether organic or inorganic'[59], such as musical instruments. I have argued that Hartley's theory of nervous vibration provided the background for the aeolian harp as an image of nervous sensitivity and suffering in Coleridge's poetry, and that musical strings survived as an analogy for the nervous system in a great deal of work in the nineteenth century. Granville employs the model of musical strings which 'vibrating at the same time, though a short distance apart, will fall into harmony', drawing also on contemporary scientific material, including John Tyndall's work with 'sensitive flames'. Sympathetic vibration leads to the suggestion that 'nervous organisms, possessing the same qualities of physical structure, should exhibit a corresponding affinity'.[60] Granville is concerned in this way with how the nervous system can be too sensitive, and thus thrown into a harmful, discordant state. 'The female organism is characterized not inaccurately,' he claims, 'though popularly, by the phrase "finely strung nerves."'[61] The hysterical, and perhaps even telepathic state to which women are supposedly prone, is seen to have its physical basis in a certain type of nervous structure. In these cases,

the nervous elements [are] especially liable to vibrate in their sheaths, and thus exposes them [women] to the risk of falling readily into any rhythm which the will, the physico-mental environment, or perhaps even the proximity of similar structures vibrating in other bodies charac-terised by the same physical organisation may suggest.[62]

Nerve disorders, according to Granville's theory, can be caused by the vibratile movement of the nervous elements being too rapid or too slow, or altogether prevented by disease. The aim of therapy then, is to stimulate the nerves with rhythmical motion, to cause them to be thrown into a healthy, harmonious state of vibration. Much as the vibrations of the railway that are propagated '*in the line*' of the spine's axis need to be counteracted by 'exciting it to vibrate in a direction *at right angles*', Granville proposes that excessively slow vibrations need be treated with fast rhythmic motions. This process of stimulation might be seen as a less violent and more elaborate manifestation of Edmund Burke's idea in the eighteenth century that disor-dered nerves should be 'shaken and worked to a proper degree' by the sublime (as discussed in Chapter One).[63] For this purpose of stimulation

Granville considers the ability to control the frequency of vibration to be very important, however, as this motion is known to have both good and bad effects. According to Granville, 'the key to the whole phenomena' is as follows:

Acute or sharp pain is, I believe, like a high note in music, produced by rapid vibrations, while a dull, heavy, or aching pain resembles a low note or tone, and is caused by comparatively slow vibrations. A slow rate of mechanical vibration will therefore interrupt the rapid nerve-vibration of acute pain, while quick mechanical vibration more readily arrests the slower.[64]

It is tempting here to associate the slow vibrations with the 'dull pain' suffered by the feminine Coleridge, who longed for the sounds of a sublime storm to make it 'move and live'.[65] According to Granville, 'a dull, heavy, or aching pain resembles a low note or tone', which seems to be sounded out in 'Dejection' where there is: 'the dull sobbing draft, that moans and rakes / Upon the strings of this Eolian lute'.[66] In contrast to the 'sharp pain' described by Granville, which is 'like a high note in music, produced by rapid vibrations', the slow vibrations of dull pain require 'quick mechanical vibration'. The storm wind can be considered an earlier form of such intervention. The sign that the sublime restores the nerve-strings of the harp is the high-pitched 'scream / Of agony by torture lengthened out', and the sound of the little child who 'now screams loud, and hopes to make her mother hear', which in turn have a therapeutic effect on Coleridge.[67]

The fundamental principles of vibration are the same, although the stimulus provided by Granville's percuteur differs from the sublime screams of the aeolian instrument in the emphasis on frequency rather than intensity, and in the intention to reduce pain, rather than increase it. The idea that it is possible to 'interrupt' an overly slow or rapid rate of nerve-vibration could have derived from the principle of 'interference' in physics. This was the basis of Thomas Young's demonstration of the wave theory of light in 1801, which showed that light waves can either reinforce or cancel each other to produce alternating bands of lightness and darkness, like sound and silence (noted above in the opening paragraph of Chapter Two).[68] In Granville's theory, mechanical vibration may 'aggravate' or 'relieve' pain in this way. The dull pain, or 'the pains of a low-pitched and slow "boring" or "grinding" sensation', may be worsened by a low speed of percussion, but interrupted or 'arrested' with rapid speeds.[69]

The principle of fixing problematic nervous vibrations with mechanical vibratory treatment features again later in a short story by Rudyard Kipling, 'In the Same Boat'. Conroy visits a nerve-specialist in the hope of finding an alternative to the drugs on which he has come to depend. His problem is a vague sense of extreme horror which comes upon him and knocks him out for days, a sense of horror that seems linked to a vibratory spasm: 'I'm no musician', says Conroy, 'but suppose you were a violin-string – vibrating – and someone put his finger on you? As if a finger were put on the naked soul! Awful!'[70] The doctor proposes that his patient undertake a long railway journey, recalling 'a case where what we'll call anaemia of the brain was masked (I don't say cured) by vibration'.[71] A little later, the doctor proposes that Conroy accompanies a women with a similar problem: she is 'a little shaken in her nerves'.[72] This couple thus proceed on several journeys – typically 'shuddering' and 'shivering' and trembling as though their nervous vibrations are so intense as to shake their whole bodies[73] – journeys which help to stave off the horror and allow them to quit the drugs. The movement of horse riding also seems to play a less formally prescribed role in all this: Conroy takes several rides on a horse at the hour he most craves his drug, during one of which he meets his companion Miss Henschil who is also on horseback, and who like himself seems to be recovering good health.[74] It is interesting to see how this story follows the fundamental principles established over a century earlier with Coleridge, with the trembling string-like nerves treated with vibratory stimuli in the external world (including mechanical vibrations, from the sounds produced by the harp to the movement of the railway). Another approach to vibratory stimulation was taken by the late eighteenth-century physician James Graham, whose 'magnetico-electrico bed', incorporating among other things large magnets and loud music, was supposed to have vibratory effects, to stimulate sexual appetites and cure impotence.[75] The notoriety of a figure like Graham seems carefully avoided in Kipling's story, however. Like Granville, Kipling goes to some lengths to convince the reader that the vibrations are not sexually stimulating: despite Conroy and Miss Henschil apparently making a handsome and financially well-off pair, they both assert that there is no sense of sexual attraction between them. Yet with Granville we see a far more controlled approach. Rather than prescribing some stormy weather or exciting sounds, or a railway or horseback journey, Granville designed his instrument for the purpose of delivering an exact quantity of rapid vibration, and was also very particular about who should use such instruments, about who should have control over such frequencies.

While the articles, letters, chapters and books about railways and bicycles argued that new speeds or frequencies of vibration were detrimental to health, the proponents of vibratory therapy aimed to increase the speed at which their instruments could operate. This form of speed was considered beneficial because it was controllable. In an environment of 'bad' vibrations, Granville warned against 'the abuse of nerve-vibration'. He claimed to have no greater dread than that his percuteur should fall into the hands of patients or their friends. 'As well, and more safely, might those gentlemen who are pursuing this course supply their clients with scalpels, galvanism, electricity in its various developments, and hypodermic injections'.[76] Although he began his investigations with women, and women were more likely to need treatment due to their finely strung nerves, Granville went on to claim that he did not treat women with his percuteur at all: 'I have avoided, and shall continue to avoid, the treatment of women by percussion, simply because I do not want to be hoodwinked, and help to mislead others, by the vagaries of the hysterical state or the characteristic phenomena of mimetic disease'.[77] This concern that vibration as therapy might somehow revert or flip back to vibration as the cause of the symptom is further evidence of the ambiguity of the phenomenon. An additional ambiguity is of course produced by the anxiety that, in relieving pain, the percuteur and its like might induce undesirable pleasures.

One possible explanation for Granville's concern about the percuteur, therefore, is that women were using such instruments not so much for medical purposes as to produce pleasurable sensations. The dangers of masturbation as set out by medical professionals in the nineteenth century are well documented, as we have seen. Rachel Maines claims that physicians became increasingly concerned to distinguish instruments like the percuteur from the models sold to the public for use at home, being 'advised to purchase professional-looking equipment, which could not be confused with consumer models', the latter being used to achieve 'titillation of the tissues'.[78] But rather than look forward with Maines to the development of the electromechanical vibrator, I have here identified a historical context for Granville's work in which the nervous system is itself described as a musical kind of mechanism, that is vulnerable to other mechanisms, which may disturb or restore a sense of neurological harmony. In response to the uncontrollable excess of vibration experienced on a train for example, which was sometimes considered a cause of both railway spine and sexual excitation, Granville and other physicians can be seen to have developed manageable, medical forms of vibration.

Vibratory energies

The ability to control the frequency of vibration, to provide 'a known number of blows per second'[79], was considered important to all kinds of vibratory therapy. Friedrich Bilz for example, who developed a foot-powered 'vibratode' – this being the vibrating end piece that was applied to the human body, and was exchangeable for different shapes – noted that this could produce 'up to 3000 vibrations in a minute'. Bilz added that an expert masseur cannot exceed 350 in the same length of time'.[80] While the new speeds or frequencies of vibration experienced by bicyclists and other travellers were considered detrimental to health, the proponents of vibratory therapy aimed to increase the speed at which their instruments could operate. M. L. H. Arnold Snow's account of a range of medical vibratory devices and practices, – including 'Headshakes', 'musical vibra-massage', 'Charcot's vibratory helmet', 'the vibratory handle', 'the vibrating table' – observed some of the speeds at which such instruments could operate, and considered that the 'essential elements of a good machine' include its controllability by an operator: 'the vibrations of uniform quality should be capable of a range from weak to strong, and the force of impulse and rate, or speed, should be under control (the rate ranging as high as 6500 per minute)'.[81] But it was electricity, not only as a way of powering mechanisms such as the percuteur and the electromechanical vibrator[82], but in its direct application to the body as a treatment for a wide range of medical complaints, including neurasthenia, skin diseases, epilepsy, ovarian tumours, menstrual pain, and impotence, which could deliver the highest rate of 'oscillations'.[83]

Granville explained that nerve-vibration acts in a different manner to electricity, which introduces a 'foreign force' to the system, whereas nerve-vibration can excite a nerve centre to perform its own activity, 'helping her [Nature] to do her work with her own forces and in her own way'.[84] Electricity was useful, however, for cases of paralysis accompanied by muscle deterioration, when Nature, as it were, has run out of steam. This idea that electricity could impart new force to a system made it possible to imagine that the exhausted might be re-energized or even the dead brought to life. Mary Shelley's *Frankenstein* most famously described this fantasy, while various other science fictions and attempts to revive corpses with electricity proliferated throughout the nineteenth century and beyond.[85] As a therapeutic tool though, according to Granville, this force should vibrate. The constant or direct current is not useful, as it simply uses the nerve as a conductor, it 'passes along without throwing it into vibration', while the alternating current 'has the power of throwing any particle of matter, whether living or inorganic, into mechanical vibration'.[86] The use of electricity was also recommended as treatment for neurasthenia, epilepsy, ovarian tumours, and numerous other complaints, in *The Medical Use of Electricity* by George Beard and Alphonso Rockwell, first published in 1867 and followed by many new editions, remaining the standard text on electric medicine through the 1880s and beyond. However, as later editions note, electricity was also used to execute criminals[87], and has been the cause of fatal accidents to workmen engaged upon electric light cables at 1,000 volts. Rockwell's experiments, and those of Nikola Tesla (inventor of the alternating current, discussed in Chapter Three), supported the use of the vibratory, alternating current, as opposed to direct current, as they 'seemed to indicate that enormous voltages were harmless to the human body if only they could be made to alternate with sufficient rapidity'.[88] Rockwell warned that the harmlessness of high frequency alteration was not yet proved, while currents of great frequency could be produced – from 'a thousand, or a million, or billion or more oscillations per second'.[89]

The vibratory energy thought to power the nervous system was just one among the various forms of energy with which physicists and others were preoccupied in the period, including light and heat, as well as electricity (as discussed extensively in Chapter Two). Medical theories about vibrating mechanisms and electricity usually involved the assumption that these various energies, or at least that electricity and nervous energy, were exchangeable. They could also come into conflict, however. As Tim Armstrong observes, there was 'a duality in electricity: seen as duplicating the motive forces of the nervous system and perhaps even the "spark" of life itself, it was at the same time becoming part of a network of power which transcended the scale of the human body and could kill'.[90] He refers to a range of practitioners for whom 'the characteristic nineteenth-century malady of nervous weakness', usually caused by the stresses and strains of modernity, 'could be cured with electricity's nerve-like energy'. Yet it was electricity that powered much of the technology which contributed to the modern mode of life – involving rapid modes of transport and information flow via telephone and other kinds of wires – that was thought to have exhausted nervous systems in the first place: 'demands on nervous energy produced by the complexity of modern life and its speed of locomotion, work, and information flow (as well as factors like the use of stimulants, luxuries, the education of women) resulted in neurasthenia'.[91] Electricity seems to problematize the boundaries between exhaustion and exhilaration, or even life and death, as Armstrong suggests. That vibration could provide the 'spark' of life for physical matter, and that sound, light, heat, electricity and nervous energy are all forms of vibration, was suggested for example by Maurice Pilgrim, as part of his theoretical justification for the medical use of 'vibratory stimulation'. Such stimulation was required, according to Pilgrim, when the nerves became 'lethargic' or 'partially unreceptive' to the ethereal stimulus:

It is generally believed and scientifically recognized, that hearing and sight, for example, are the results of rapid vibrations in the universal ether. Physicists say that the ether here referred to, is a medium filling all space through which the vibrations of light, radiant heat, and electric energy are propagated. This medium, whose existence most authorities now consider to be established, is thought to be more elastic than any ordinary form of matter and to exist throughout all known space, even within the densest bodies. Electric and magnetic phenomena are explained as due to strains and pulsations in the ether. Why may it not be reasonably supposed that the *vis a tergo* – the vitalizing force behind the anatomical structure of a nerve and which "makes it go," – is a part of this same operating cause? Nerves must draw their vitality from some never-failing reservoir, otherwise the breaks in the continuity of physical life would be of such frequent occurrence as would very soon complete the extinction of the human race.[92]

This understanding of life as dependent on the nervous system being 'powered' by, or drawing its vitality from, an external vibratory force, seemed to make it vulnerable on the one hand to any fluctuations in that force, which could cause 'the extinction of the human race', and on the other to make it the potential beneficiary of 'vibratory stimulation'. But Pilgrim did not see 'the rapidity of the vibrations' – most instruments ranging from the rate of 1,750 to 2,500 per minute – as important as their 'length'. 'The general "shake-up" of the entire body, such as some vibration instruments are constructed to give,' he claimed, 'is neither desirable nor productive of satisfactory results'.[93]

Vibrations after death

The idea that electricity might have the power to bring inanimate matter, nerve-like strings and wires, or stitched-together corpses, to life, seems to have been familiar at least since *Frankenstein*. Once alive, according to the theories of spiritualist practitioners of vibratory therapy, it may be that nothing ever dies. The first law of thermodynamics, that of the conservation of energy, was central to much spiritualist theory through the second half of the nineteenth century, as we have seen. Energy, it was argued, is transmitted and transformed, rather than created or destroyed. Nervous and other human kinds of energy are of course also subject to this principle, according to theorists such as Gustav Fechner, who was one of the earliest to explore connections between energy physics and religious ideas. In *On Life After Death* Fechner described activity in the nerves as vibratory, and vibration as energy that never dies. Later in the century, the law of energy conservation was used to explain the benefits of vibratory therapy. For George Henry Taylor, inventor of a range of therapeutic, vibratory mechanisms like 'the manipulator', this law explained how massage could heal people:

> Motor energy is transmitted to the vital tissues and the fluids which pervade them in the form of *waves*, whose length and depth are determined by the amount of pressure and extent of motion the hand affords. But it no longer remains motor energy; neither is it lost or even diminished, force or energy being in its nature indestructible. It simply assumes other forms, which, together, are the exact equivalent of that transmitted.[94]

In other words, massage generates energy within the usually female body – considering the 'fearful increase among females of a great variety of nervous disorders'[95] – the beneficial consequences of which, as energy never dies or is 'diminished', being 'indestructible', start to seem limitless in their potential. Taylor goes on to observe the parallel between the vibrations observed by physicists, and the waves and vibrations produced by his mechanisms, which make it possible to deliver massage at even higher rates, beyond 'those natural for the hand of an operator to supply', beyond 'the narrow line of human capability'[96]:

> We have been shown that what to our senses are the far differing phenomena of light, heat, electricity, motion, and other forms of energy, are but variations of *rate* and *degree* of essentially the same thing – differing forms and conditions, modified by material agents, of wave-like or vibratory motions. By the aid of appropriate apparatus, we may also investigate the consequences of vibratory or wave-like motions, at their different rates, when transmitted to the complex components, vital and non-vital of the organism, and learn what we may of the laws governing this procedure and the objects attainable thereby – matters which are as a sealed book to those whose observations have been limited to the degrees and rates of motor energy which emanate from the masseur.[97]

Taylor invented several instruments for applying vibrations to the body at 'degrees and rates' that exceed the limited capacity of the masseur. One such mechanism worked by turning a wheel that in turn turned a smaller wheel, for increased rapidity, which was connected to a rod that moved to and fro with each rotation.[98] The 'Manipulator' involved a padded table with a hole in it, under which the vibrating mechanism was placed. The patient lay on the table to have her pelvic area massaged.[99]

The idea of energy conservation may also have supported Taylor's belief in the powers of the legendary spiritualist medium, Katie Fox, whose career in receiving spirit messages began as a child in 1848 during the internationally reported 'Rochester Rappings'. She was treated by Taylor at various times through the 1870s and 1880s and on hundreds of occasions performed as the medium at séances with the doctor and his wife. *Katie Fox: Epochmaking Medium and the Making of the Fox-Taylor Record*, written by their son, William George Langworthy Taylor, reports that 'Katie was, during psychic activity, a dweller at the sanatorium' at which his father performed his therapies.[100] The energetic principle of spiritualism – of a 'logic of continuity' – is set out in the introduction.[101]

The various forms of vibratory energy in which the Taylors were interested, then, included the spiritual frequencies to which Fox was considered highly sensitive. As both a patient and a medium, she was appropriately nervous and delicately feminine, like 'a quivering leaf'.[102] As well as feeling sensitive to Taylor's mechanisms, which could deliver at the rate of 'up to 1,600 vibrations per minute'[103], she felt herself sensitive to the even higher frequencies observed by spiritualists such as William Crookes, in whose experiments she participated during the 1870s.[104] Crookes, as we have seen, was interested in how the scale of vibration extends beyond the sensory thresholds, ranging from sound, heat, light up to X-rays, an orgasmic '2,305763,009213,693952 per second or even higher', beyond which lies the realm of spiritual vibrations, as he explained in 1897. He observes that some animals, like sensitive mediums, 'probably hear sounds too acute for our organs; that is, sounds which vibrate at a higher rate'.[105]

More and more vibration, beyond the thresholds of hearing, was generated in the nineteenth century. Ultrasonic forms of energy, brain waves and radio waves radiated through the atmosphere, while the palpable vibrations of railway trains, sewing machines, bicycles, and medical mechanisms became increasingly rapid, extending beyond the limits of consciousness. Vibration, it seems, can both harm and heal, cause and cure nervous illnesses, and can even bring inanimate matter to life, and go on after death. Women seem especially sensitive to the threats and thrills of all such vibrations – ranging from the spiritual to the mechanical varieties – due to their inherently delicate nerves which the medical profession claimed should be protected from the industrial workplace, from the hazardous machines of the modern world beyond the domestic realm. Mechanical vibrations thus appear to pose a particular threat to the female body, and yet that body could be treated by these same vibrations *if* controlled, managed by the medical profession. Because vibration, with all its potential benefits and dangers, seems able to trigger such a vast range of mental experiences and behaviours, of pains and pleasures, fantasies and practices of control are not unusual in the increasingly technological world of the late nineteenth and early twentieth centuries. Much of this book has documented the range of attempts to count and to manage vibrations, including those of the railway and of street musicians, and to produce very specific frequencies of vibration with such mechanisms as the percuteur, the vibratode, and manipulator. Katie Fox was thus not only sensitive to the extrasensory world of spiritual communications, but also had access to the energizing thrills of vibratory medical techniques – presumably an attempt to manage, to harness the uncontrolled frequencies of spirits. The threat to femininity came from women who themselves used the vibrating machines – who travelled by railway and bicycle, who worked at the sewing machine, and who stole Granville's percuteurs for self-application – while their health could be restored, it seems, by medical intervention, by therapeutic practices such as Taylor's. In contrast to the sewing machinists and 'The New Woman', then, Katie Fox seems appropriately, quiveringly feminine.

By the early twentieth century, vibrating mechanisms were sold directly to women, but still carefully presented in terms of their medical benefits, rather than their potential as providers of pleasurable sensations. Physicians became increasingly concerned to distinguish their professional-looking equipment from the consumer models sold to health spas, beauty parlours, and individuals for self-treatment at home.[106] Both physicians and advertisers continued to conceive of vibration in medical terms as a kind of energy, the electric vibrator for home-use being promoted in one women's magazine, *Modern Priscilla*, as the provider of no less than life itself.[107] Under the large title 'Vibration is Life', the advertisement begins: 'The secret of the ages has been discovered in *Vibration*. Great scientists tell us that we owe not only our health but even our life strength to this wonderful force. Vibration promotes life and vigor, strength and beauty'. The potential conflict between the health benefits of vibration and the dangers of mechanical stimulation seems here to be successfully staved off, the emphasis on the former being used to override the dangers. The medical construction of self-stimulation as harmful seems thus to be shifting, albeit cautiously: vibration may be both pleasurable *and* healthy. It is only after several paragraphs about its benefits to health that the advertisement alludes to the vibrator's ability to produce pleasurable sensations: 'It makes you fairly tingle with the joy of living'.[108]

AFTERWORD

In recent excursions to a number of universities throughout Britain, I noticed the recurrent use of the word 'vibrant' in their promotional descriptions. The marketing departments of some universities choose to describe the city in which they are located, and to which they claim to be central, as vibrant. For the University of Liverpool, for instance, 'Liverpool is a thriving vibrant city – and the University has been at the heart of city life since it was founded'.[1] Birkbeck, University of London, pushes the idea a little further, that it is the university itself that is vibrant: 'Birkbeck is a world-class research and teaching institution, a vibrant centre of academic excellence and London's only specialist provider of evening higher education'.[2] Other universities, both in the UK and the US, place more emphasis on the vibrancy of the student community, as at the University of Exeter's Cornwall Campus, where there is a 'vibrant mixture of students from science, engineering, humanities and arts backgrounds'.[3] Brown and Harvard University similarly describe their communities as vibrant:

> Brown's vibrant, diverse community consists of 6,000 undergraduates, 2,000 graduate students, 400 medical school students, and nearly 700 faculty members. Brown students come from all 50 states and more than 100 countries.
>   Harvard is home to a vibrant and dedicated community which celebrates, interrogates, and practices art.[4]

The use of the word 'vibrant' in these and many comparable descriptions seems to belong to the discursive rather than the material, in that there is no actual vibration going on. If the city of Liverpool, or Birkbeck's buildings, were actually vibrating they would be in danger of falling down, which is precisely the opposite of the claims that these promotional blurbs are trying to get across. The University of Liverpool is in fact emphasising its 'key role in the economic development of the region', and this language of vibration is similarly employed in the discourse of the public 'regeneration' of buildings and communities. The current issue of my council's quarterly magazine describes the '£1.5bn regeneration' of a local area: 'Work is underway to transform the area into a vibrant central London destination, with better transport links, affordable homes, green spaces, new shops and leisure facilities'.[5] University promoters are picking up on a more widespread sense of vibrancy, that is also used by councils and politicians. In a speech in 2004, Tony Blair claimed that the success of the Labour party had generated, among other things, a new vibrancy: 'Full employment has transformed regions of the country left behind in the 80s. Across Britain's cities, city centres and riversides that had become drab, empty at night, are now vibrant'.[6] Vibrancy is often associated with money, with economic opportunity or wealth, or with multiculturalism or other factors that seem able most crucially to generate a sense of life, to create lively, 'vibrant communities'.[7]

Earlier senses of vibration nevertheless survive in the current usage of 'vibrant'. I have jumped about a hundred years, from 1910 to the present, and in keeping with my earlier arguments against disruptive breaks (circa 1800 and 1900) I wish briefly to indicate how this book could provide what my introduction called the 'prehistory' of more recent senses of vibration. Stringed instruments have provided a refrain through much of this book, as vibrating mechanisms which preceded more recent technologies. Stringed instruments provided a way of comprehending and controlling the vibratory movements of the human body and its world. Before telephone wires, physiologists and poets used strings as a model for the nerves of the body, nerves that were in turn considered sensitive to the sounds of stringed instruments. Before the percuteur or vibrator, strings produced harmonious vibrations but also sublime, even painful noises which could be a beneficial, healing or even life-giving influence on the body and mind, according to some physicians, though beyond certain limits they might also be harmful. Figured as a passive mechanism, the body could be brought to life by vibration.

It is the positive aspects of vibration – its stimulating, energetic, healthy, and pleasurable qualities – that seem to be carried forward in the recent widespread use of the word 'vibrant'. The idea that vibrancy is a measure of economic success occludes its pathological resonances in the nineteenth century. It is a simplification that serves Blair's ideological vision of neo-liberal progress, a vision that is entirely unambiguous, in contrast to the ambivalence around capitalist development and destruction that we see in Dickens's work (as I discussed in Chapter Four). With the development of the vibrator as a technology that was promoted primarily in terms of the enormous medical benefits of vibratory energy, but also, more cautiously, its production of pleasurable sensations, we began to see the emerging sense in which vibration could be shifted decisively out of its association with pain and pathology. Numerous earlier technologies, from the aeolian harp strings to the fantastic inventions of science fiction, from measuring instruments like the siren to the development of smoother rail travel, paved the way in their attempts to organize, to measure, to control the good and bad affects of vibration on the human body and mind. But it is the vibrator that brings together the sense of health and pleasure, drawing on the theoretical physics and spiritualism of extrasensory energy in order to over-ride the sense that mechanical sexual excitation is unhealthy. And it is this sense that vibration is simultaneously energy and life itself, pleasurable and sensual, and even spiritually meaningful, that come together in the word 'vibrant'. It is perhaps the spiritual sense of 'good vibes' that is at work in the University of Hull's 'vibrant University atmosphere'.[8]

Since the harp and vibrator, new technologies have continued to control vibration, to harness its potential and to manage its movement between pleasure and pain. Vibration remains a problem to be eliminated or reduced in some fields, especially transport, noise control, and engineering, but it is also amplified and harmonized, turned into the 'good vibrations' of the Beach Boys, the bass sounds of the 1990s and beyond. The 'vibrant' nature of universities is at first sight entirely unrelated to any material movement or bodily sensation, but its prehistory is bound up with both the theories and practices, science and technologies of the nineteenth century and with the ongoing production of good vibrations.

NOTES

Notes to Introduction

1   Derek Walmsley, 'The Primer: Dubstep', *The Wire* 279 (May 2007), 44.

2   Chris Jackson-Jones, Fabric review, accessed 20 July 2009, http://www.
viewlondon.co.uk/review_608.html.

3   The Guittammer Company, 'ButtKicker: Home Theater' (2011), accessed
21 July 2011, http://www.thebuttkicker.com/home_theater/index.htm.

4   For a short video of a cat sitting on a vibrating speaker, which persists with
grooming itself while its entire body is shaken up and down, see 'Subwoofer
Cat', accessed 20 July 2011, www.youtube.com/watch?v=zmRTGRbrATs.

5   'White Lives on Speaker', accessed 20 July 2009, www.wlos.jp/about.html.

6   For a 'movie' of the 'white lives' stimulated firstly by a constant sound
frequency and then by brain waves see www.wlos.jp/movie.html, accessed
20 July 2011.

7   Hermann Helmholtz, 'On the Physiological Causes of Harmony in Music',
in *Popular Lectures on Scientific Subjects*, 1st series, trans. E. Atkinson
(London: Longmans, Green, & Co, 1895), 53–93 (56).

8   Ibid.

9   Walter Benjamin, 'The Work of Art in the Age of Mechanical Reproduction',
in *Illuminations* (London: Collins / Fontana Books, 1973), pp. 219–44 (238).
Benjamin's ideas are taken further by Rosalind Krauss, who develops much
more extensive analyses of the links between an optical and psychoanalytic
unconscious, in *The Optical Unconscious* (Cambridge, Massachusetts and
London, England: The MIT Press, 1994).

10   Ibid., 239.

11   Steve Goodman explores the violent and threatening dimension of sound as
vibration, mainly in a contemporary political context, in his *Sonic Warfare:
Sound, Affect, and the Ecology of Fear* (Cambridge, Massachusetts and
London, England: The MIT Press, 2010). Goodman makes a strong case for
attending to vibration, arguing that many discussions of sound and music
cultures, 'in their amnesia of vibration, have a missing dimension' (xiv),
and that vibration can problematize the 'boundaries of the auditory' (xvi).
Like Goodman, I am keen to move beyond the analysis of 'sonic and music
culture as text, plunging instead into the materiality of sensation' (endnote 6,
199), as I will indicate further in the second section of this introduction. But

rather than being orientated around sound culture and 'affective tonality' (or even 'the *not yet audible*', which is still to conceive of vibration in terms of sound) (xviii), my study argues that sound becomes just one among multiple forms of vibration over the course of the nineteenth century, moving across a broad range of both sonorous and non-sonorous vibrations and their pervasive cultural affects.

12 See H. F. Cohen, *Quantifying Music: The Science of Music at the First Stage of the Scientific Revolution, 1580–1650* (Dordrecht, Boston, and Lancaster: D. Reidel, 1984), 75–114; Penelope Gouk, *Music, Science, and Natural Magic in the Seventeenth Century* (London: Warburg Institute, 1999), 170–8.

13 For details of the corpuscular theory of sound see Cohen, *Quantifying Music*, 77 & 120–61. Gouk notes that in the later seventeenth-century English natural philosophers generally agreed that 'sound consists in an undulating motion of the air', *Music, Science, and Natural Magic*, 248. Curtis Roads reviews theories of sound and light since antiquity, noting that after the mid-seventeenth century sound was viewed as a wave form with few exceptions, until the twentieth century since which he and others have studied sound particles, in *Microsound* (Cambridge, Massachusetts and London, England: The MIT Press, 2001), 50–3.

14 Art and sound historians have observed similar shifts to subjectivity, whose work I will engage with in later chapters, including Jonathan Crary's *Techniques of the Observer: On Vision and Modernity in the Nineteenth Century* (Cambridge, Massachusetts & London, England: MIT, 1992), and Jonathan Sterne's *The Audible Past: Cultural Origins of Sound Reproduction* (Durham: Duke University Press, 2003).

15 Helmholtz, 'On the Physiological Causes', 59.

16 Ibid., 92.

17 Beer, '"Authentic Tidings of Invisible Things": Vision and the Invisible in the later Nineteenth Century', in *Vision in Context: Historical and Contemporary Perspectives on Sight*, ed. Teresa Brennan and Martin Jay (New York & London: Routledge, 1996), 85–94 (85).

18 For example David Howes, *The Empire of the Senses: The Sensual Culture Reader* (Oxford & New York: Berg, 2005); Mark M. Smith, *Sensory History* (Oxford & New York: Berg, 2007); Jonathan Crary, *Suspensions of Perception: Attention, Spectacle, and Modern Culture* (Cambridge, Massachusetts, & London, England: MIT, 2000).

19 See, for example, Marshall McLuhan, *Understanding Media: The Extensions of Man* (London: Routledge, 2001). See also Walter Ong, *Orality and Literacy* (London and New York: Routledge, 2002).

20 For such critiques see, for example, Gouk, *Music, Science, and Natural Magic*, pp. 14–19; Smith, *Sensory History*, pp. 8–18, Sterne, *The Audible Past*, 16–19; Veit Erlmann, *Reason and Resonance: A History of Modern Aurality* (New York: Zone Books, 2010), 14–15.

21 G. S. Rousseau, *Nervous Acts: Essays on Literature, Culture and Sensibility*

(Basingstoke: Palgrave, 2004); Laura Salisbury and Andrew Shail (eds), *Neurology and Modernity: A Cultural History of Nervous Systems, 1800–1950* (Basingstoke: Palgrave, 2010).

22   Jonathan Crary's and Friedrich Kittler's are among the best–known investigations of the sensory experience as embodied and technological, and their work will be taken up here (in chapters 1, 2, & 5), especially Crary's *Techniques of the Observer*, and Kittler's *Discourse Networks, 1800 / 1900*, trans. Michael Metteer and Chris Cullens (Stanford, California: Stanford University Press, 1990). William A. Cohen is one of the more recent critics to provide an account of the senses, focusing most closely and explicitly on the nineteenth-century view of the senses as embodied, in *Embodied: Victorian Literature and the Senses* (Minneapolis & London: University of Minnesota Press, 2009).

23   Brown, *A Sense of Things: The Object Matter of American Literature* (Chicago: University of Chicago Press, 2003), 3.

24   Buckland, 'Thomas Hardy, Provincial Geology, and the Material Imagination', *19: Interdisciplinary Studies in the Long Nineteenth Century* 6 (2008), accessed 18 July 2011, http://19.bbk.ac.uk/index.php/19/article/viewFile/469/329.

25   Flint, Introduction to special issue of *Romanticism and Victorianism on the Net* 53 (2009), 'Materiality and Memory', accessed 18 July 2011, http://www.erudit.org/revue/ravon/2009/v/n53/029895ar.html. For studies of glass, gas, and dust, see Isobel Armstrong, *Victorian Glassworlds: Glass Culture and the Imagination 1830–1880* (Oxford: Oxford University Press, 2008); Steven Connor, 'Gasworks', *19: Interdisciplinary Studies in the Long Nineteenth Century* 6 (2008), accessed 18 July 2011, http://19.bbk.ac.uk/index.php/19/article/viewFile/469/329; Marilena Parlati, 'Beyond Inchoate Debris: Dust in Contemporary Culture', *European Journal of English Studies* 15: 1 (2011), 73–84.

26   Steven Connor, *The Matter of Air: Science and Art of the Ethereal* (London: Reaktion, 2010), 148–72. Ether and vibration, however, seem to collapse into each other: 'As the bearer of vibrations – or the ur-form of the vibration, since it is so very hard to know in what the ether consists apart from the vibrations it transmits, the ether is a kind of symbol of … "the *universality of rhythm*"', 168.

27   Buckland, 'Thomas Hardy', 5.

28   Brown, 'Thing Theory', *Critical Inquiry* 28: 1 (2001), 1–22 (3–4).

29   Daniel Miller (ed.), *Materiality* (Durham and London: Duke University Press, 2005). The introduction contains a section entitled 'The Tyranny of the Subject'.

30   Latour, *We Have Never Been Modern*, trans. Catherine Porter (Cambridge, Massachusetts: Harvard University Press, 1993), 55.

31   For references to Latour see for example Brown, 'Thing Theory', 12; Miller, *Materiality*, 11–15; Bennett, *Vibrant Matter: A Political Ecology of Things* (Durham and London: Duke University Press, 2010). Brown, in *The Sense*

of Things, develops his analysis of how 'things seem slightly human and humans seem slightly thing-like' (13).

32   Bennett, 10.

33   Ibid., xiii.

34   *The Shorter Oxford English Dictionary on Historical Principles*, 3rd edn. (Oxford: Clarendon Press, 1955), 2353.

35   Bissell, 'Vibrating materialities: mobility–body–technology relations', *Area* 42 (2010), 479–86 (481).

36   Nancy, *Listening*, trans. Charlotte Mandell (New York: Fordham University Press, 2007), 2.

37   Latour, *Politics of Nature: How to Bring the Sciences into Democracy*, trans. Catherine Porter (Cambridge, MA and London, England: Harvard University Press, 2004), 76.

38   For two accounts of this gradual and irregular shift, involving the nervous system, see George Rousseau, *Nervous Acts: Essays on Literature, Culture and Sensibility* (Basingstoke: Palgrave, 2004); Roy Porter, *Flesh in the Age of Reason: How the Enlightenment Transformed the Way We See Our Bodies and Souls* (London: Penguin, 2004). For an important account of the role of sympathetic vibration in Enlightenment thinking, and how it involves the conjunction of subject and object, 'or the collapse of the boundary between perceiver and perceived', which has points of resonance with my own, see Veit Erlman, *Reason and Resonance* (10).

39   Steven Connor, 'Isobel Armstrong's Material Imagination' (2002) accessed 22 April 11, http://stevenconnor.com/isobel/.

40   Jason R. Rudy considers how nineteenth-century poets used electricity as a model for overcoming boundaries through their language, including boundaries between individuals, in utopian fantasies of interpersonal connection and communication, in *Electric Meters: Victorian Physiological Poetics* (Athens: Ohio University Press, 2009). There are some rich points of connection between our studies, as well as differences including Rudy's focus on poetry in contrast to my discussion also of other kinds of literary narrative (especially short stories and novels). My study also explores utopian fantasies of communication which ultimately do away with literary texts, in the imagination of unmediated communication, whereas Rudy concentrates more closely on the relationship between texts and readers.

41   Erle and Garrison, Introduction to special issue of *Romanticism and Victorianism on the Net* 52 (2008), 'Science, Technology and the Senses', accessed 18 July 2011, http://www.erudit.org/revue/ravon/2008/v/n52/019801ar.html.

42   William A. Cohen, *Embodied: Victorian Literature and the Senses* (Minneapolis and London: University of Minnesota Press, 2009). For related discussions see, for example, Rick Rylance, who observes that concepts of mind were constantly shifting and disputed in the nineteenth century, the materialist view of mind being an important strand of thought among this, in *Victorian Psychology and British Culture, 1850–1880* (Oxford: Oxford

University Press, 2000). Jenny Bourne Taylor and Sally Shuttleworth consider how mental science involved a materialist rejection of the dualism between mind and body, moving away from disembodied concepts of mind and towards physiology, in the introduction to *Embodied Selves: An Anthology of Psychological Texts, 1830–1890* (Oxford: Clarendon Press, 1998), xiii–xviii.

43   Teresa Brennan has explored how affects are materially transmissable between people and the environment, as opposed to the concept of humans as self-contained, bounded individuals, in *The Transmission of Affect* (Ithaca and London: Cornell University Press, 2004). In contrast to the usual understanding of sight as the sense that separates, or that plays into the distinction between object and subject, she writes that: 'Visual images, like auditory traces, also have a direct physical impact; their reception involves the activation of neurological networks, stimulated by spectrum vibrations at various frequencies. These also constitute transmissions breaching the bounds between individual and environment' (10). Brennan also notes that eighteenth-century notions of animal magnetism as a form of affect transmission contributed to variants of the idea becoming feminized (17), an idea which I will return to later in this book (especially chapters two, three, and five). For discussion of the transmission of affect which focuses on the materiality of sound vibration in a contemporary Jamaican music scene see Julian Henriques, 'The Vibrations of Affect and their Propagation on a Night Out on Kingston's Dancehall Scene', *Body & Society* 16: 1 (2010), 57–89.

44   See Pamela Thurschwell, *Literature, Technology and Magical Thinking, 1880–1920* (Cambridge: Cambridge University Press, 2001).

Notes to Chapter 1

1   The Aeolian harp was invented in the mid-seventeenth century by Athanasius Kircher. It is a stringed instrument played by the wind. The traditional form is a wooden box across which strings are stretched between two bridges. It is usually placed in a window, so that the wind can blow across the strings, thus vibrating them, to produce harmonic sounds. More information about this instrument will follow.

2   James Thomson, *Complete Poetical Works of James Thomson*, ed. J. Logie Robertson (London: Oxford UP, 1951), 266.

3   For discussion of its use in acoustics as well as its representation in British poetry see Hankins and Silverman, 'The Aeolian Harp and the Romantic Quest of Nature', in *Instruments and the Imagination* (Princeton, New Jersey: Princeton University Press, 1995), 86–112. For connections between the instrument and Romanticism see also Erhardt-Sietbold, 'Some Inventions of the Pre-Romantic Period and their Influence upon Literature', *Englische Studien*, 66 (1931–2), 347–63.

4   See for example Robert Jütte's discussion of Julien Offray de La Mettrie and

others in *A History of the Senses, from Antiquity to Cyberspace*, trans. James Lynn (Cambridge and Malden: Polity, 2005), 126–33.

5   For a recent example see Rosemary Ashton, 'England and Germany', in *A Companion to Romanticism*, ed. Duncan Wu (Maldon, Oxford, and Carlton: Blackwells, 1999), 499–500.

6   For examples of this debate in relation to associationism see Katherine Wheeler, *The Creative Mind in Coleridge's Poetry* (London: Heinemann, 1981); Jerome Christensen, *Coleridge's Blessed Machine of Language* (London: Cornell University Press, 1981); David Vallins, *Coleridge and the Psychology of Romanticism: Feeling and Thought* (London: MacMillan Press, 2000).

7   Alan Richardson, *British Romanticism and the Science of the Mind* (Cambridge: Cambridge University Press, 2001).

8   The most influential early exception is probably G. S. Rousseau, 'Nerves, Spirits, and Fibres: Towards Defining the Origins of Sensibility', in *Studies in the Eighteenth Century III*, eds. R. F. Brissenden and J. C. Eade (Toronto and Buffalo: University of Toronto Press, 1976), 137–57. For a review of the recent interest in the Romantic body, and how this contrasts with earlier work, see Alan Richardson, 'Romanticism and the Body', *Literature Compass* 1 (2004), 1–14.

9   Crary, *Techniques of the Observer: On Vision and Modernity in the Nineteenth Century*. (Cambridge, Massachusetts and London, England: MIT, 1992), 16.

10 Kittler, *Optical Media*, trans. Anthony Enns (Cambridge and Malden: Polity, 2010), 34.

11 As noted in Coleridge, 'Biographia Literaria', in *Samuel Taylor Coleridge: The Major Works*, ed. H. J. Jackson (Oxford: Oxford UP, 1985), 155–482 (250).

12 Ibid., 215

13 Vallins, *Coleridge and the Psychology of Romanticism*. Further exceptions to the view that Coleridge's rejection of Hartley was final include Thomas McFarland, *Coleridge and the Pantheist Tradition* (Oxford: Oxford University Press, 1969), 166–77; Jerome Christensen, *Coleridge's Blessed Machine of Language*.

14 Rick Rylance, *Victorian Psychology and British Culture: 1850–1880* (Oxford: Oxford University Press, 2000), 84. For Rylance's account of Coleridge's criticism of associationism, see 46–55, 63–5. For Richardson's account of Coleridge's criticism see *British Romanticism and the Science of the Mind*, 9–12.

15 This doctrine, along with associationism, is introduced in the opening section of Chapter One, 'Of the Doctrines of Vibrations and Association in General', in David Hartley, *Observations on Man, His Frame, His Duty, and His Expectations*, 2 vols (London: Joseph Johnson, 1791); repr. as *Observations on Man*, 2 vols (Poole: Woodstock Books, 1998), 1, iii and 5–6. Hereafter cited in text as *OM*.

16 For discussion of Hartley's attempt to develop a physical or material understanding of the psychology of associationism see for example Richardson, *British Romanticism*, 9; Roy Porter, *Flesh in the Age of Reason: How the Enlightenment Transformed the Way We See Our Bodies and Souls* (London: Penguin, 2004), 349–50.

17 Penelope Gouk, 'Raising Spirits and Restoring Souls: Early Modern Medical Explanations for Music's Effects', in *Hearing Cultures: Essays on Sound, Listening and Modernity*, ed. Veit Erlmann (Oxford and New York: Berg, 2004), 87–105 (98).

18 Ibid., 97. See also Penelope Gouk, *Music, Science, and Natural Magic in the Seventeenth Century* (London: Warburg Institute, 1999), 272–3.

19 Gouk, 'Raising Spirits and Restoring Souls', 97. See also Bruce Smith, 'Listening to the Wild Blue Yonder: The Challenges of Acoustic Ecology', in *Hearing Cultures: Essays on Sound, Listening and Modernity*, ed. Veit Erlman (Oxford and New York: Berg, 2004), 37–8.

20 Edwin Clarke, 'The Doctrine of the Hollow Nerve in the Seventeenth and Eighteenth Centuries', in *Medicine, Science, and Culture*, ed. Lloyd Stevenson and Robert Multhauf (Baltimore, Maryland: The Johns Hopkins Press, 1968), 123–41 (123–4). For details of this debate see also for example W. Wightman, 'Wars of Ideas in Neurological Science – from Willis to Bichat and from Locke to Condillac', in *The History and Philosophy of Knowledge of the Brain and its Functions* (Oxford: Blackwell Scientific Publications, 1958), 135–53.

21 Roach, *The Player's Passion: Studies in the Science of Acting* (Ann Arbor: University of Michigan Press, 1993), 105.

22 Ibid., 97. (Roach here paraphrases Fouquet's claims.)

23 Ibid., 104. See also Paul Goring, *The Rhetoric of Sensibility in Eighteenth-Century Culture* (Cambridge: Cambridge UP, 2005), 25.

24 Joseph Priestley, *Hartley's Theory of the Human Mind, on the Principle of the Association of Ideas; with Essays Relating to the Subject of it* (London, 1790), xii.

25 The preface explains the purposes of the edition, Priestley, *Hartley's Theory*, iii–iv.

26 Robert Miles, *Anne Radcliffe: The Great Enchantress* (Manchester and New York: Manchester University Press, 1995), 49.

27 Ibid., 51.

28 Ibid., 49. The phrases quoted by Miles are from Nathaniel Drake's *Literary Hours, or Sketches Critical and Narrative*, 2nd edn, 2 vols. (New York: Garland Publishing, 1970), 360. First published in 1800.

29 See for example Robert Bloomfield, 'Nature's Music. Consisting of Extracts from Several Authors with Practical Observations and Poetical Testimonies in Honour of the Harp of Aeolus', in *The Remains of Robert Bloomfield*, ed. Joseph Weston, 2 vols (London: Baldwin, Craddock and Joy, 1824), 1, 93–143.

30 Hankins and Silverman, *Instruments and the Imagination*, 110.

31 Samuel Taylor Coleridge, 'The Eolian Harp', in *Samuel Taylor Coleridge: The Major Works*, ed. H. J. Jackson (Oxford: Oxford University Press, 1985), 27–9, quotes are from lines 1–11. Hereafter cited in text as *AH* with line numbers.

32 Timothy Morton, 'Of Matter and Meter: Environmental Form in Coleridge's "Effusion 35" and "The Eolian Harp"', *Literature Compass* 5: 2 (2008), 310–35.

33 See for example M. H. Abrams, 'Coleridge's "A Light in Sound"', in *The Correspondent Breeze: Essays on English Romanticism* (New York: W. W. Norton and Company, 1984), 158–91. Hankins and Silverman refer to Boehme and Schelling but also William Jones, who argued that the Eolian harp works because air contains music just as light contains colours, *Instruments and the Imagination*, 93–106.

34 Erika Erhardt-Sietbold, 'Some Inventions of the Pre-Romantic Period and their Influence upon Literature', 347–8.

35 This query from Newton's *Opticks* is discussed in Joseph Priestley, *Hartley's Theory of the Human Mind*, x; and *The History and Present State of Discoveries Relating to Vision, Light and Colours*, 2 vols (London: J. Johnson, 1772), 2, 782. The original version is query 13 in Isaac Newton, *Opticks: Or, A Treatise of the Reflections, Refractions, Inflections and Colours of Light*, 3rd edn (London: William and John Innys, 1721), 320, where it is put slightly differently: 'Do not several sorts of Rays make Vibrations of several bignesses, which according to their bignesses excite sensations of several Colours much after the manner that the Vibrations of the Air, according to their several bignesses excite sensations of several sounds?'

36 Joseph Priestley, *Experiments and Observations on Different Kinds of Air*, 2 vols (London, 1774), 1, xxiii.

37 George Dekker, *Coleridge and the Literature of Sensibility* (London: Vision Press Limited, 1978), 114.

38 M. H. Abrams, *The Mirror and the Lamp: Romantic Theory and the Critical Tradition* (London, Oxford, and New York: Oxford University Press, 1953), 57.

39 Crary, *Techniques*, 9.

40 Ibid.

41 See for example Walter Ong, *The Presence of the Word: Some Prolegomena for Religious and Cultural History* (New Haven and London: Yale University Press, 1967), 66–76. Among the poets, Ong quotes Blake for his awareness of the elimination of 'oral residue' at this time, 71.

42 Coleridge, 'Biographia Literaria', 476–7

43 See Tim Fulford, 'Conducting the Vital Fluid: The Politics and Poetics of Mesmerism in the 1790s', *Studies in Romanticism* 43: 1 (2004), 57–78.

44 Ibid., 63.

45 Franz Anton Mesmer, trans. George Bloch, in *Mesmerism, A Translation of the Original Scientific and Medical Writings of F. A. Mesmer* (Los Altos, California: William Kaufmann, 1980), 19.

46 Conder, review of William Wordsworth's 'The White Doe of Rylstone; or the Fate of the Nortons', *Eclectic Review*, 2nd series, 5 (London, January 1816), 33–45 (33). Thomas McCarthy explores the sympathetic relation between poet and audience, in *Relationships of Sympathy: The Writer and the Reader in British Romanticism* (Aldershot: Scolar Press, 1997). See also Jason R. Rudy's fine analysis of the electrical communication of affect in Romantic period (though his broader argument concerning the poetry of this period differs considerably from mine) in the first chapter of *Electric Meters: Victorian Physiological Poetics* (Athens: Ohio University Press, 2009), 17–43.

47 See for example Thomas McFarland, *Coleridge and the Pantheist Tradition*.

48 Hartley develops his religious theory in the second volume of *Observations on Man*. Porter gives an account of this development (352–60).

49 For discussion, in particular, of Mary Robinson's concept of affective community, see Jason R. Rudy, *Electric Meters: Victorian Physiological Poetics*.

50 Samuel Taylor Coleridge, 'Dejection: An Ode', in *Samuel Taylor Coleridge: The Major Works*, ed. H. J. Jackson (Oxford: Oxford University Press, 1985), pp.114–18 (114, lines 6–8). Hereafter cited in text as *D* with line numbers.

51 Burke, *A Philosophical Enquiry into the Sublime and Beautiful, and Other Pre-Revolutionary Writings* (London: Penguin, 1998), 86, 164.

52 Ibid., 164.

53 Ibid., 165.

54 Vickers, *Coleridge and the Doctors, 1795–1806* (Oxford: Clarendon Press, 2004), 31.

55 Coleridge, review of *The Monk* first published in *Critical Review*, 19 (1797); repr. in *Gothic Documents: A Sourcebook 1700–1820*, ed. E. J. Clery and Robert Miles (Manchester and New York: Manchester University Press, 2000), 185–9 (187).

56 Ibid., 188.

57 See Gavin Budge, '"Art's Neurosis": Medicine, Mass Culture and the Romantic Artist in William Hazlitt', Romanticism and Victorianism on the Net 49 (2008).

58 Miles, *Anne Radcliffe*, 49, 50. For further discussion of how sensibility was redescribed as pathological in the later eighteenth and the nineteenth centuries see, for example, Janet Todd, *Sensibility: An Introduction* (London and New York: Methuen, 1986). The various categories of attack on sensibility are quite comprehensively discussed in the introduction to Chris Jones, *Radical Sensibility: Literature and Ideas in the 1790s* (London and New York: Routledge, 1993).

59 Whytt, 'Observations on the Nature, Causes, and Cure of those Diseases which are Commonly called Nervous, Hypochondriac, or Hysteric; To which

are Prefixed some Remarks on the Sympathy of the Nerves', in *The Works of Robert Whytt* (Edinburgh: Balfour, Auld, and Smellie, 1768), 583.

60 Ibid., 581.

61 Ibid., 540.

62 Smith, *A Dissertation upon the Nerves; Containing an Account: 1/ of the Nature of Man 2/ of the Nature of Brutes 3/ of the Nature and Connection of Soul and Body 4/ of the Threefold Life of Man 5/ of the Symptoms, Causes and Cure of all Nervous Diseases* (London, 1768), 147.

63 Ibid., 191.

64 Coleridge, entry in 'Notebooks' for December 1829, in *Samuel Taylor Coleridge: The Major Works*, ed. H. J. Jackson (Oxford: Oxford University Press, 1985), 560.

65 George S. Rousseau, *Nervous Acts: Essays on Literature, Culture and Sensibility* (Basingstoke: Palgrave, 2004), 213, 233.

66 Smith, *A Dissertation upon the Nerves*, 191.

67 Sarafianos, 'Pain, Labor, and the Sublime: Medical Gymnastics and Burke's Aesthetics', Representations 91 (2005), 58–83 (75).

68 Vickers, 49. James Graham, a student of Robert Whytt, had experimented earlier, in the 1770s, with 'airs' or gases as well as other stimulants, including music and his more renowned 'celestial bed', as noted by Lydia Syson, *Doctor of Love: James Graham and His Celestial Bed* (Surrey: Alma Books, 2008), 18, 86, 148–52, 182–6. Although further discussion of the 'celestial or magnetico-electrico bed' would lead me to stray from the focus of this chapter, this therapeutic technology, with its albeit vague vibratory affects (see, for example, 184–5), is relevant as another form of medical stimulus, which was in this case supposed to stimulate sexual desire and to cure infertility. I will return to the topic of sexual health in Chapter Five (see p. 142 for specific brief reference to Graham's bed).

69 See Sharon Ruston, *Shelley and Vitality* (Basingstoke: Palgrave, 2009), 34–7.

70 See John Beer, Coleridge's Poetic Intelligence (London and Basingstoke: MacMillan, 1977), 200.

71 Sarafianos, 67–8.

72 Burke, *A Philosophical Enquiry*, 102, 106.

73 Ibid., 106.

74 Ibid., 101, 165.

75 Coleridge, 'Biographia Literaria', 218–19.

76 Ibid., 219.

77 Discussed for example by Aidan Day, *Romanticism* (London and New York: Routledge, 1996), 54–7.

78 Abrams, *The Correspondent Breeze*, 27; *The Mirror and the Lamp*, 67.

79 Burke, *A Philosophical Enquiry*, 123–4.

80 Ibid., 155–6

81   Ibid., 168.

82   Ibid., 180.

83   See, for example, Lewis's *The Monk* (Oxford and New York: Oxford University Press, 1995), 275, 276 (the trembling monk), 316 (Antonia). Trembling heroines had become familiar enough by the end of the century to feature in Jane Austen's satirical pastiche of 'horrid' novels in *Northanger Abbey* (London: Penguin, 1994), 148–55.

84   Vickers discusses theories about convulsions in his final chapter (134–66).

85   Bloomfield, 'Nature's Music', 100.

86   For associations between strings and health, wind instruments and disorder see for example Penelope Gouk, *Musical Healing in Cultural Contexts* (Aldershot, Singapore, and Sydney: Ashgate, 2000), 15. For examples from the eighteenth and early nineteenth centuries of music as therapeutic see Christian Uvedale, *The Construction of the Nerves, and the Causes of Nervous Disorders, Practically Explained* (London: R. Baldwin, 1758), 31; Smith, *A Dissertation*, 116, 191; James Mason Cox, *Practical Observations on Insanity* (London, 1804), 166.

87   James Beattie, *Essays in Poetry and Music* (London, 1779), 139.

88   Percy Shelley, 'Ode to the West Wind', in *The Complete Poetical Works of Percy Bysshe Shelley*, ed. Thomas Hutchinson (London: Oxford University Press, 1935), 573–4.

89   Abrams, *The Correspondent Breeze*, 58

90   Vickers makes the comparison between Beddoes's use of air and electricity in Frankenstein (34).

91   Ruston, *Shelley and Vitality*, 25. Vibratory energies continued to be seen as life-giving throughout the nineteenth century and into the twentieth, as the following chapters will document.

Notes to Chapter 2

1   For Young's own account of his early work on sound and light (and water) waves see Thomas Young, 'Experiments and Calculations Relative to Physical Optics', in *The Wave Theory of Light: Memoirs by Huygens, Young and Fresnel*, ed. Henry Crew (New York: American Book Company, 1900), 68–76 (74).

2   Robert Purrington provides more details about the development of the wave theory of light and heat, in *Physics in the Nineteenth Century* (New Brunswick, New Jersey, and London: Rutgers University Press, 1997), 79.

3   Sterne, *The Audible Past: Cultural Origins of Sound Reproduction* (Durham: Duke University Press, 2003), 23.

4   Hermann Helmholtz, 'On the Physiological Causes of Harmony in Music', in *Popular Lectures on Scientific Subjects*, 1st series, trans. E. Atkinson (London: Longmans, Green and Co, 1895), 53–93 (61).

5 Ibid., 92.

6 Gillian Beer, '"Authentic Tidings of Invisible Things": Vision and the Invisible in the later Nineteenth Century', in *Vision in Context: Historical and Contemporary Perspectives on Sight*, ed. Teresa Brennan and Martin Jay (New York and London: Routledge, 1996), 85–94 (85).

7 Hermann Helmholtz, 'The Conservation of Force', in *Hermann von Helmholtz: Science and Culture, Popular and Philosophical Essays*, ed. David Cahan (Chicago: University of Chicago Press, 1995), 96–126 (118). For discussion of Helmholtz's place in the development of the law of energy conservation see for example Yehuda Elkana, *The Discovery of the Conservation of Energy* (London: Hutchinson Educational, 1974); P. M. Harmans, *Energy, Force, and Matter: The Conceptual Development of Nineteenth-Century Physics* (Cambridge: Cambridge University Press, 1982), 41–4.

8 Hermann Helmholtz, 'On the Origin of the Planetary System', in *Popular Lectures on Scientific Subjects*, 2nd series, trans. E. Atkinson (London: Longmans, Green and Co, 1895), 152–95 (194).

9 For example William Barrett, *Sensitive Flames as Illustrative of Sympathetic Vibration* (London, 1879). See Richard Noakes for discussion of 'sensitive flames' and the links with spiritualism (to be discussed below), 'The "Bridge which is between Physical and Psychical Research": William Fletcher Barrett, Sensitive Flames, and Spiritualism', *History of Science* 42 (2004), 419–64.

10 Hermann Helmholtz, *On the Sensations of Tone as a Physiological Basis for the Theory of Music* (New York: Dover Publications, 1954). This is a recurring theme in Helmholtz's work; discussed further below.

11 Hereafter cited as *LV*.

12 Hereafter cited as *AE*.

13 Fechner's approach was developed by Hermann Ebbinghaus and others later in the nineteenth century. For discussion of Fechner as a founder of scientific psychology see Edwin Boring, *A History of Experimental Psychology* (New Jersey: Prentice-Hall, 1950), whose work in turn has influenced other historians of psychology, including Robert Thompson, *The Pelican History of Psychology* (Harmondsworth: Penguin, 1968), 54–61; L. S. Hearnshaw, *The Shaping of Modern Psychology* (London and New York: Routledge, 1987), 127–9; Thomas Leahey, *A History of Psychology: Main Currents in Psychological Thought*, 5th ed. (New Jersey: Prentice Hall, 2000), 229–30. Fechner's work also became important to Sigmund Freud in his attempts to identify the physiological processes behind mental phenomena, as discussed by Henri Ellenberger, 'Fechner and Freud', in *Beyond the Unconscious: Essays of Henri F. Ellenberger*, ed. Mark Micale (Princeton, New Jersey: Princeton University Press, 1993), 89–103; Michael Heidelberger, *Nature from Within: Gustav Theodor Fechner and His Psychophysical Worldview*, trans. Cynthia Klohr (Pittsburgh: University of Pittsburgh Press, 2004), 260–71.

14 Gustav Theodor Fechner, *Elements of Psychophysics*, trans. Helmut Adler,

ed. David Howes and Edwin Boring (New York, Chicago, San Francisco, Toronto, and London: Holt, Rineheart and Winston, 1966), 8. Hereafter cited as *EP*.

15 Ibid., 215.

16 Ibid., 217.

17 Helmholtz, 'On the Physiological Causes of Harmony in Music', 61.

18 Ibid.

19 James Ward uses this terminology, 'An Attempt to Interpret Fechner's Law', in *Mind: A Quarterly Review of Psychology and Philosophy*, 1 (London and Edinburgh: Williams and Norgate, 1876), 452–66 (462).

20 Hermann Helmholtz, 'The Facts of Perception', in *Selected Writings of Hermann von Helmholtz*, ed. Russell Kahl (Middletown, Connecticut: Wesleyan University Press, 1971), 366–408 (371).

21 William Thomson, 'The Wave Theory of Light', *Popular Lectures and Addresses*, 2nd edn, 3 vols. (London: Macmillan and Co., 1891), 1, 307–55 (308).

22 Ibid., 327.

23 Gustav Fechner, *On Life After Death* (London: Searle and Rivington, 1882), 54. Fechner speculates less about what he came to term 'inner psychophysics' in *Elements of Psychophysics*, but continues to describe physiological processes in terms of energy throughout much of the latter text.

24 Fechner, *Psychophysics*, 10.

25 Many histories of psychology note this, for example Graham Richards, *Mental Machinery, Part 1: The Origins and Consequences of Psychological Ideas from 1600 to 1850* (London: The Athlone Press, 1992), 304; Edward Reed, *From Soul to Mind: The Emergence of Psychology, from Erasmus Darwin to William James* (New Haven and London: Yale University Press, 1997), 84, 90–1.

26 Helmholtz, *On the Sensations of Tone*, 7.

27 Helmholtz, 'On Goethe's Scientific Researches', in *Popular Lectures on Scientific Subjects*, First series, trans. E. Atkinson (London: Longmans, Green and Co, 1895), 29–51 (45–6).

28 William Thomson, *The Six Gateways of Knowledge* (Birmingham: Osborne and Son, 1883), 9–10.

29 Ibid., 17–18.

30 Jonathan Crary, *Suspensions of Perception: Attention, Spectacle, and Modern Culture* (Cambridge, Massachusetts and London, England: The MIT Press, 1999), 12.

31 Ibid., 40.

32 Helmholtz, *Sensations of Tone*, 129. See also 147–9 for discussion of Muller's theory of specific energies in this context.

33 Friedrich Kittler, *Discourse Networks, 1800 / 1900*, trans. Michael Metteer

and Chris Cullens (Stanford, California: Stanford University Press, 1990), 183–4.

34   Crary, *Suspensions of Perception*, 42.

35   Kittler, *Optical Media: Berlin Lectures 1999*, trans. Anthony Enns (Cambridge and Malden, MA: Polity, 2010), 148.

36   John Tyndall, 'Radiation', part 2, in *Fragments of Science: A Series of Detached Essays, Addresses, and Reviews*, 7th edn, 2 vols (London: Longmans, Green and Co., 1889), 2, 28–73, (28, 72–3).

37   John Tyndall, *Sound: A Course of Eight Lectures* (London: Longmans, Green and Co., 1867), 324.

38   Ibid., 3.

39   Gustav Fechner, *On Life After Death* (London: Searle and Rivington, 1882), 54.

40   Gustav Fechner, 'Nanna oder das Seelenleben der Pflanzen', in *Religion of a Scientist: Selections from Gustav Theodor Fechner*, trans. and ed. Walter Lowrie (New York: Pantheon, 1946), 174.

41   Ibid., 182.

42   Gretchen Finney, *Musical Backgrounds for English Literature: 1580–1650* (New Brunswick, New Jersey: Rutgers University Press, 1961), 9 (sensitivity) and 4 (sympathy).

43   Fechner, *On Life After Death*, 54. Hereafter cited in text as *LD*.

44   See, for example, Janet Oppenheim, *The Other World: Spiritualism and Psychical Research in England, 1850–1914* (Cambridge: Cambridge University Press); Roger Luckhurst, *The Invention of Telepathy: 1870–1901* (Oxford: Oxford University Press, 2002); Pamela Thurschwell, *Literature, Technology and Magical Thinking, 1880–1920* (Cambridge: Cambridge University Press, 2001).

45   Janet Oppenheim, *The Other World*, 200.

46   Marilyn Marshall, 'Physics, Metaphysics, and Fechner's Psychophysics', in *The Problematic Science: Psychology in Nineteenth-Century Thought*, ed. William Woodward and Mitchell Ash (New York: Praeger Publishing, 1982), 65–87 (70).

47   Boring, for example, documents how Ebbinghaus acquired Fechner's *Elements of Psychophysics* and ideas of British associationists, *A History of Experimental Psychology*, 387.

48   Henri Ellenberger, *Beyond the Unconscious: Essays of Henri F. Ellenberger in the History of Psychiatry*, ed. Mark Micale (Princeton, New Jersey: Princeton University Press, 1993), 97.

49   Coleridge's references to mesmerism are discussed above: ch.1. It is seen as the first popular science, followed by spiritualism and psychical research by Leahey, *A History of Psychology*, 216–19.

50   Anne Harrington, 'Hysteria, Hypnosis, and the Lure of the Invisible: The Rise of Neo-Mesmerism in *fin-de-siècle* French Psychiatry', in *The Anatomy*

of Madness, vol. 3: The Asylum, ed. W. F. Bynum, Roy Porter and Michael Shepherd (London: Routledge, 1988), 226–46 (237).

51   Ibid., 230.

52   F. de Courmelles, *Hypnotism*, trans. L. Ensor (London: George Routledge and Sons, 1891), 48.

53   Edmund Gurney, *Phantasms of the Living*, ed. Edmund Gurney, Frederic Myers, and Frank Podmore, 2 vols (Florida: Scholars' Facsimiles and Reprints, 1970), 1, 111–12.

54   For example: Thurschwell, *Literature, Technology and Magical Thinking*; Jeffrey Sconce, *Haunted Media: Electronic Presence from Telegraphy to Television* (Durham and London: Duke University Press, 2000); more examples will follow in this chapter and Chapter Three.

55   Roger Luckhurst, *The Invention of Telepathy: 1870–1901* (Oxford: Oxford University Press, 2002).

56   William Crookes, in *Presidential Addresses to the Society for Psychical Research 1882-1911* (Glasgow: Robert Maclehose, 1912), 86–103 (98, 100).

57   Ibid., 100, 101.

58   Crookes, in *Presidential Addresses*, 100.

59   Hanson Hey, 'The Seven Principles of Spiritualism, with a Brief History of the Spiritualists' National Union' (Halifax: Spiritualists' National Union, 1910), 13.

60   Ibid., 16.

61   Leahey, *A History of Psychology*, 218. Janet Oppenheim also opens her authoritative and comprehensive account of spiritualism with the claim that many Victorian people turned to spiritualism in an effort to counter the insecurity of religion in their time, and later goes on to consider the spiritualist engagement with science, in *The Other World*, 1,199 *ff.*

62   Beer, 'Authentic Tidings of Invisible Things', 87.

63   Hugo Wernicke, 'Preface' to *On Life After Death*, 26.

64   Pamela Thurschwell, *Literature, Technology and Magical Thinking*, 33.

65   See Sally Shuttleworth, *George Eliot and Nineteenth-Century Science: The Make Believe of a Beginning* (London, New York, New Rochelle, Melbourne and Sydney: Cambridge University Press, 1984); Gillian Beer, *Darwin's Plots: Evolutionary Narrative in Darwin, George Eliot and Ninteenth-Century Fiction* (London: Ark, 1983). For discussions of science and contemporary theories of phrenology and mesmerism in relation to 'The Lifted Veil' see Beryl Gray, 'Pseudoscience and George Eliot's "The Lifted Veil"', *Nineteenth-Century Fiction* 36, 407–23; Terry Eagleton, 'Power and Knowledge in "The Lifted Veil"', *Literature and History* 9, 52–61; Jane Wood, 'Scientific Rationality and Fanciful Fiction: Gendered Discourse in *The Lifted Veil*', *Women's Writing*, 3 (1996), 161–76.

66   See George Lewes, *Problems of Life and Mind*, 3 vols (London: Trübner and Co., 1874), 3, part 1: 'The Physical Basis of Mind', 3–27, 56.

Lewes's journal records reading Fechner's work between 1869–74, which is also mentioned in a letter, included in appendix 4 in Anthony McCobb, *George Eliot's Knowledge of German Life and Letters* (Salzburg, Austria: Institut für Anglistik und Amerikanistik, Universitat Salzburg, 1982), 334.

67   George Eliot, letter to Harriet Beecher Stowe, 11 July 1869, in *The George Eliot Letters, vol. 5: 1869–1873*, ed. Gordon S. Haight (London: Oxford University Press, 1955), 48.

68   George Levine, 'George Eliot's Hypothesis of Reality', *Nineteenth-Century Fiction*, 35 (1980), 1–28 (2, 3).

69   Ibid., 7.

70   George Eliot, *Middlemarch* (London: Penguin, 1994), 144.

71   Samuel Taylor Coleridge, 'Dejection: An Ode', in *Samuel Taylor Coleridge: The Major Works*, ed. H. J. Jackson (Oxford: Oxford University Press, 1985), pp. 114–18 (114, lines 6–8).

72   Jane Wood, 'Scientific Rationality and Fanciful Fiction: Gendered Discourse in *The Lifted Veil*', *Women's Writing*, 3 (1996), 161–76 (163).

73   *Proceedings of the Society for Psychical Research*, 1 (1882), 3.

74   Kittler, *Discourse Networks*, 183–4.

75   Wood, 'Scientific Rationality and Fanciful Fiction', 170.

76   Eliot, *Middlemarch*, p. 709.

77   See for example Edmund Gurney, *The Power of Sound* (New York: Basic Books, 1966), 25, 29.

78   Tyndall, 'Radiation', part 2, 66.

79   Eliot, *Middlemarch*, 189.

80   Josephine McDonagh, *George Eliot* (Plymouth, U.K.: Northcote House Publishers, 1997), 44.

81   Feuerbach's *The Essence of Christianity* quoted in McDonagh, *George Eliot*, 44.

82   Eliot, *Adam Bede* (London: Penguin, 1985), 141.

83   Thurschwell, *Literature, Technology and Magical Thinking*, 37.

84   Wilkie Collins, *The Woman in White* (London: Penguin, 1985), 242.

85   Ibid., 67.

86   Ibid., 243.

87   Ibid., 310.

88   Coleridge, entry in 'Notebooks' for December 1829, in *Samuel Taylor Coleridge: The Major Works*, ed. H. J. Jackson (Oxford: Oxford University Press, 1985), 560. See above, Chapter One, fn. 64.

89   Samuel Taylor Coleridge, 'The Eolian Harp', in *Samuel Taylor Coleridge: The Major Works*, ed. H. J. Jackson (Oxford: Oxford University Press, 1985), 27–9, lines 14–15.

90 Friedrich Schiller, 'Honor to Woman', *Poems of Schiller* (Boston: S. E. Cassino and Co., 1884), 237–8.

91 See Finney, *Musical Backgrounds for English Literature*, 76–100; Gouk, *Musical Healing in Cultural Contexts*, 20. Another instrument with sympathetic strings, used in music in the late eighteenth and early nineteenth centuries, was the viola d'amore. This has seven strings touched by a bow, and seven strings which lie beneath them which vibrate sympathetically to the sounds of the upper set. See for example Arthur Jacobs, *A New Dictionary of Music* (Harmondsworth: Penguin Books Ltd, 1958), 398.

92 Collins, *The Woman in White*, 178, 179.

93 Ibid., 75. D. A. Miller notes this, in '*Cage aux Folles*: Sensation and Gender in Wilkie Collins's *The Woman in White*', in ed. Stephen Regan, *The Nineteenth-Century Novel: A Critical Reader* (Oxon: Routledge, 2001), 426. Miller proposes that a major purpose of the novel is to oversee Walter's progression from immature sensitive quiverer to a suitably masculine figure who upholds heterosexual norms by marrying Laura.

94 Collins, *The Woman in White*, 228. As Nicholas Daly among a number of critics have discussed, 'nerves are everywhere aquiver in this novel. Moreover, the effect of the novel seems to be to set the reader's nerves jangling in sympathetic vibration', *Literature, Technology, and Modernity, 1860–2000* (Cambridge: Cambridge University Press, 2004), 36.

95 Wood, 'Scientific Rationality and Fanciful Fiction', 166.

96 Alex Owen, *The Darkened Room* (Chicago: University of Chicago Press, 2004), 7, 10; Judith Walkowitz, 'Science and the Séance: Transgressions of Gender and Genre in Late Victorian London', *Representations* 22 (1988), 3–29 (9).

97 Wood, 'Scientific Rationality and Fanciful Fiction', 167.

98 Walkowitz, 'Science and the Séance, 5.

99 Owen, *The Darkened Room: Women, Power, and Spiritualism in Late Victorian England* (Chicago and London: University of Chicago Press, 1989), 10.

100 The sympathy between Walter and Laura is discussed in depth by Rachel Ablow, 'Good Vibations: The Sensationalization of Masculinity in *The Woman in White*', in *Novel: A Forum in Fiction* 37 (2003), 158–80.

101 Cohen, *Embodied: Victorian Literature and the Senses* (Minneapolis: University of Minnesota Press, 2009), 15.

102 For discussion of homosexuality specifically in *The Woman in White* see D. A. Miller, '*Cage aux Folles*: Sensation and Gender in Wilkie Collins's *The Woman in White*'.

103 See Alan Sinfield, *The Wilde Century: Effeminacy, Oscar Wilde and the Queer Moment* (New York: Cassell, 1994).

104 For discussion of this with respect to Wilde see Joseph Bristow, 'Wilde, *Dorian Gray*, and gross indecency', in *Sexual Sameness: Textual Differences in Lesbian and Gay Writing* (London and New York: Routledge, 1992), 44–63.

105 See Noakes, 'Instruments to Lay Hold of Spirits', 125–63.

106 William Carpenter, 'Spiritualism', *Spectator* (14 October 1876), 1282.

107 William Crookes, 'Spiritualism Viewed by the Light of Modern Science', *Quarterly Journal of Science* 7 (1870), 316–21 (317–19).

108 Forbes, B. C., 'Edison Working on How to Communicate with the Next World', *American Magazine* 90: 10/11 (1920), 85.

109 Enns, 'Voices of the Dead: Transmission/Translation/Transgression', *Culture, Theory and Critique* 46 (2005), 11–27 (19).

110 Edison, Thomas, 'The Perfected Phonograph', *North American Review* 146 (1888), 641–50 (642).

111 Enns, 'Voices of the Dead', 20.

112 Villiers de L'Isle-Adam, *Tomorrow's Eve*, trans. Robert Martin Adams (Urbana, Chicago, and London: University of Illionis Press, 2001), 10.

113 Connor, *Dumbstruck – A Cultural History of Ventriloquism* (Oxford: OUP, 2000), 359–61. Douglas Kahn also elaborates on the connection between Edison's ideas and McLandburgh's tale, *Noise, Water, Meat* (Cambridge, Massachusetts and London, England: MIT, 1999), 212*ff*.

114 Gurney, *Phantasms of the Living*, 1, 536.

115 Le Fanu, 'The Familiar', in *Irish Ghost Stories* (Hertfordshire: Wordsworth Editions, 2005), 41–78 (41–2).

116 As articulated in Todorov, *The Fantastic: A Structural Approach to a Literary Genre* (New York: Cornell UP, 1975).

117 Frances Ridley Havergal, 'The Message of An Aeolian Harp', in *The Poetical Works of Frances Ridgley Havergal*, 2 vols (London: James Nisbet and Co., 1884), 2, 159.

118 Havergal, 'The Message of An Aeolian Harp', 162.

Notes to Chapter 3

1 See for example Morton Schatzman, *Soul Murder: Persecution in the Family* (London: Allen Lane, 1973).

2 Mark S. Roberts, 'Wired: Schreber As Machine, Technophobe, and Virtualist', *TDR: The Drama Review*, 40 (1996) 31–46; repr. in *Experimental Sound and Radio*, ed. Allen S. Weiss (Cambridge, Massachusetts and London, England: MIT Press, 2001), 27–41 (28).

3 As well as Roberts, see for example Friedrich Kittler, *Discourse Networks: 1800 / 1900*, trans. Michael Metteer, with Chris Cullens (Stanford: Stanford University Press, 1990), 293–304.

4 Enns, 'Voices of the Dead', 13.

5 Enns, 11.

6 Daniel Paul Schreber, *Memoirs of My Nervous Illness* (New York: New York

Review of Books, 2000), 19–20. Hereafter cited in text as *NI* with page numbers.

7   Hermann Helmholtz, *On the Sensations of Tone as a Physiological Basis for the Theory of Music* (New York: Dover Publications, 1954), 149.

8   Elizabeth Musselman, 'The Governor and the Telegraph: Mental Management in British Natural Philosophy', in *Bodies / Machines*, ed. Iwan Morus (Oxford and New York: Berg, 2002), 67–92 (68). For other discussions of the connections drawn between the nervous system and telegraph/telephone networks see, for example, Anthony Enns, 'Psychic Radio: Sound Technologies, Ether Bodies and Spiritual Vibrations', *Senses and Society* 3 (2008), special issue, ed. Shelley Trower, 'Vibratory Movements', 137–52.

9   David Hartley, *Observations on Man*, 2 vols (Poole: Woodstock Books, 1998), 1, 28.

10   Laura Otis, 'The Other End of the Wire: Uncertainties of Organic and Telegraphic Communication', in *Configurations: A Journal of Literature, Science, and Technology*, 9 (2001), 181–206 (190).

11   For discussions of the 'electric body' see for example Carolyn Marvin, *When Old Technologies Were New: Thinking About Electric Communication in the Late Nineteenth Century* (Oxford: Oxford University Press, 1988); Tim Armstrong, *Modernism, Technology and the Body: A Cultural Study* (Cambridge: Cambridge University Press, 1998).

12   Richard Noakes, '"Instruments to Lay Hold of Spirits": Technologizing the Bodies of Victorian Spiritualism', in ed. Iwan Morus, *Bodies / Machines* (Oxford and New York: Berg, 2002), 125–63 (125).

13   Peter Widmer, 'A Misrecognised Object in Psychoanalysis: the Voice', trans. Hanjo Berressem, *Literature and Psychology*, 37 (1991), 1–8 (5).

14   Musselman, 'The Governor and the Telegraph', 82, 83.

15   Gurney, *Phantasms of the Living*, 2 vols (Florida: Scholars' Facsimiles and Reprints, 1970), 1, 536.

16   Emil Kraepelin, 'Dementia Praecox', in *Abnormal Psychology: Selected Readings*, ed. Max Hamilton, (Harmondsworth: Penguin, 1967), 11–81 (14).

17   Emil Kraepelin, *Lectures on Clinical Psychiatry*, trans. T. Johnstone (London: Balliere, Tindall and Cox, 1906), 222.

18   Kraepelin, 'Dementia Praecox', 15, 18.

19   See Carolyn Marvin for some examples, *When Old Technologies Were New*, 132–3; and Enns, 'Voices of the Dead', 11–27.

20   See for example L. S. Forbes Winslow, 'Spiritualistic Madness', in *1900: A Fin-de-Siècle Reader*, ed. Mike Jay and Michael Neve (London: Penguin, 1999), 118–19.

21   James Mackay, *Sounds Out of Silence: A Life of Alexander Graham Bell* (Edinburgh and London: Mainstream Publishing, 1997), 230.

22   Mackay, *Sounds Out of Silence*, 157.

23 Enns, 'Voices of the Dead', 16.

24 Ronell, *The Telephone Book*, 261.

25 Anon., *The Voice by Wire and Post-Card: All About the Telephone and Phonograph. Containing Description of Bell's and Dolbear's Telephones and Edison's Phonograph. History of the Discovery. Details of Construction and Interesting Experiments* (London: Ward, Lock and Co., 1878), 55.

26 Herbert Casson, *The History of the Telephone* (New York: Books for Libraries Press, 1910), 237, 295–6.

27 Steven Connor, *Dumbstruck: A Cultural History of Ventriloquism* (Oxford: Oxford University Press, 2000), 357.

28 Carolyn Marvin, *When Old Technologies Were New*, 191.

29 As well as the studies by Musselman and Otis, this is observed for example by Patrick Brantlinger, 'Mass Media and Culture in *Fin-de-Siècle* Europe', in *Fin de Siècle and its Legacy*, ed. Mikuláš Teich and Roy Porter (Cambridge: Cambridge University Press, 1990), 98–113.

30 Casson, *The History of the Telephone*, 121.

31 Ronell, *The Telephone Book*, 259.

32 As Barbara Will observes, 'Nervous Systems, 1880–1915', in *American Bodies*, ed. Tim Armstrong (Sheffield: Sheffield Academic Press, 1996), 86–100 (97).

33 Anne Harrington, 'Hysteria, Hypnosis, and the Lure of the Invisible: The Rise of Neo-Mesmerism in *Fin-de-siècle* French Psychiatry', in *The Anatomy of Madness, vol. 3: The Asylum*, ed. W. F. Bynum, Roy Porter and Michael Shepherd (London: Routledge, 1988), 226–46 (239).

34 See Jeffrey Sconce, *Haunted Media: Electronic Presence from Telegraphy to Television* (Durham and London: Duke University Press, 2000), 47–52.

35 Discussed by various commentators on the science of the new technologies, for example the anonymous writer of *The Voice by Wire and Post-Card*, 14–16.

36 Patricia Fara, *Sympathetic Attractions: Magnetic Practices, Beliefs, and Symbolism in Eighteenth-Century England* (Princeton, New Jersey: Princeton University Press, 1996), 150–1, 174–5, 190–3.

37 See Alison Winter, *Mesmerized: Powers of Mind in Victorian Britain* (Chicago and London: University of Chicago Press, 1998), 54.

38 Ibid., 215.

39 Alex Owen, *The Darkened Room: Women, Power and Spiritualism in Late Victorian England* (London: Virago Press, 1989), 10.

40 Judith Walkowitz, 'Science and Séance: Transgressions of Gender and Genre in Late Victorian London', *Representations*, 22 (1988), 3–29 (9).

41 Winter, *Mesmerized*, 235

42 Ibid., 238–9.

43 Ibid., 339–40.

44   As I mentioned at the beginning of this chapter. See also, for example, Maurits Katan, 'Schreber's Hereafter: Its Building-Up (Aufbau) and its Downfall', in *The Schreber Case: Psychoanalytic Profile of a Paranoid Personality*, ed. William Niederland (New York: Quadrangle / The New York Times Book Company, 1974), 146, 148.

45   For thorough consideration not only of the differences between *Trilby* and *The Picture of the Dorian Gray* but also how '*Trilby's* popularity set the stage for Wilde's demonization', see Pamela Thurschwell, *Literature, Technology and Magical Thinking, 1880–1930* (Cambridge: Cambridge University Press), 50–64.

46   Janet Oppenheim discusses Carpenter's ideas about suggestion, *The Other World: Spiritualism and Psychical Research in England, 1850–1914* (Cambridge: Cambridge University Press, 1985), 241–4.

47   Carpenter, 'On the Influence of Suggestion Modifying and Directing Muscular Movement, Independently of Volition', *Proceedings, Royal Institution of Great Britain*, 1 (1851–4), 147–53 (147).

48   Carpenter, *Principles of Mental Physiology, with Their Applications to the Training of the Mind, and the Study of its Morbid Conditions* (London, 1875), 628.

49   Henry Maudsley's *Mental Physiology* quoted by William Barrett, 'On Some Phenomena Associated with Abnormal Conditions of Mind', *Proceedings of the Society of Psychical Research*, 1 (1882), 238.

50   Barrett, 'On Some Phenomena Associated with Abnormal Conditions of Mind', 240.

51   See Noakes, 'Instruments to Lay Hold of Spirits', 125–63.

52   William Barrett, 'Science and Spiritualism', *Light*, 13 (1894), 583–5 (585).

53   William Carpenter, 'Spiritualism', *Spectator* (14 October 1876), 1282.

54   See Jeffrey Sconce, *Haunted Media: Electronic Presence from Telegraphy to Television* (Durham and London: Duke University Press, 2000), 60–1.

55   Sigmund Freud, 'Psycho-analytic Notes on an Autobiographical Account of a Case of Paranoia (Dementia Paranoides)', in *Standard Edition of the Complete Psychological Works of Sigmund Freud*, ed. James Strachey, 24 vols (London: Vintage, 2001), 7, 9–82. Morton Schatzman's argument in *Soul Murder* is that the persecutory child-rearing practices of Schreber's father resulted in the son's paranoia, and are illustrative of a wider context of authoritarian rule in Germany at the time which supported the development of Nazism, but Niederland in *The Schreber Case* suggests that the idea that parental upbringing can cause schizophrenia has led to the 'scapegoating' of parents, becoming yet another 'conspirational theory' which echoes Schreber's paranoia (109). Santner reviews the debate around Schreber's father, psychiatry, and the genesis of Nazism, in *My Own Private Germany*, arguing that an examination of this case offers a key to understanding the 'paranoid core of National Socialist ideology' and its success in mobilizing the population (ix).

56   Sconce, *Haunted Media*, 63–4.

57   Ibid., 63.

58   Enns, 'Psychic Radio', 142; Wolfgang Hagen, *Das Radio: Zur Geschichte und Theorie des Hörfunks–Deutschland/USA* (München: Wilhelm Fink Verlag, 2005).

59   Luckhurst, *Invention of Telepathy*, 88.

60   Kraepelin, 'Dementia Praecox', 18, 20.

61   Thomas Watson, *Exploring Life: The Autobiography of Thomas A. Watson* (New York: D. Appleton, 1926), 98–9.

62   Steven Connor, 'Modernism in Midair' (2003), accessed 21 July 2011, http://www.bbk.ac.uk/english/skc/midair/.

63   Nikola Tesla, 'On the Roentgen Streams', *Electrical Review* (1 December 1896), repr. in *Nikola Tesla, 1856–1943: Lectures, Patents, Articles*, eds. Vojin Pović, Radoslav Horvat, and Nikola Nikolić (Beograd, Yugoslavia: Nikola Tesla Museum, 1956), A-58-61.

64   Nikola Tesla, 'On the Hurtful Actions of Lenard and Roentgen Tubes', *Electrical Review* (5 May 1897), repr. in *Nikola Tesla, 1856–1943: Lectures, Patents, Articles*, eds. Vojin Pović, Radoslav Horvat, and Nikola Nikolić (Beograd, Yugoslavia: Nikola Tesla Museum, 1956), A–62.

65   Ibid., A–65.

66   Marvin, *When Old Technologies Were New*, 127.

67   Cheney writes, 'Today it is known that thermonuclear reaction on the sun causes the radiation of X rays, ultraviolet, visible, and infrared rays as well as radio waves and solar particles at the rate of 64 million watts (or volt-amperes) per square meter of the sun's surface', in *Tesla: Man Out of Time* (New York: Delta, 1981), 67.

68   Nikola Tesla, 'The Problem of Increasing Human Energy, with Special References to the Harnessing of the Sun's Energy', *Century* (June 1900), 175–216; repr. in *Nikola Tesla, 1856–1943: Lectures, Patents, Articles*, eds. Vojin Pović, Radoslav Horvat, and Nikola Nikolić (Beograd, Yugoslavia: Nikola Tesla Museum, 1956), A–128.

69   Ibid., A–149.

70   Nikola Tesla, *My Inventions: The Autobiography of Nikola Tesla*, ed. Ben Johnston (New York: Barnes and Noble, 1982), 95, 101.

71   Tesla, 'Problem of Increasing Human Energy', A–150, 151. Paul Fayter discusses both scientific and popular reports of the spectroscopically seen surface and life on Mars during the 1890s, in Europe and America, 'Strange New Worlds of Space and Time: Late Victorian Science and Science Fiction', *Victorian Science in Context* (Chicago and London: The University of Chicago Press, 1997), 256–74.

72   Cheney, *Tesla*, 51–4.

73   Ibid., 283.

74   Tesla, 'Problem of Increasing Human Energy', A–120.

75 Wells, Interview with the *Weekly Sun Literary Supplement*, 1 December 1895; from Steven Mclean, *The Early Fiction of H. G. Wells: Fantasies of Science* (Basingstoke: Palgrave Macmillan, 2009), 1.

76 Wells, *The War of the Worlds* (London: Heinemann Educational Books, 1951), 22.

77 Wells refers directly to Tesla's work in the context of communicating with Mars in *The First Men in the Moon*, ed. Patrick Parrinder (London: Penguin, 2005), 162–3. For discussions of X-ray vision and communication technologies in Wells's work in a post-imperial context see Keith Williams, 'Alien Gaze: Postcolonial Vision in *The War of the Worlds*, in ed. Steven McLean, *H. G. Wells: Interdisciplinary Essays* (Cambridge: Cambridge Scholars, 2008), 49–73; and Aaron Worth, 'Imperial Transmissions: H. G. Wells, 1897–1901', *Victorian Studies* 52 (2010), 65–89.

78 Ibid., A–122–123.

79 Ibid.

80 Tesla, *My Inventions*, 59–60.

81 Villiers de l'Isle-Adam, *Tomorrow's Eve*, trans. Robert Martin Adams (Urbana, Chicago and London: University of Illinois Press, 2001), 60.

82 Ibid., 213.

83 Thurschwell, *Literature, Technology and Magical Thinking, 1880–1920* (Cambridge: Cambridge University Press, 2001), 29.

84 Frederic Stimson, 'Dr. Materialismus', in *Future Perfect: American Science Fiction of the Nineteenth Century* (London, Oxford and New York: Oxford University Press, 1978), 169–87 (175).

85 Ibid., 175–6.

86 Ibid., 179.

87 Ibid., 182.

88 Ibid., 183.

89 H. G. Wells, 'The New Accelerator', in *The Country of the Blind and Other Selected Stories*, ed. Patrick Parrinder (London: Penguin, 2007), 296–310 (302, 304).

Notes to Chapter 4

1 *Oxford English Dictionary*, 2nd edn, 20 vols (Oxford: Clarendon Press, 1989), 15, 293.

2 David Hartley, *Observations on Man, His Frame, His Duty, and His Expectations*, 2 vols (London: Joseph Johnson, 1791); repr. as *Observations on Man*, 2 vols (Poole: Woodstock Books, 1998), 1, 11 (prop. 5).

3 Hartley, *Observations on Man*, 133.

4 Rousseau, *Nervous Acts: Essays on Literature, Culture and Sensibility* (Basingstoke: Palgrave, 2004), 27.

5   Psychophysics and the pathology of shock are rarely discussed together, as historians of psychology and medicine tend to focus on either experimental psychology or psychopathology, though Graham Richards comments on the university-centred work in Germany, noting that a more industrialized England used mechanical metaphors for mind, *Mental Machinery*, 291–2. Wolfgang Schivelbusch argues that medical attention to train accident victims began in England, *The Railway Journey: The Industrialization of Time and Space in the 19th Century* (Berkeley and Los Angeles: University of California Press, 1986), 136–7.

6   Schivelbusch, *The Railway Journey*, 114.

7   Daly, *Literature, Technology, and Modernity, 1860–2000* (Cambridge: Cambridge University Press, 2004), 36, 44.

8   Ibid., 39.

9   Examples in which railway spine features include Ian Hacking, *Rewriting the Soul: Multiple Personality and the Sciences of Memory* (Princeton: Princeton University Press, 1995), 183–6; Roger Luckhurst, 'Traumaculture', in *New Formations*, Special Issue, *Remembering the 1990s*, ed. Joe Brooker and Roger Luckhurst, 50 (2003), 33–4.

10 Allan Young, *The Harmony of Illusions: Inventing Post-Traumatic Stress Disorder* (Princeton: Princeton University Press, 1995), 13–38.

11 Tim Armstrong, 'Two Types of Shock in Modernity', *Critical Quarterly*, 42 (2000), 61–73 (60).

12 Gillian Beer, *Open Fields: Science in Cultural Encounter* (Oxford: Clarendon Press, 1996), 296.

13 Hermann Helmholtz, 'On the Physiological Causes of Harmony in Music', in *Popular Lectures on Scientific Subjects*, 1st series, trans. E. Atkinson (London: Longmans, Green and Co, 1895), 53–93 (59).

14 John Eric Erichsen, *On Concussion of the Spine, Nervous Shock, and Other Obscure Injuries of the Nervous System, in Their Medical and Medico-Legal Aspects* (London, 1875), 194. This was a considerably enlarged and revised version of his earlier collection of lectures, *On Railway and Other Injuries of the Nervous System* (London: Walton and Maberly, 1866).

15 See, for example, Luckhurst, 34.

16 'Compensation for Railway Accidents', *Times* (16 December 1870), 11; 'Compensation After Railway Accident', *Times* (23 November 1883), 9.

17 William Cox, 'Cox v. The Midland Railway Company', letter to the *Lancet* (1 December 1849), 589; see also J. Davies, 'Cox, Davies, and Silk *versus* the Midland Counties Railway Company', 589–90. The next case (Wraith v. Lancashire and Yorkshire Railway Company) refers back to the earlier report, 'Preston County Court. – Important Decision to Railway Companies', *Lancet* (9 April 1853), 352–3. General criticism of rail companies and the frequency of accidents appear every year from January 1857.

18 'The Influence of Railway Travelling on Public Health', *Lancet* (4 January 1862), part 1, 15, 17.

19   Ibid., 17.

20   Ibid.

21   William Crookes, in *Presidential Addresses to the Society for Psychical Research 1882–1911* (Glasgow: Robert Maclehose, 1912 [1897]), 86–103 (98).

22   'Influence of Railway Travelling', *Lancet* (8 March 1862), part 8, 258.

23   J. Russell Reynolds, 'Travelling: Its Influence on Health', in *The Book of Health*, ed. Malcolm Morris (London, Paris, and Melbourne: Cassell and Co., 1883), 554–84 (581).

24   Mark Turner, 'Periodical Time in the Nineteenth Century', *Media History*, 8 (2002), 183–96 (187–9).

25   'Influence of Railway Travelling', *Lancet* (1 March 1862), part 7, 234.

26   'Influence of Railway Travelling', *Lancet* (11 January 1862), part 2, 48.

27   *Bradshaw's Railway Guide (London,* January 1860), 84–5. I used the enquiry service at the National Railway Museum in York for this information, provided by Philip Atkins.

28   See Crosbie Smith for example, for the argument that the energy concept in physics was constructed through successful attempts to secure legitimacy, in *The Science of Energy: Cultural History of Energy Physics in Victorian Britain* (Chicago and London: Chicago University Press, 1999). Alison Winter discusses how 'alternative' psychologies sought legitimacy in 'The Construction of Orthodoxies and Heterodoxies in the Early Victorian Life Sciences', ed. Bernard Lightman, *Victorian Science in Context* (Chicago and London: University of Chicago Press, 1997), 24–50.

29   See for example Walter Ong, *Hopkins, the Self, and God* (Toronto, Buffalo and London: University of Toronto Press, 1986), 13.

30   *Techniques of the Observer: On Vision and Modernity in the Nineteenth Century* (Cambridge, MA and London: MIT, 1992), and *Suspensions of Perception: Attention, Spectacle, and Modern Culture* (Cambridge, MA and London: MIT, 1999).

31   'The Narcotic Influence of Railway Travelling', *Lancet* (24 July 1875), 139.

32   'Influence of Railway Travelling', *Lancet* (11 January 1862), part 2, 52.

33   'Influence of Railway Travelling', *Lancet* (1 February 1862), part 5, 130.

34   John Tyndall, *Sound: A Course of Eight Lectures* (London: Longmans, Green and Co., 1867), 324.

35   See for example Edmund Gurney, *The Power of Sound* (New York: Basic Books, 1966), 25, 29.

36   John Tyndall, 'Radiation', part 2, in *Fragments of Science: A Series of Detached Essays, Addresses, and Reviews*, 7th edn, 2 vols (London: Longmans, Green and Co., 1889), 2, 66.

37   *Oxford English Dictionary*, 15, 293.

38   William Shakespeare, *King Richard III*, ed. Antony Hammond (London and New York: Methuen, 1981), pp. 308, 313 (Act 5, Scene 3, lines 10–11, 94).

39   Schivelbusch, *The Railway Journey*, 151, 152.

40   Ibid., 160.

41   Tyndall, *Sound*, 49–50.

42   Max Nordau, *Degeneration* (Lincoln and London: University of Nebraska Press, 1993), 39, 41.

43   Ibid., 38.

44   'Influence of Railway Travelling', *Lancet* (4 January 1862), part 1, 16.

45   'Influence of Railway Travelling', *Lancet* (11 January 1862), part 2, 48.

46   Ibid., 52.

47   R. Stewart, letter to the *Lancet* (7 August 1875), 232.

48   'Influence of Railway Travelling', part 2, 48–9.

49   Ibid., 49.

50   Charles Babbage, *Passages from the Life of a Philosopher* (London: Longman, Roberts and Green, 1864), 320.

51   Ibid., 321.

52   Babbage, *Passages*, 339.

53   Ibid., 345.

54   Ibid., 353.

55   'Vexatious Noises', *Lancet* (23 June 1877), 920.

56   'Bell Nuisance', *Lancet* (24 June 1880), 142–3.

57   Michael Bass, *Street Music in the Metropolis: Correspondence and Observations on the Existing Law, and Proposed Amendments* (London: John Murray, 1864).

58   See 'Monkey Tricks: How They Are Trained for Hand Organ Service. Attending a Monkey Sale. Teaching Him to Fire a Gun and Other Well Known Tricks. A Complete Review of His School Days.', *The Harrisburg Patriot* (July 11, 1889), accessed 15 April 2010, www.floraco.com/organs/monkey/ and http://www.floraco.com/organs/monkey/page2.html.

59   Much as Thomas Beddoes, George Cheyne and others in the eighteenth century conceived of nervous disorders as an affliction of cultivated sensibility (see above Chapter One), writers like George Beard in the 1880s thought 'neurasthenia' a disease of affluent people who participated fully in the stressful tempo of modern civilization, as discussed by Janet Oppenheim, *"Shattered Nerves": Doctors, Patients and Depression in Victorian England* (New York and Oxford: Oxford University Press, 1991), 90–109. However, as Oppenheim shows, much of the medical profession disagreed, seeing nervous exhaustion as common among all social classes.

60   Picker, *Victorian Soundscapes* (Oxford: Oxford University Press, 2003), 62.

61 Charles Manby Smith, 'Music-Grinders of the Metropolis', *Chambers's Edinburgh Journal*, n.s., 17 (1852), 197–201 (199).

62 Charles Babbage, 'On the Advantage of a Collection of Numbers, to be Entitled the Constants of Nature and Art', *The Edinburgh Journal of Science*, n.s., 6 (1832), 334–40 (334).

63 Harriet Ritvo, 'Zoological Nomenclature and the Empire of Victorian Science', in *Victorian Science in Context*, ed. Bernard Lightman (Chicago and London: University of Chicago Press, 1997), 334–53 (349).

64 Gustav Fechner, *On Life After Death* (London: Searle and Rivington, 1882), 54.

65 Charles Babbage, *The Ninth Bridgewater Treatise*, 2nd edn., (London: John Murray, 1838), 111–12.

66 Picker, *Victorian Soundscapes*, 16.

67 Babbage, *Passages from the Life of a Philosopher*, 320.

68 Ibid.

69 Charles Dickens, *Dombey and Son*, ed. Alan Horsman (Oxford: Oxford University Press, 1974), 861.

70 W. Bolton Tomson, 'The General Appreciation of Vibration as a Sense Extraordinary', *Lancet* (14 June 1890), 1299.

71 Picker, *Victorian Soundscapes*, 27.

72 Charles Dickens, *Dombey and Son*, ed. Alan Horsman (Oxford: Oxford University Press, 1974), 16. Hereafter cited in text as *DS* with page numbers.

73 That Dickens read Lyell's work is noted by James Secord in his preface to *Principles of Geology* (London: Penguin, 1997), ix–xliii.

74 Michael Freeman, *Railways and the Victorian Imagination* (New Haven and London: Yale University Press, 1999); Ian Carter, *Railways and Culture in Britain: The Epitome of Modernity* (Manchester & New York: Manchester University Press, 2001), 77. Carter notes Humphrey House's earlier observations in *The Dickens World*, second edn. (London: Oxford University Press, 1942), 145, 139, about the novel's reflection of the new interest in stratiographic geology.

75 *Dombey and Son*, 68. For discussions of Lyell's work in relation to nineteenth-century geology, consisting of various branches of which the study of earthquakes was one, see Karl Alfred von Zittel's *History of Geology and Palaeontology to the End of the Nineteenth Century*, trans. Maria Ogilvie-Gordon (London: Walter Scott, 1901); Mott Greene, *Geology in the Nineteenth Century: Changing Views of a Changing World* (Ithaca and London: Cornell University Press, 1982). To trace the connections between geology and the literature on vibration, particularly the physics of sound, light and heat, the work of John William Strutt, Lord Rayleigh, is a useful starting point. Like Helmholtz and others, Rayleigh spanned a range of topics including acoustics and optics; publications include *The Theory of Sound*, 2 vols (London: Macmillan, 1877–8) and *The Collected Optics Papers of Lord Rayleigh*, 2 vols (Washington, D.C.: Optical Society

of America, 1996). From sound waves Rayleigh moved onto 'surface waves' which he thought probably played a part in earthquakes, 'On Waves Propagated Along the Plane Surface of an Elastic Solid', *Proceedings of the London Mathematical Society*, 17 (1885), 4–11. The wave form identified in this paper came to be named after the author; the term 'Rayleigh waves' is routinely used in seismology.

76   Buckland, '"The Poetry of Science": Charles Dickens, Geology, and Visual and Material Culture in Victorian London', *Victorian Literature and Culture* 35 (2007), 679–94 (681).

77   *Principles of Geology*, 134.

78   See Harlan Nelson for example, for a view of the railway in *Dombey and Son* as destructive, 'Stagg's Gardens: The Railway through Dickens' World', *Dickens Studies Annual*, 3 (1974), 43–52. For an account of railway development in terms of progress, see Michael Slater, *An Intelligent Person's Guide to Dickens* (London: Duckbacks, 1999), 99–101. Ian Carter reviews the mass of criticism on this matter, in his chapter 'Eight Great Pages: *Dombey and Son*', in *Railways and Culture in Britain: The Epitome of Modernity* (Manchester and New York: Manchester University Press, 2001), pp. 71–91. My following position about opposition between the extremes drew on my reading of Steven Connor, *Charles Dickens* (Oxford: Basil Blackwell, 1985).

79   Buckland, 680.

80   My reading here draws on Steven Connor, *Charles Dickens* (Oxford: Basil Blackwell, 1985).

81   Carter reviews the criticism and observes how Carker's last seconds before he is run down by the train, as well as the rhythm of Dombey's journey, convey this tempo, in *Railways and Culture in Britain*, 71–91.

82   'The Influence of Railway Travelling on Public Health', *Lancet* (1 March 1862), part 7, 234.

83   'Electric Railways and Vibration', *Lancet* (22 December 1900), 1826.

84   A. Mallock, 'The Study of Vibration', *Pearson's Magazine* 23 (March 1907), 322–8 (322).

85   Ibid., 323–5.

86   Ibid., 324.

87   Ibid., 328.

88   Julie Wosk, *Women and the Machine: Representations from the Spinning Wheel to the Electronic Age* (Baltimore and London: Johns Hopkins University Press, 2001), xvii.

89   Benjamin Wooley, *The Bride of Science: Romance, Reason and Byron's Daughter* (London: Macmillan, 1999), 4.

90   Nordau, *Degeneration*, 5.

91   Karl Marx and Friedrich Engels, *The Communist Manifesto* (London: Penguin, 1967), 55 & 66.

92 Daniel Pick, *Faces of Degeneration: A European Disorder, c. 1848–c. 1918* (Cambridge: Cambridge University Press, 1989), 21–2, 224.

93 Pick mentions the circular motions in *Faces of Degeneration*, 22.

94 Marx and Engels, *Communist Manifesto*, 83.

95 Charles Dickens, 'An Unsettled Neighbourhood', first published in *Household Words*, 10 (1855), 289–92; repr. in *The Railway Through Dickens's World: Texts from* Household Words *and* All the Year Round, ed. Ewald Mengel (Frankfurt am Main: Peter Lang, 1989), 180–6 (182).

96 Marx and Engels, *Communist Manifesto*, 86.

97 Dickens, 'Unsettled Neighbourhood', 183.

98 Ibid., 184.

99 'Railway Noise and Vibration and their Effect upon Health', *Lancet* (24 July 1897), 211.

100 Turner, 'Periodical Time in the Nineteenth Century', 187–9.

101 Andrew Sanders, *Dickens and the Spirit of the Age* (Oxford: Oxford University Press, 1999), 43.

102 Ewald Mengel discusses this in the introduction to *The Railway Through Dickens's World*, 3–27.

103 Sanders, *Dickens and the Spirit of the Age*, 70–1.

104 Ibid., 44.

105 For an account of this see Steven Connor, 'The Shakes: Conditions of Tremor', *The Senses and Society* 3: 2 (2008), 205–20.

106 Joseph Conrad, *The Secret Agent* (London: Penguin, 1963), 162.

107 Ibid., 232.

108 Ibid., 236–7.

109 Ibid., 261.

110 Sanders, *Dickens and the Spirit of the Age*, 63.

111 For example see Daly, *Literature, Technology, and Modernity*. This idea has also helped to underpin more recent ideas of 'trauma'. See for example Cathy Caruth, *Unclaimed Experience: Trauma, Narrative, and History* (Baltimore and London: Johns Hopkins University Press, 1996), 6.

112 Several historians and critics have discussed Dickens's accident, including Schivelbusch, *The Railway Journey*, 137–40; Michael Trimble, *Post-Traumatic Neurosis: from Railway Spine to Whiplash* (Chichester, New York, Brisbane and Toronto: John Wiley and Sons, 1981), 27–8; Jill Matus, 'Trauma, Memory, and Railway Disaster: The Dickensian Connection', *Victorian Studies*, 43 (2001), 413–36; Daly, *Literature, Technology, and Modernity*, 34–5.

113 A number of commentators have also observed the widespread ambivalence and contradictory views of the railway as a symbol of progress that was simultaneously associated with death and disaster, including Ian Carter, *Railways and Culture in Britain*, and Matthew Beaumont and Michael

Freeman, eds. *The Railway and Modernity: Time, Space, and the Machine Ensemble* (Oxford: Peter Lang, 2007), who also note that 'satanic imagery' was assigned to the technology while it was viewed in 'utopian anticipation', 11.

Notes to Chapter 5

1   See, for example, Tim Armstrong, 'Two Types of Shock in Modernity', *Critical Quarterly*, 42 (2000), 61–73; Mark S. Micale, 'Jean-Martin Charcot and *les névroses traumatiques*: From Medicine to Culture in French Trauma Theory of the Late Nineteenth Century', in *Traumatic Pasts: History, Psychiatry, and Trauma in the Modern Age, 1870-1930*, ed. Mark S. Micale and Paul Lerner (Cambridge: Cambridge University Press, 2001), 115–39. I also discussed railways as 'traumatic' in Chapter Four.

2   Daly, *Literature, Technology, and Modernity, 1860–2000* (Cambridge: Cambridge University Press, 2004), 44. For examples of physicians who saw railway vibrations as a cause of sexual excitation see Rachel Maines's commentary, *The Technology of Orgasm: 'Hysteria,' the Vibrator, and Women's Sexual Satisfaction* (Baltimore, Maryland: Johns Hopkins UP, 1999), 90–1. For psychoanalytic perspectives see Wolfgang Schivelbusch, *The Railway Journey: The Industrialization of Time and Space in the 19th Century* (Berkeley: California UP, 1986), 77–9.

3   George Gissing, *The Odd Women* (Oxford: Oxford University Press), 108.

4   Bailey, 'Adventures in Space: Victorian Railway Erotics, or Taking Alienation for a Ride', *Journal of Victorian Culture* 9 (2004), 1–21 (10, 11).

5   Sally Ledger, 'Gissing, the Shopgirl and the New Woman', *Women: A Cultural Review* 6 (1995), 268–70.

6   Ibid., 270, 272.

7   See, for example, Jill Matus, *Unstable Bodies: Victorian Representations of Sexuality and Maternity* (Manchester and New York: Manchester University Press, 1995); Andrew Miller and James Adams (eds.), *Sexualities in Victorian Britain* (Bloomington and Indianapolis: Indiana University Press, 1996). Jane Wood mentions some of the feminist work on medicine as a dominant discourse with its ideologies of femininity and though she distances herself from the more extreme polemics develops a strong analysis of the relationship between female pathologies and 'the angel in the house', in *Passion and Pathology in Victorian Fiction* (Oxford: Oxford University Press, 2001), especially 8–27.

8   Robert Ellis, 'The Effects of Railway Travelling upon Uterine Diseases', letter to the *Lancet* (15 February 1862), 184. See also reference to young women's alleged susceptibility to 'spinal irritation', in Thomas Keller, 'Railway Spine Revisited: Traumatic Neurosis or Neurotrauma?', *Journal of the History of Medicine and Allied Sciences* 50 (1995), 507–24 (513).

9   Ibid.

10   Charles Dickens, *The Life and Adventures of Martin Chuzzlewit* (London: Everyman's, 1994), 626.

11   As Wood also observes, *Passion and Pathology*, 10.

12   For discussion of Browning's resistance to male traditions see Susan Brown, 'The Victorian poetess', in *The Cambridge Companion to Victorian Poetry*, ed. Joseph Bristow (Cambridge: Cambridge University Press, 2000), 180–202 (193).

13   Barrett Browning, *Aurora Leigh* (Oxford: Oxford UP, 1993), 235.

14   Jason R. Rudy considers Barrett Browning's work as part of his own discussion of electrical poetics with references to other critics, and to her spiritualist activities (briefly alluded to above in Chapter Three), in *Electric Meters: Victorian Physiological Poetics* (Athens: Ohio University Press, 2009), 176–83.

15   Ellis, *Studies in the Psychology of Sex, volume 1: The Evolution of Modesty; The Phenomena of Sexual Periodicity; Auto-Eroticism*, 3rd edn., (Philadelphia: F. A. Davis Company, 1910), 175–6.

16   Rachel Maines, *The Technology of Orgasm: 'Hysteria' the Vibrator, and Women's Sexual Satisfaction* (Baltimore, Maryland: The Johns Hopkins University Press, 1999), 89.

17   See Sarah Wintle, 'Horses, Bikes and Automobiles: New Woman on the Move', in ed. Angelique Richardson and Chris Willis, *The New Woman in Fiction and Fact* (Basingstoke: Palgrave, 2001), 66–78 (p. 67). For further commentary on dress see Alison Matthews David, 'Victorian Riding Habits and the Fashionable Horsewoman', *Victorian Literature and Culture* 30 (2002), 179–210.

18   Thomas Hardy, *Far from the Madding Crowd* (Hertfordshire: Wordsworth Editions., 1993), 14.

19   Ibid., 16.

20   George Eliot, *Middlemarch* (London: Penguin, 1994), 12.

21   This is Havelock Ellis's term, used in *Studies in the Psychology of Sex, volume 1*.

22   Mentioned above in Chapter Two, p. 60. Feminist critics have debated whether Dorothea is a precursor to the New Woman or is problematically traditional in this respect. See, for example, Gillian Beer, Chapter Six, '*Middlemarch* and "The Woman Question'', in *George Eliot* (Sussex: Harvester Press, 1986), 147–99. With regard to the horse riding scene, Kathleen Blake argues that Dorothea's 'energy' is evident at this point as at others, an energy that is stifled by social pressures, while the energy of the narrator – her strong narrative control – succeeds, in '*Middlemarch* and the Woman Question', *Nineteenth Century Fiction* 31 (1976), 285–312.

23   J. Langdon Down, 'On the Influence of the Sewing-Machine on Female Health', *British Medical Journal* (12 January 1867), 26.

24   Ibid, 26.

25 Ibid., 27.

26 Ellis, *Studies in the Psychology of Sex, volume 1*, 176.

27 Ibid., 176–7. Cites Pouillet, *L'Onanisme chez la Femme* (Paris, 1880).

28 Coffin, 'Credit, Consumption, and Images of Women's Desires: Selling the Sewing Machine in Late Nineteenth-Century France', *French Historical Studies* 18 (1994), 749–83 (761).

29 Ibid., 767.

30 The New Woman was sometimes constructed as having dangerous sexual appetites, as Sally Ledger also observes in 'The New Woman and the crisis of Victorianism', in ed. Ledger and Scott McCracken, *Cultural Politics at the Fin de Siècle* (Cambridge: Cambridge UP, 1995), 30. (I will pick up on this point again shortly.)

31 Ibid., 27.

32 For examples of the debate see the letters by Isaac Baker Brown, *British Medical Journal* (5 January 1867), 18; Robert Harling, who reported that the state of a woman subjected to the operation 'worsened', and Robert Greenhalgh, who claimed 'women have been made victims' of it (12 January 1867), 40–1.

33 'The Sewing-Machine', *British Medical Journal* (18 February 1871), 173. See also M. Guibout, 'Sewing Machines a Cause of Uterine Disorders', *Lancet* (2 January 1869), 23. For discussion of the range of reasons for objection to this procedure see Ornella Moscucci, 'Cliterodectomy, Circumcision, and the Politics of Sexual Pleasure in Mid-Victorian Britain', in eds. Andrew Miller and James Adams, *Sexualities in Victorian Britain* (Bloomington and Indianapolis: Indiana University Press, 1996), 59–78.

34 For a feminist view of clitoridectomy see for example Elaine Showalter, *The Female Malady* (New York: Virago, 1987), 74–8.

35 See Michael Mason, *The Making of Victorian Sexuality* (Oxford: Oxford University Press, 1994), 205. For wider discussions of masturbation and its challenge to social norms see Michel Foucault, *The History of Sexuality: The Will to Knowledge, vol. 1* (London: Penguin, 1998); Foucault, *Abnormal: Lectures at the College de France 1974–1975* (London and New York: Verso, 2003), 231–90; Thomas Laqueur, *Making Sex: Body and Gender from the Greeks to Freud* (Cambridge, Massachusetts, and London, England: Harvard University Press, 1990); Thomas Laqueur, *Solitary Sex: A Cultural History of Masturbation* (New York: The MIT Press, 2003)

36 Moscucci, 'Cliterodectomy, Circumcision, and the Politics of Sexual Pleasure in Mid-Victorian Britain', 71. As did Sigmund Freud, *Three Essays on the History of Sexuality* (1905), trans. James Strachey (New York: Avon, 1962). Laqueur discusses Freud's work in this context, *Making Sex*, 193–243.

37 See, for example, Michael Mason, 205–15; Ben Barker Benfield, 'The Spermatic Economy: A Nineteenth Century View of Sexuality', *Feminist Studies* 1 (1972), 45–74; Diane Mason, *The Secret Vice: Masturbation in*

Victorian Fiction and medical culture (Manchester: Manchester University Press, 2008), 12–26.

38 Mason, 16.

39 Anon., 'The Surgery of Bicycles', *Lancet* (5 June 1868), 794.

40 J. S. Boothroyd, letter to the *Lancet* (4 October 1884), 616.

41 Strahan, 'Bicycle Riding and Perineal Pressure', *Lancet* (20 September 1884), 490–1.

42 Hunt, 'The Great Masturbation Panic and the Discourses of Moral Regulation in Nineteenth- and Early Twentieth-Century Britain', *Journal of the History of Sexuality* 8 (1998), 575–615 (610).

43 See, for example, Sally Ledger and Roger Luckhurst (eds.), *The Fin de Siècle: A Reader in Cultural History, c. 1880–1900* (Oxford: Oxford University Press, 2000). See also my discussion of Max Nordau in Chapter Four.

44 George Herschell, 'Bicycle Riding and Perineal Pressure: Their Effect on the Young', letter to the *Lancet* (18 October 1884), 708.

45 Ibid. For further concerns with bicycles and sexual excitation see Edward Semple and James Taylor, 'On Certain Symptoms of Spinal Cord Affection in Bicycle Riders', *Lancet* (17 April 1897), 1085.

46 'New Inventions: The "Christy" Anatomical Bicycle Saddle', *Lancet* (23 October 1897), 1053; see also 'A New Bicycle Saddle', invented by Walter Wiglesworth, *Lancet* (19 March 1898), 796.

47 Ellis, *Studies in the Psychology of Sex, volume 1*, 178.

48 See, for example, Maines, 57, 89–90.

49 Wosk, *Women and the Machine*, 103.

50 Ibid., 73.

51 Coffin, 779.

52 'The New Woman', 30–1. See also Wood, 'New Women and Neurasthenia: Nervous Degeneration and the 1890s', Chapter Four of *Passion and Pathology in Victorian Fiction* (Oxford: Oxford University Press, 2001), 163–214.

53 For discussion of the use of musical strings since antiquity as an image for the body whose 'harmony' is upset in illness, and the adaptation of this context for nineteenth-century medical treatments, see Shelley Trower, '"Nerve-Vibration": Therapeutic Technologies in the 1880s and 1890s', in *Neurology and Modernity: A Cultural History of Nervous Systems, 1800–1950*, ed. Laura Salisbury and Andrew Shail (Basingstoke: Palgrave, 2010), 148–62.

54 Joseph Mortimer Granville, 'Treatment of Pain by Mechanical Vibrations', *Lancet* (19 February 1881), 286–8 (286).

55 For discussion of the medical practices and of their ideological context in terms of gender see Mary Poovey, 'Scenes of an Indelicate Character: The Medical Treatment of Victorian Women', which is Chapter 2 of *Uneven*

Developments: The Ideological Work of Gender in Mid-Victorian England (London: Virago, 1989), 24–50.

56 Granville, 'Treatment of Pain', 287.

57 Granville, *Nerve-Vibration and Excitation as Agents in the Treatment of Functional Disorder and Organic Disease* (London: J. and A. Churchill, 1883), 24–5, 58.

58 Joseph Mortimer Granville, 'A New Treatment for Certain Forms of Neurasthenia Spinalis', *Lancet* (15 October 1881), 671.

59 Granville, *Nerve-Vibration*, 13.

60 Ibid., 27.

61 Granville, 'Treatment of Pain by Mechanical Vibrations', 288; repeated in *Nerve-Vibration*, 28.

62 Granville, 'Treatment of Pain by Mechanical Vibrations', 288.

63 Edmund Burke, *A Philosophical Enquiry into the Sublime and Beautiful, and Other Pre-Revolutionary Writings* (London: Penguin, 1998), 165.

64 Ibid.

65 Samuel Taylor Coleridge, 'Dejection: An Ode', in *Samuel Taylor Coleridge: The Major Works*, ed. H. J. Jackson (Oxford: Oxford University Press, 1985), 114–18 (line 20).

66 Ibid., lines 6–8.

67 Ibid., lines 97–8 (agony by torture) and 125 (hopes to make her mother hear).

68 Thomas Young, 'Experiments and Calculations Relative to Physical Optics', in *The Wave Theory of Light: Memoirs by Huygens, Young and Fresnel*, ed. Henry Crew (New York: American Book Company, 1900), 68–76 (74).

69 Granville, 'Treatment of Pain by Mechanical Vibrations', 287.

70 Kipling, 'In the Same Boat', in *Strange Tales*, ed. David Stuart Davies (London: Wordsworth Editions, 2006), 85–104 (85).

71 Ibid., 86.

72 Ibid., 87.

73 Ibid., 87, 90, 91.

74 Ibid., 97.

75 Mentioned in an endnote to Chapter One, see p. 164. See also Tim Fulford, 'The Electrifying Mrs Robinson', *Women's Writing* 9 (2002), 23–35.

76 Granville, 'Nerve-Vibration: A Caution', *Lancet* (16 September 1882), p. 465; see also *Nerve-Vibration and Excitation*, 36.

77 Granville, *Nerve-Vibration and Excitation*, 57.

78 Maines, *Technology of Orgasm*, 95, 100.

79 Granville, 'Treatment of Pain', 287.

80 Friedrich Eduard Bilz, *The New Natural Method of Healing* (London: A. Bilz, 1898), 1816.

81 Snow, Mary Lydia Hastings Arnold, *Mechanical Vibration* (2005), Early
    American Manual Therapy Version 5.0, accessed 17 June 2010, http://www.
    meridianinstitute.com/eamt/files/snow/mvch2.htm.

82 Electromechanical vibrators were first used in medicine in 1878, according to
    Alphonso Rockwell, on hysterical women at the Salpêtrière, see *The Medical
    and Surgical Uses of Electricity: New Edition* (New York: E. B. Treat, 1903),
    635, 641.

83 See George Beard and Alphonso Rockwell, *The Medical Use of Electricity,
    with Special Reference to General Electrization as a Tonic in Neuralgia,
    Rheumatism, Dyspepsia, Chorea, Paralysis, and Other Affections associated
    with General Debility* (New York: William Wood and Co., 1867); Alphonso
    Rockwell, *Medical and Surgical Uses of Electricity: New Edition* (London,
    1896).

84 Granville, *Nerve-Vibration and Excitation*, 12.

85 For an account of this see Armstrong, *Modernism, Technology and the Body*
    (Cambridge: Cambridge University Press, 1998), 13–41.

86 Ibid.

87 The first chapter of Armstrong's *Modernism, Technology and the Body*
    begins by describing two executions, one by hanging after which friends
    tried to revive the corpse with electricity, and the other in the electric chair
    (13–14), and goes on to discuss how electricity is used both to kill and to
    heal, which is to be considered further below.

88 Rockwell, *Medical and Surgical Uses of Electricity*, 177.

89 Ibid., 178 ('not yet proved'), 355 ('billion or more').

90 Armstrong, *Modernism, Technology and the Body*, 14.

91 Ibid., 15, 17.

92 Maurice Pilgrim, *Vibratory Stimulation, its Theory and Application in the
    Treatment of Disease* (New York: Metropolitan Publishing, 1903), 106–7.

93 Ibid., 118–21.

94 George Henry Taylor, *Mechanical Aids in the Treatment of Chronic Forms of
    Disease* (New York: George W. Rodgers, 1893), 38.

95 Taylor, *Diseases of Women: Their Causes, Prevention, and Radical Cure*
    (Philadelphia, New York and Boston: Geo. MacLean, 1871), 20.

96 Taylor, *Mechanical Aids*, 48.

97 Ibid., 49–50.

98 Taylor, *An Illustrated Sketch of the Movement Cure: Its Principles, Methods
    and Effects* (New York, 1866), 18–19.

99 Taylor, *Pelvic and Hernial Therapeutics* (New York: J. B. Alden, 1885),
    187–90.

100 W. G. Langworthy Taylor, *Katie Fox: Epochmaking Medium and the Making
    of the Fox-Taylor Record* (New York and London: G. P. Putman's Sons,
    1933), viii.

101 Ibid., 1–28.

102 Ibid., 149.

103 Taylor, *Illustrated Sketch of the Movement Cure*, 18.

104 Recorded by William Crookes, 'Notes of an Enquiry into the Phenomena called Spiritual During the Years 1870–1873', *The Quarterly Journal of Science*, 11 (1874), 77–97.

105 Crookes, in *Presidential Addresses to the Society for Psychical Research 1882–1911* (Glasgow: Robert Maclehose, 1912), 86–103 (98).

106 Maines, 95–100.

107 For scientific medical discussions of vibration as energy or life see, for example, Samuel Spencer Wallian, *Rhymotherapy: A Discussion of the Physiologic Basis and Therapeutic Potency of Mechano-Vital Vibration* (Chicago: The Ouellette Press, 1906); D. T. Smith, *Vibration and Life* (Boston: Gorham Press, 1912).

108 'Vibration is Life', advertisement for Lindstrom Smith's White Cross Vibrator, *Modern Priscilla* (1910), repr. in Rachel Maines, *The Technology of Orgasm*, 106 (Fig. 25).

Notes to Afterword

1 University of Liverpool, 'Working at the University', accessed 1 August 2011, http://www.liv.ac.uk/working/.

2 Birkbeck, University of London, homepage, last modified 29 July 2011, accessed 1 August 2011, http://www.birkbeck.ac.uk/.

3 University of Exeter, 'About the Cornwall Campus', accessed 1 August 2011, http://www.exeter.ac.uk/cornwall/about/.

4 Brown University, 'About Brown University', © 2011, accessed 1 August 2011, http://brown.edu/about; Harvard University, 'Harvard Arts: Welcome', © 2011, accessed 1 August 2011, http://arts.harvard.edu/.

5 'The Elephant regeneration marches forward', *Southwark Life* (London: Southwark Council, Summer 2011), 4. Also available at 'Southwark Council: Southwark Life', accessed 1 August 2011, http://www.southwark.gov.uk/downloads/download/2502/southwark_life.

6 Tony Blair, speech to the TUC conference in 2004. Full text published in the *Guardian* (13 September 2004), accessed 2 August 2011, http://www.guardian.co.uk/society/2004/sep/13/publicservices.speeches.

7 See, for example, a recent interview in which Ed Miliband said that 'The Muslim community provides a huge vibrancy and richness to British life', the *Muslim News* 262 (25 February 2011), accessed 2 August 2011, http://www.muslimnews.co.uk/paper/index.php?article=5120. In a speech Ed Miliband argues that 'vibrant communities' depend on protection from the free market,

'Ed Miliband: Social Democracy', accessed 2 August 2011, http://edmiliband. org/speeches/4-the-state-and-social-democracy/.

8   University of Hull, 'Hull Campus', last modified 4 June 2011, accessed 1 August 2011, http://www2.hull.ac.uk/theuniversity/hull_campus.aspx.

BIBLIOGRAPHY

Ablow, Rachel, 'Good Vibrations: The Sensationalization of Masculinity in *The Woman in White*', *Novel: A Forum in Fiction*, 37 (2003), 158–80.

Abrams, M. H., *The Mirror and the Lamp: Romantic Theory and the Critical Tradition* (London, Oxford and New York: Oxford University Press, 1953).

—*The Correspondent Breeze: Essays on English Romanticism* (New York: W. W. Norton and Company, 1984).

Annual Register for 1757 (London, 1758); *The Annual Register* (British Library). <http://historyonline.chadwyck.co.uk/ar> [consulted 16.6.2004].

Anon., 'Preston County Court. – Important Decision to Railway Companies', *Lancet* (9 April 1853), 352–3.

Anon., 'The Surgery of Bicycles', *Lancet* (5 June 1868), 794.

Anon., 'Compensation for Railway Accidents', *The Times* (16 December 1870), 11.

Anon., 'The Sewing-Machine', *British Medical Journal* (18 February 1871), 173.

Anon., 'The Narcotic Influence of Railway Travelling', *Lancet* (24 July 1875), 139.

Anon., 'Vexatious Noises', *Lancet* (23 June 1877), 920.

Anon., *The Voice by Wire and Post-Card: All About the Telephone and Phonograph. Containing Description of Bell's and Dolbear's Telephones and Edison's Phonograph. History of the Discovery. Details of Construction and Interesting Experiments* (London: Ward, Lock and Co., 1878).

Anon., 'Bell Nuisance', *Lancet* (24 June 1880), 142–3.

Anon., 'Compensation after Railway Accident', *The Times* (23 November 1883), 9.

Anon., 'Monkey Tricks: How They Are Trained for Hand Organ Service. Attending a Monkey Sale. Teaching Him to Fire a Gun and Other Well Known Tricks. A Complete Review of His School Days.', *The Harrisburg Patriot* (11 July 1889), accessed 15 April 2010, www.floraco.com/organs/monkey/ and http://www.floraco.com/organs/monkey/page2.html.

Anon., 'Railway Noise and Vibration and their Effect upon Health', *Lancet* (24 July 1897), 211.

Anon., 'New Inventions: The "Christy" Anatomical Bicycle Saddle', *Lancet* (23 October 1897), 1053.

Anon., 'A New Bicycle Saddle', *Lancet* (19 March 1898), 796.

Anon., 'Electric Railways and Vibration', *Lancet* (22 December 1900), 1826.

Armstrong, Isobel, *Victorian Glassworlds: Glass Culture and the Imagination 1830–1880* (Oxford: Oxford University Press, 2008).

Armstrong, Tim, *Modernism, Technology and the Body: A Cultural Study* (Cambridge: Cambridge University Press, 1998).

—'Two Types of Shock in Modernity', *Critical Quarterly*, 42 (2000), 61–73.

Ashton, Rosemary, 'England and Germany', in Duncan Wu ed. *A Companion to Romanticism* (Maldon, Oxford and Carlton: Blackwells, 1999), 499–500.

Austen, Jane, *Northanger Abbey* (London: Penguin, 1994).

Babbage, Charles, 'On the Advantage of a collection of Numbers, to be Entitled the Constants of Nature and Art', *The Edinburgh Journal of Science*, new series, 6, (1832), 334–40.

—*The Ninth Bridgewater Treatise*, 2nd edn (London: John Murray, 1838).

—*Passages from the Life of a Philosopher* (London: Longman, Roberts and Green, 1864).

Bailey, Peter, 'Adventures in Space: Victorian Railway Erotics, or Taking Alienation for a Ride', *Journal of Victorian Culture*, 9 (2004), 1–21.

Barker Benfield, Ben, 'The Spermatic Economy: A Nineteenth Century View of Sexuality', *Feminist Studies*, 1 (1972), 45–74.

Barrett Browning, Elizabeth, *Aurora Leigh* (Oxford: Oxford UP, 1993).

Barrett, William, *Sensitive Flames as Illustrative of Sympathetic Vibration* (London, 1879).

—'On Some Phenomena Associated with Abnormal Conditions of Mind', *Proceedings of the Society of Psychical Research*, 1 (1882), 238–44.

Bass, Michael, *Street Music in the Metropolis: Correspondence and Observations on the Existing Law, and Proposed Amendments* (London: John Murray, 1864).

Beard, George, and Alphonso Rockwell, *The Medical Use of Electricity, with Special Reference to General Electrization as a Tonic in Neuralgia, Rheumatism, Dyspepsia, Chorea, Paralysis, and Other Affections associated with General Debility* (New York: William Wood and Co., 1867).

Beattie, James, *Essays in Poetry and Music* (London, 1779).

Beaumont, Matthew, and Michael Freeman (eds), *The Railway and Modernity: Time, Space, and the Machine Ensemble* (Oxford: Peter Lang, 2007).

Beer, Gillian, *Darwin's Plots: Evolutionary Narrative in Darwin, George Eliot and Nineteenth-Century Fiction* (London: Ark, 1983).

—*George Eliot* (Sussex: Harvester Press, 1986).

—'"Authentic Tidings of Invisible Things": Vision and the Invisible in the later Nineteenth Century', in Teresa Brennan and Martin Jay (eds), *Vision in Context: Historical and Contemporary Perspectives on Sight* (New York and London: Routledge, 1996), 85–94.

—*Open Fields: Science in Cultural Encounter* (Oxford: Clarendon Press, 1996).

Beer, John, *Coleridge's Poetic Intelligence* (London and Basingstoke: MacMillan, 1977).

Benjamin, Walter, *Illuminations* (London: Collins / Fontana Books, 1973).

Bennett, Jane, *Vibrant Matter: A Political Ecology of Things* (Durham and London: Duke University Press, 2010).

Bilz, Friedrich Eduard, *The New Natural Method of Healing* (London: A. Bilz, 1898).

Bissell, David, 'Vibrating materialities: mobility–body–technology relations', *Area*, 42 (2010), 479–86.

Blake, Kathleen, '*Middlemarch* and the Woman Question', *Nineteenth Century Fiction*, 31 (1976), 285–312.

Bloomfield, Robert, 'Nature's Music. Consisting of extracts from several authors with practical observations and poetical testimonies in honour of the harp of Aeolus', in *The Remains of Robert Bloomfield*, Joseph Weston ed. 2 vols (London: Baldwin, Craddock and Joy, 1824), 1, 93–143.

Boothroyd, J. S., letter to the *Lancet* (4 October 1884), 616.

Boring, Edwin, *A History of Experimental Psychology* (New Jersey: Prentice-Hall, 1950).

Bourne Taylor, Jenny, and Sally Shuttleworth, *Embodied Selves: An Anthology of Psychological Texts, 1830–1890* (Oxford: Clarendon Press, 1998).

Bradshaw's Railway Guide (London, January 1860).

Brantlinger, Patrick, 'Mass Media and Culture in *Fin-de-Siècle* Europe', in Mikuláš Teich and Roy Porter (eds), *Fin de Siècle and its Legacy* (Cambridge: Cambridge University Press, 1990), 98–113.

Brennan, Teresa, *The Transmission of Affect* (Ithaca and London: Cornell University Press, 2004).

Bristow, Joseph, 'Wilde, *Dorian Gray*, and gross indecency', in *Sexual Sameness: Textual Differences in Lesbian and Gay Writing* (London and New York: Routledge, 1992), 44–63.

Brown, Bill, 'Thing Theory', *Critical Inquiry*, 28: 1 (2001), 1–22.

—*A Sense of Things: The Object Matter of American Literature* (Chicago: University of Chicago Press, 2003).

Brown, Isaac Baker, *On the Curability of Certain Forms of Insanity, Epilepsy, Catalepsy, and Hysteria in Females* (London: Robert Hardwicke, 1866).

—'Clitoridectomy', letter to the *British Medical Journal* (5 January 1867), 18.

Brown, Susan, 'The Victorian poetess', in Joseph Bristow ed. *The Cambridge Companion to Victorian Poetry* (Cambridge: Cambridge University Press, 2000), 180–202.

Buckland, Adelene, '"The Poetry of Science": Charles Dickens, Geology, and Visual and Material Culture in Victorian London', *Victorian Literature and Culture*, 35 (2007), 679–94.

—'Thomas Hardy, Provincial Geology, and the Material Imagination', *19: Interdisciplinary Studies in the Long Nineteenth Century* 6 (2008), accessed 18 July 2011, http://19.bbk.ac.uk/index.php/19/article/viewFile/469/329.

Budge, Gavin, '"Art's Neurosis": Medicine, Mass Culture and the Romantic Artist in William Hazlitt', *Romanticism and Victorianism on the Net* 49 (2008).

Burke, Edmund, *A Philosophical Enquiry into the Sublime and Beautiful, and Other Pre-Revolutionary Writings* (London: Penguin, 1998).

Carpenter, William, 'On the Influence of Suggestion Modifying and Directing Muscular Movement, Independently of Volition', *Proceedings, Royal Institution of Great Britain*, 1 (1852), 147–53.

Carter, Ian, *Railways and Culture in Britain: The Epitome of Modernity* (Manchester and New York: Manchester University Press, 2001).

Caruth, Cathy, *Unclaimed Experience: Trauma, Narrative, and History* (Baltimore and London: Johns Hopkins University Press, 1996).

Casson, Herbert, *The History of the Telephone* (New York: Books for Libraries Press, 1910).

Cheney, Margaret, *Tesla: Man Out of Time* (New York: Delta, 1981).

Christensen, Jerome, *Coleridge's Blessed Machine of Language* (London: Cornell University Press, 1981).

Clarke, Edwin, 'The Doctrine of the Hollow Nerve in the Seventeenth and Eighteenth Centuries', in Lloyd Stevenson and Robert Multhauf (eds), *Medicine, Science, and Culture* (Baltimore, Maryland: The Johns Hopkins Press, 1968), 123–41.

Coffin, Judith, 'Credit, Consumption, and Images of Women's Desires: Selling the Sewing Machine in Late Nineteenth-Century France', *French Historical Studies*, 18 (1994), 749–83.

Cohen, H. F., *Quantifying Music: The Science of Music at the First Stage of the Scientific Revolution, 1580–1650* (Dordrecht, Boston, and Lancaster: D. Reidel Publishing Company, 1984).

Cohen, William A., *Embodied: Victorian Literature and the Senses* (Minneapolis and London: University of Minnesota Press, 2009).

Coleridge, Samuel Taylor, review of *The Monk*, first published in *Critical Review*, 19 (1797); reprinted in E. J. Clery and Robert Miles (eds), *Gothic Documents: A sourcebook 1700–1820* (Manchester and New York: Manchester University Press, 2000), 185–9.

—'Biographia Literaria; or Biographical Sketches of My Literary Life and Opinions', in H. J. Jackson ed. *Samuel Taylor Coleridge: The Major Works*, edn (Oxford: Oxford University Press, 1985), 155–482.

—'Dejection: An Ode', in H. J. Jackson ed. *Samuel Taylor Coleridge: The Major Works* (Oxford: Oxford University Press, 1985), 114–18.

—'The Eolian Harp', in H. J. Jackson ed. *Samuel Taylor Coleridge: The Major Works* (Oxford: Oxford University Press, 1985), 27–9.

—'Notebooks', in H. J. Jackson ed. *Samuel Taylor Coleridge: The Major Works* (Oxford: Oxford University Press, 1985), 543–63.

Collins, Wilkie, *The Woman in White* (London: Penguin, 1985).

Conder, Josiah, review of William Wordsworth's 'The White Doe of Rylstone; or the Fate of the Nortons', *Eclectic Review*, 2nd series, 5 (London, January 1816), 33–45.

Connor, Steven, *Charles Dickens* (Oxford: Basil Blackwell, 1985).

—*Dumbstruck: A Cultural History of Ventriloquism* (Oxford: Oxford University Press, 2000).

—'Isobel Armstrong's Material Imagination' (2002), accessed 22 April 11, http://stevenconnor.com/isobel/.

—'Modernism in Midair' (2003), accessed 21 July 2011, http://www.bbk.ac.uk/english/skc/midair/.

—'Gasworks', *19: Interdisciplinary Studies in the Long Nineteenth Century* 6 (2008), accessed 18 July 2011, http://19.bbk.ac.uk/index.php/19/article/viewFile/469/329.

—'The Shakes: Conditions of Tremor', *The Senses and Society* 3: 2 (2008), 205–20.

—*The Matter of Air: Science and Art of the Ethereal* (London: Reaktion, 2010), 148–72.

Conrad, Joseph, *The Secret Agent* (London: Penguin, 1963).

Courmelles, F. de, *Hypnotism*, trans. L. Ensor (London: George Routledge and Sons, 1891).

Cox, James Mason, *Practical Observations on Insanity* (London, 1804).

Cox, William, 'Cox *v*. The Midland Railway Company', letter to the *Lancet* (1 December 1849), 589.

Crary, Jonathan, *Techniques of the Observer: On Vision and Modernity in the Nineteenth Century* (Cambridge, Massachusetts and London, England: MIT, 1992).

—*Suspensions of Perception: Attention, Spectacle, and Modern Culture* (Cambridge, Massachusetts and London, England: The MIT Press, 1999).

Crookes, William, 'Spiritualism Viewed by the Light of Modern Science', *Quarterly Journal of Science*, 7 (1870), 316–21.

—'Notes of an Enquiry into the Phenomena called Spiritual During the Years 1870–1873', *The Quarterly Journal of Science*, 11 (1874), 77–97.

—in *Presidential Addresses to the Society for Psychical Research 1882–1911* (Glasgow: Robert Maclehose, 1912), 86–103.

Daly, Nicholas, *Literature, Technology, and Modernity, 1860–2000* (Cambridge: Cambridge University Press, 2004).

Davies, J., 'Cox, Davies, and Silk *versus* the Midland Counties Railway Company', letter to the *Lancet* (1 December 1849), 589–90.

Day, Aidan, *Romanticism* (London and New York: Routledge, 1996).

Dekker, George, *Coleridge and the Literature of Sensibility* (London: Vision Press Limited, 1978).

Dickens, Charles, 'An Unsettled Neighbourhood', *Household Words*, 10 (1855), 289–92; repr. in *The Railway Through Dickens's World: Texts from Household Words and All the Year Round* (Frankfurt am Main: Peter Lang, 1989), 180–6.

—*Dombey and Son*, Alan Horsman ed. (Oxford: Oxford University Press, 1974).

—*The Life and Adventures of Martin Chuzzlewit* (London: Everyman's, 1994).

Down, J. Langdon, 'On the Influence of the Sewing-Machine on Female Health', *British Medical Journal* (12 January 1867), 26–7.

Drake, Nathanial, *Literary Hours, or Sketches Critical and Narrative*, 2nd edn, 2 vols. (New York: Garland Publishing, 1970).

Eagleton, Terry, 'Power and Knowledge in "The Lifted Veil"', *Literature and History*, 9 (1983), 52–61.

Edison, Thomas, 'The Perfected Phonograph', *North American Review*, 146 (1888), 641–50.

Eliot, George, *The George Eliot Letters*, Gordon S. Haight ed. 7 vols (London: Oxford University Press, 1955).

—*Adam Bede* (London: Penguin, 1985).

—*Middlemarch* (London: Penguin, 1994).

—*The Lifted Veil, and Brother Jacob,* Helen Small ed. (Oxford: Oxford Paperbacks, 1999).

Elkana, Yehuda, *The Discovery of the Conservation of Energy* (London: Hutchinson Educational, 1974).

Ellenberger, Henri, *Beyond the Unconscious: Essays of Henri F. Ellenberger in the History of Psychiatry*, Mark Micale ed. (Princeton, New Jersey: Princeton University Press, 1993).

Ellis, Havelock, *Studies in the Psychology of Sex, volume 1: The Evolution of Modesty; The Phenomena of Sexual Periodicity; Auto-Eroticism*, 3rd edn (Philadelphia: F. A. Davis Company, 1910).

Ellis, Robert, 'The Effects of Railway Travelling upon Uterine Diseases', letter to the *Lancet* (15 February 1862), 184.

Enns, Anthony, 'Voices of the Dead: Transmission/Translation/Transgression', *Culture, Theory and Critique*, 46 (2005), 11–27.

—'Psychic Radio: Sound Technologies, Ether Bodies and Spiritual Vibrations', *Senses and Society* 3 (2008), special issue, Shelley Trower ed. 'Vibratory Movements', 137–52.

Erhardt-Sietbold, Erika von, 'Some Inventions of the Pre-Romantic Period and their Influence upon Literature', *Englische Studien*, 66 (1931–2), 347–63.

Erichsen, John Eric, *On Railway and Other Injuries of the Nervous System* (London: Walton and Maberly, 1866).

—*On Concussion of the Spine, Nervous Shock, and Other Obscure Injuries of the Nervous System, in Their Medical and Medico-Legal Aspects* (London, 1875).

Erle, Sibylle, and Laurie Garrison, special issue of *Romanticism and Victorianism on the Net* 52 (2008), 'Science, Technology and the Senses', accessed 18 July 2011, http://www.erudit.org/revue/ravon/2008/v/n52/019801ar.html.

Erlman, Veit, *Hearing Cultures: Essays on Sound, Listening and Modernity* (Oxford and New York: Berg, 2004).

—*Reason and Resonance: A History of Modern Aurality* (New York: Zone Books, 2010).

Fanu, Sheridan Le, 'The Familiar', in *Irish Ghost Stories* (Hertfordshire: Wordsworth Editions, 2005).

Fara, Patricia, *Sympathetic Attractions: Magnetic Practices, Beliefs, and Symbolism in Eighteenth-Century England* (Princeton, New Jersey: Princeton University Press, 1996).

Fayter, Paul, 'Strange New Worlds of Space and Time: Late Victorian Science and Science Fiction', *Victorian Science in Context*, Bernard Lightman ed. (Chicago and London: The University of Chicago Press, 1997), 256–74.

Fechner, Gustav, *On Life after Death* (London: Searle and Rivington, 1882).

—'Nanna oder das Seelenleben der Pflanzen', in *Religion of a Scientist: Selections from Gustav Theodor Fechner*, Walter Lowrie (trans. and ed.) (New York: Pantheon, 1946).

—*Elements of Psychophysics*, trans. Helmut Adler, David Howes and Edwin Boring (New York, Chicago, San Francisco, Toronto, London: Holt, Rineheart and Winston Inc., 1966).

Finney, Gretchen, *Musical Backgrounds for English Literature: 1580–1650* (New Brunswick, New Jersey: Rutgers University Press, 1961).

Flint, Kate, Introduction to special issue of *Romanticism and Victorianism on the Net*, 53 (2009), 'Materiality and Memory', accessed 18 July 2011, http://www.erudit.org/revue/ravon/2009/v/n53/029895ar.html.

Forbes, B. C., 'Edison Working on How to Communicate with the Next World', *American Magazine* 90: 10/11 (1920).

Foucault, Michel, *The History of Sexuality: The Will to Knowledge, vol. 1* (London: Penguin, 1998).

—*Abnormal: Lectures at the College de France 1974–1975* (London and New York: Verso, 2003), 231–90.

Freeman, Michael, *Railways and the Victorian Imagination* (New Haven and London: Yale University Press, 1999).

Freud, Sigmund, 'Psycho-analytic Notes on an Autobiographical Account of a Case of Paranoia (Dementia Paranoides)', in *Standard Edition of the Complete*

Psychological Works of Sigmund Freud, James Strachey ed. 24 vols (London: Vintage, 2001), 7, 9–82.

Fulford, Tim, 'The Electrifying Mrs Robinson', *Women's Writing*, 9 (2002), 23–35.

—'Conducting the Vital Fluid: The Politics and Poetics of Mesmerism in the 1790s', *Studies in Romanticism*, 43: 1 (2004), 57–78.

Gissing, George, *The Odd Women* (Oxford: Oxford University Press).

Goodman, Steve, *Sonic Warfare: Sound, Affect, and the Ecology of Fear* (Cambridge, Massachusetts and London, England: The MIT Press, 2010).

Goring, Paul, *The Rhetoric of Sensibility in Eighteenth-Century Culture* (Cambridge: Cambridge University Press, 2005).

Gouk, Penelope, *Music, Science, and Natural Magic in the Seventeenth Century* (London: Warburg Institute, 1999).

—*Musical Healing in Cultural Contexts* (Aldershot, Brookfield USA, Singapore, Sydney: Ashgate, 2000).

—'Raising Spirits and Restoring Souls: Early Modern Medical Explanations for Music's Effects', in Veit Erlmann ed. *Hearing Cultures: Essays on Sound, Listening and Modernity*, (Oxford and New York: Berg, 2004), 87–105.

Granville, J. Mortimer, 'Treatment of Pain by Mechanical Vibrations', *Lancet* (19 February 1881), 286–8.

—'A New Treatment for Certain Forms of Neurasthenia Spinalis', *The Lancet* (15 October 1881), 671.

—'Nerve-Vibration: A Caution', *The Lancet* (16 September 1882), 465.

—*Nerve-Vibration and Excitation as Agents in the Treatment of Functional Disorder and Organic Disease* (London: J. and A. Churchill, 1883).

Gray, Beryl, 'Pseudoscience and George Eliot's "The Lifted Veil"', *Nineteenth-Century Fiction*, 36, 407–23.

Greene, Mott, *Geology in the Nineteenth Century: Changing Views of a Changing World* (Ithaca and London: Cornell University Press, 1982).

Guibout, M., 'Sewing Machines a Cause of Uterine Disorders', *The Lancet* (2 January 1869), 23.

Guitammer Company, 'Buttkicker: Home Theater' (2011), accessed 21 July 2011, http://www.thebuttkicker.com/home_theater/index.htm.

Gurney, Edmund, *The Power of Sound* (New York: Basic Books, 1966).

Gurney, Edmund, Frederic Myers and Frank Podmore, (eds) *Phantasms of the Living*, 2 vols (Florida: Scholars' Facsimiles and Reprints, 1970).

Hacking, Ian, *Rewriting the Soul: Multiple Personality and the Sciences of Memory* (Princeton: Princeton University Press, 1995).

Hagen, Wolfgang, *Das Radio: Zur Geschichte und Theorie des Hörfunks–Deutschland/USA* (München: Wilhelm Fink Verlag, 2005).

Hankins, Thomas and Robert Silverman, *Instruments and the Imagination* (Princeton, New Jersey: Princeton University Press, 1995).

Hardy, Thomas, *Far from the Madding Crowd* (Hertfordshire: Wordsworth Editions, 1993).

Harling, Robert, letter to *British Medical Journal* (12 January 1867), 40.

Harmans, P. M., *Energy, Force, and Matter: The Conceptual Development of Nineteenth-Century Physics* (Cambridge: Cambridge University Press, 1982).

Harrington, Anne, 'Hysteria, Hypnosis, and the Lure of the Invisible: the Rise of Neo-Mesmerism in *fin-de-siècle* French Psychiatry', in W. F. Bynum, Roy

Porter and Michael Shepherd (eds), *The Anatomy of Madness*, 3 vols (London: Routledge, 1988), 3: *The Asylum*, 226–46.

Hartley, David, *Observations on Man, His Frame, His Duty, and His Expectations*, 2 vols. (London: Joseph Johnson, 1791); repr. as *Observations on Man*, 2 vols (Poole: Woodstock Books, 1998).

Havergal, Frances Ridley, 'The Message of An Aeolian Harp', in *The Poetical Works of Frances Ridgley Havergal*, 2 vols (London: James Nisbet and Co., 1884), 2, 159–62.

Hearnshaw, L. S., *The Shaping of Modern Psychology* (London and New York: Routledge, 1987).

Heidelberger, Michael, *Nature from Within: Gustav Theodor Fechner and His Psychophysical Worldview*, trans. Cynthia Klohr (Pittsburgh: University of Pittsburgh Press, 2004).

Helmholtz, Hermann, 'On the Physiological Causes of Harmony in Music', in *Popular Lectures on Scientific Subjects*, 1st series, trans. E. Atkinson (London: Longmans, Green and Co, 1895), 53–93.

—'On Goethe's Scientific Researches', in *Popular Lectures on Scientific Subjects*, 1st series, trans. E. Atkinson (London: Longmans, Green and Co, 1895), 29–51.

—'On the Origin of the Planetary System', in *Popular Lectures on Scientific Subjects*, 2nd series, trans. E. Atkinson (London: Longmans, Green and Co, 1895), 152–95.

—*On the Sensations of Tone as a Physiological Basis for the Theory of Music* (New York: Dover Publications, 1954).

—'The Facts of Perception', in Russell Kahl ed. *Selected Writings of Hermann von Helmholtz* (Middletown, Connecticut: Wesleyan University Press, 1971), 366–408.

—'The Conservation of Force', in David Cahan ed. *Hermann von Helmholtz: Science and Culture, Popular and Philosophical Essays*, (Chicago: University of Chicago Press, 1995), 96–126.

Henriques, Julian, 'The Vibrations of Affect and their Propagation on a Night Out on Kingston's Dancehall Scene', *Body and Society*, 16: 1 (2010), 57–89.

Herschell, George, 'Bicycle Riding and Perineal Pressure: Their Effect on the Young', letter to the *Lancet* (18 October 1884), 708.

Hey, Hanson, 'The Seven Principles of Spiritualism, with a brief History of the Spiritualists' National Union' (Halifax: Spiritualists' National Union, 1910).

Howes, David, *The Empire of the Senses: The Sensual Culture Reader* (Oxford and New York: Berg, 2005).

Hunt, Alan, 'The Great Masturbation Panic and the Discourses of Moral Regulation in Nineteenth- and Early Twentieth-Century Britain', *Journal of the History of Sexuality*, 8 (1998), 575–615.

'The Influence of Railway Travelling on Public Health', *Lancet*, part 1 to 8 (4 January to 8 March 1862).

L'Isle-Adam, Villiers de, *Tomorrow's Eve*, trans. Robert Martin Adams (Urbana, Chicago and London: University of Illinois Press, 2001).

Jackson-Jones, Chris, Fabric review, accessed 20 July 2009, http://www.viewlondon.co.uk/review_608.html.

Jacobs, Arthur, *A New Dictionary of Music* (Harmondsworth: Penguin Books Ltd, 1958).

James, William, *The Varieties of Religious Experience: a Study in Human Nature* (New York: Touchstone, 1997).

Jones, Chris, *Radical Sensibility: Literature and Ideas in the 1790s* (London and New York: Routledge, 1993).

Jütte, Robert, *A History of the Senses, from Antiquity to Cyberspace*, trans. James Lynn (Cambridge and Malden: Polity, 2005).

Kahn, Douglas, *Noise, Water, Meat: A History of Sound in the Arts* (Cambridge, Massachusetts and London, England: The MIT Press, 1999).

Katan, Maurits, 'Schreber's Hereafter: Its Building-Up (Aufbau) and its Downfall', in William Niederland ed. *The Schreber Case: Psychoanalytic Profile of a Paranoid Personality*, (New York: Quadrangle / The New York Times Book Company, 1974).

Kato, Yoshimasa, and Yuichi Ito, 'White Lives on Speaker', accessed 20 July 2009, www.wlos.jp/about.html.

Keller, Thomas, 'Railway Spine Revisited: Traumatic Neurosis or Neurotrauma?', *Journal of the History of Medicine and Allied Sciences*, 50 (1995), 507–24.

Kipling, Rudyard, 'In the Same Boat', in *Strange Tales*, ed. David Stuart Davies (Hertfordshire: Wordsworth Editions, 2006), 85–104.

Kittler, Friedrich, *Discourse Networks, 1800 / 1900*, trans. Michael Metteer and Chris Cullens (Stanford, California: Stanford University Press, 1990).

—*Optical Media*, trans. Anthony Enns (Cambridge and Malden: Polity, 2010).

Kraepelin, Emil, *Lectures on Clinical Psychiatry*, trans. T. Johnstone (London: Balliere, Tindall and Cox, 1906).

—'Dementia Praecox', in Max Hamilton ed. *Abnormal Psychology: Selected Readings* (Harmonsdworth: Penguin, 1967), 11–81.

Krauss, Rosalind, *The Optical Unconscious* (Cambridge, Massachusetts and London, England: The MIT Press, 1994).

Laquer, Thomas, *Making Sex: Body and Gender from the Greeks to Freud* (Cambridge: Harvard University Press, 1990).

—*Solitary Sex: A Cultural History of Masturbation* (New York: The MIT Press, 2003).

Latour, Bruno, *We Have Never Been Modern*, trans. Catherine Porter (Cambridge, Massachusetts: Harvard University Press, 1993).

—*Politics of Nature: How to Bring the Sciences into Democracy*, trans. Catherine Porter (Cambridge, Massachusetts and London, England: Harvard University Press, 2004).

Leahey, Thomas, *A History of Psychology: Main Currents in Psychological Thought*, 5th edn (New Jersey: Prentice Hall, 2000).

Ledger, Sally, 'Gissing, the Shopgirl and the New Woman', *Women: A Cultural Review* 6 (1995), 268–70.

—'The New Woman and the crisis of Victorianism', in Sally Ledger and Scott McCracken, (eds), *Cultural Politics at the* Fin de Siecle (Cambridge: Cambridge UP, 1995).

Ledger, Sally, and Roger Luckhurst (eds), *The Fin de Siecle: A Reader in Cultural History, c. 1880–1900* (Oxford: Oxford University Press, 2000).

Levine, George, 'George Eliot's Hypothesis of Reality', *Nineteenth-Century Fiction*, 35 (1980), 1–28.

Lewes, George Henry, *Problems of Life and Mind*, 3 vols (London: Trubner and Co., 1874, 1877, 1879).

Lewis, Matthew, *The Monk* (Oxford and New York: Oxford University Press, 1995).

Luckhurst, Roger, *The Invention of Telepathy* (Oxford: Oxford University Press, 2002).

—'Traumaculture', *New Formations*, Special Issue, ed. Joe Brooker and Roger Luckhurst, *Remembering the 1990s*, 50 (2003), 28–47.

Lyell, Charles, *Principles of Geology* (London: Penguin, 1997).

Mackay, James, *Sounds Out of Silence: A Life of Alexander Graham Bell* (Edinburgh and London: Mainstream Publishing, 1997).

Maines, Rachel P., *The Technology of Orgasm: 'Hysteria,' the Vibrator, and Women's Sexual Satisfaction* (Baltimore, Maryland: The Johns Hopkins University Press, 1999).

Mallock, A., 'The Study of Vibration', *Pearson's Magazine*, 23 (March 1907), 322–8.

Marshall, Marilyn, 'Physics, Metaphysics, and Fechner's Psychophysics', in William Woodward and Mitchell Ash (eds), *The Problematic Science: Psychology in Nineteenth-Century Thought* (New York: Praeger Publishing, 1982), 65–87.

Marvin, Carolyn, *When Old Technologies Were New: Thinking About Electric Communication in the Late Nineteenth Century* (Oxford: Oxford University Press, 1988).

Marx, Karl, and Friedrich Engels, *The Communist Manifesto* (London: Penguin, 1967).

Mason, Diane, *The Secret Vice: Masturbation in Victorian Fiction and medical culture* (Manchester: Manchester University Press, 2008).

Mason, Michael, *The Making of Victorian Sexuality* (Oxford: Oxford University Press, 1994).

Matthews David, Alison, 'Victorian Riding Habits and the Fashionable Horsewoman', *Victorian Literature and Culture* 30 (2002), 179–210.

Matus, Jill, *Unstable Bodies: Victorian Representations of Sexuality and Maternity* (Manchester and New York: Manchester University Press, 1995).

—'Trauma, Memory, and Railway Disaster: The Dickensian Connection', *Victorian Studies*, 43 (2001), 413–36.

McCarthy, Thomas, *Relationships of Sympathy: The Writer and the Reader in British Romanticism* (Aldershot: Scolar Press, 1997).

McCobb, Anthony, *George Eliot's Knowledge of German Life and Letters* (Salzburg, Austria: Institut für Anglistik und Amerikanistik, Universitat Salzburg, 1982).

McDonagh, Josephine, *George Eliot* (Plymouth, U.K.: Northcote House Publishers, 1997).

McFarland, Thomas, *Coleridge and the Pantheist Tradition* (Oxford: Oxford University Press, 1969).

McLandburgh, Florence, 'The Automaton-Ear', *Scribner's Monthly*, 5 (1873), 711–20; repr. as 'The Automaton Ear', in *The Automaton Ear, and Other Sketches* (Chicago: Jansen, McClurg and Co., 1876), 7–43.

McLean, Steven, *H. G. Wells: Interdisciplinary Essays* (Cambridge: Cambridge Scholars, 2008).

—*The Early Fiction of H. G. Wells: Fantasies of Science* (Basingstoke: Palgrave Macmillan, 2009).

McLuhan, Marshall, *Understanding Media: The Extensions of Man* (London: Routledge, 2001).

Mesmer, Franz Anton, *Mesmerism, A Translation of the Original Scientific and Medical Writings of F. A. Mesmer*, trans. George Bloch (Los Altos, California: William Kaufmann, 1980).

Micale, Mark S., 'Jean-Martin Charcot and *les névroses traumatiques*: From Medicine to Culture in French Trauma Theory of the Late Nineteenth Century', in Mark S. Micale and Paul Lerner (eds), *Traumatic Pasts: History, Psychiatry, and Trauma in the Modern Age, 1870–1930* (Cambridge: Cambridge University Press, 2001), 115–39.

Miles, Robert, *Anne Radcliffe: The Great Enchantress* (Manchester and New York: Manchester University Press, 1995).

Miller, Andrew, and James Adams (eds), *Sexualities in Victorian Britain* (Bloomington and Indianapolis: Indiana University Press, 1996).

Miller, D. A., '*Cage aux Folles*: Sensation and Gender in Wilkie Collins's *The Woman in White*', in Stephen Regan ed. *The Nineteenth-Century Novel: A Critical Reader* (Oxon: Routledge, 2001), 424–9.

Miller, Daniel ed. *Materiality* (Durham and London: Duke University Press, 2005).

Morton, Timothy, 'Of Matter and Meter: Environmental Form in Coleridge's "Effusion 35" and "The Eolian Harp"', *Literature Compass*, 5: 2 (2008), 310–35.

Moscucci, Ornella, 'Cliterodectomy, Circumcision, and the Politics of Sexual Pleasure in Mid-Victorian Britain', in (eds) Andrew Miller and James Adams, *Sexualities in Victorian Britain* (Bloomington and Indianapolis: Indiana University Press, 1996), 59–78.

Musselman, Elizabeth, 'The Governer and the Telegraph: Mental Management in British Natural Philosophy', in Iwan Morus ed. *Bodies / Machines*, (Oxford and New York: Berg, 2002), 67–92.

Nancy, Jean Luc, *Listening*, trans. Charlotte Mandell (New York: Fordham University Press, 2007).

Nelson, Harlan, 'Stagg's Gardens: The Railway through Dickens' World', *Dickens Studies Annual*, 3 (1974), 43–52.

Newton, Isaac, *Opticks: Or, A Treatise of the Reflections, Refractions, Inflections and Colours of Light*, 3rd edn (London: William and John Innys, 1721).

Niederland, William, *The Schreber Case: Psychoanalytic Profile of a Paranoid Personality* (New York: Quadrangle / The New York Times Book Company, 1974).

Noakes, Richard, '"Instruments to Lay Hold of Spirits": Technologizing the Bodies of Victorian Spiritualism', in Iwan Morus ed. *Bodies / Machines* (Oxford and New York: Berg, 2002), 125–63.

—'The "Bridge which is between Physical and Psychical Research": William Fletcher Barrett, Sensitive Flames, and Spiritualism', *History of Science*, 42 (2004), 419–64.

Ong, Walter, *The Presence of the Word: Some Prolegomena for Religious and Cultural History* (New Haven and London: Yale University Press, 1967).

—*Hopkins, the Self, and God* (Toronto, Buffalo and London: University of Toronto Press, 1986).

—*Orality and Literacy* (London and New York: Routledge, 2002).

Oppenheim, Janet, *The Other World: Spiritualism and Psychical Research in England, 1850–1914* (Cambridge: Cambridge University Press, 1985).

—'*Shattered Nerves': Doctors, Patients and Depression in Victorian England* (New York and Oxford: Oxford University Press, 1991).

Otis, Laura, 'The Other End of the Wire: Uncertainties of Organic and Telegraphic Communication', *Configurations: A Journal of Literature, Science, and Technology*, 9 (2001), 181–206.

Owen, Alex, *The Darkened Room: Women, Power and Spiritualism in Late Victorian England* (London: Virago Press, 1989).

Oxford English Dictionary, 2nd edn, 20 vols (Oxford: Clarendon Press, 1989).

Parlati, Marilena, 'Beyond Inchoate Debris: Dust in Contemporary Culture', *European Journal of English Studies*, 15: 1 (2011), 73–84.

Pick, Daniel, *Faces of Degeneration: A European Disorder, c. 1848–c. 1918* (Cambridge: Cambridge University Press, 1989).

—*Svengali's Web: The Alien Enchanter in Modern Culture* (New Haven and London: Yale University Press, 2000).

Picker, John, *Victorian Soundscapes* (Oxford: Oxford University Press, 2003).

Pilgrim, Maurice, *Vibratory Stimulation, its Theory and Application in the Treatment of Disease* (New York: Metropolitan Publishing, 1903).

Poovey, Mary, *Uneven Developments: The Ideological Work of Gender in Mid-Victorian England* (London: Virago, 1989).

Porter, Roy, *Flesh in the Age of Reason: How the Enlightenment Transformed the Way We See Our Bodies and Souls* (London: Penguin, 2004).

Priestley, Joseph, *The History and Present State of Discoveries Relating to Vision, Light and Colours*, 2 vols (London: J. Johnson, 1772).

—*Experiments and Observations on Different Kinds of Air*, 2 vols (London, 1774).

—*Hartley's Theory of the Human Mind, on the Principle of the Association of Ideas; with Essays Relating to the Subject of it* (London, 1790).

Proceedings of the Society for Psychical Research, 1 (London, Trübner and Co., 1882).

Purrington, Robert, *Physics in the Nineteenth Century* (New Brunswick, New Jersey and London: Rutgers University Press, 1997).

Rayleigh, Lord (John William Strutt) *The Theory of Sound*, 2 vols (London: Macmillan, 1877–8).

—'On Waves Propagated Along the Plane Surface of an Elastic Solid', *Proceedings of the London Mathematical Society*, 17 (1885), 4–11.

—*The Collected Optics Papers of Lord Rayleigh*, 2 vols (Washington, D.C.: Optical Society of America, 1996).

Reed, Edward, *From Soul to Mind: The Emergence of Psychology, from Erasmus Darwin to William James* (New Haven and London: Yale University Press, 1997).

Reynolds, J. Russell, 'Travelling: Its Influence on Health', in Malcolm Morris (ed), *The Book of Health* (London, Paris and Melbourne: Cassell and Co., 1883), 554–84.

Richards, Graham, *Mental Machinery, Part 1: The Origins and Consequences of Psychological Ideas from 1600 to 1850* (London: The Athlone Press, 1992).

Richardson, Alan, *British Romanticism and the Science of the Mind* (Cambridge: Cambridge University Press, 2001).

—'Romanticism and the Body', *Literature Compass*, 1 (2004), 1–14.

Ridley Havergal, Frances, 'The Message of An Aeolian Harp', in *The Poetical Works of Frances Ridgley Havergal*, 2 vols (London: James Nisbet and Co., 1884), 159–62.

Ritvo, Harriet, 'Zoological Nomenclature and the Empire of Victorian Science', in Bernard Lightman ed. *Victorian Science in Context*, (Chicago and London: University of Chicago Press, 1997), 334–53.

Roach, Joseph, *The Player's Passion: Studies in the Science of Acting* (Ann Arbor: University of Michigan Press, 1993).

Roads, Curtis, *Microsound* (Cambridge, Massachusetts and London, England: The MIT Press, 2001).

Roberts, Mark S., 'Wired: Schreber As Machine, Technophobe, and Virtualist', *TDR: The Drama Review*, 40 (1996) 31–46; repr. in Allen S. Weiss ed. *Experimental Sound and Radio* (Cambridge, Massachusetts and London, England: MIT Press, 2001), 27–41.

Rockwell, Alphonso, *Medical and Surgical Uses of Electricity: New Edition* (London, 1896).

—*The Medical and Surgical Uses of Electricity: New Edition* (New York: E. B. Treat, 1903).

Ronell, Avital, *The Telephone Book: Technology, Schizophrenia, Electric Speech* (Lincoln: University of Nebraska Press, 1989).

Rousseau, G. S., 'Nerves, Spirits, and Fibres: Towards Defining the Origins of Sensibility', in R. F. Brissenden and J. C. Eade (eds), *Studies in the Eighteenth Century III* (Toronto and Buffalo: University of Toronto Press, 1976), 137–57.

—*Nervous Acts: Essays on Literature, Culture and Sensibility* (Basingstoke: Palgrave, 2004).

Rudy, Jason R., *Electric Meters: Victorian Physiological Poetics* (Athens: Ohio University Press, 2009).

Ruston, Sharon, *Shelley and Vitality* (Basingstoke: Palgrave, 2009).

Rylance, Rick, *Victorian Psychology and British Culture: 1850–1880* (Oxford: Oxford University Press, 2000).

Salisbury, Laura, and Andrew Shail (eds), *Neurology and Modernity: A Cultural History of Nervous Systems, 1800–1950* (Basingstoke: Palgrave, 2010).

Sanders, Andrew, *Dickens and the Spirit of the Age* (Oxford: Oxford University Press, 1999).

Santner, Eric, *My Own Private Germany: Daniel Paul Schreber's Secret History of Modernity* (Princeton, New Jersey: Princeton University Press, 1996).

Sarafianos, Aris, 'Pain, Labor, and the Sublime: Medical Gymnastics and Burke's Aesthetics', *Representations*, 91 (2005), 58–83.

Schatzman, Morton, *Soul Murder: Persecution in the Family* (London: Allen Lane, 1973).

Schiller, Friedrich, 'Honor to Woman', *Poems of Schiller* (Boston: S. E. Cassino and Co., 1884), 237–8.

Schivelbusch, Wolfgang, *The Railway Journey: The Industrialization of Time and*

Space in the 19th Century (Berkeley and Los Angeles: University of California Press, 1986).

Schreber, Daniel Paul, *Memoirs of My Nervous Illness* (New York: New York Review of Books, 2000).

Sconce, Jeffrey, *Haunted Media: Electronic Presence from Telegraphy to Television* (Durham and London: Duke University Press, 2000).

Secord, James, preface to Charles Lyell, *Principles of Geology* (London: Penguin, 1997), ix–xliii.

Semple, Edward, and James Taylor, 'On Certain Symptoms of Spinal Cord Affection in Bicycle Riders', *Lancet* (17 April 1897), 1085.

Shakespeare, William, *King Richard III*, ed. Antony Hammond (London and New York: Methuen, 1981).

Shelley, Percy, 'Ode to the West Wind', in *The Complete Poetical Works of Percy Bysshe Shelley*, ed. Thomas Hutchinson (London: Oxford University Press, 1935), 573–4.

Showalter, Elaine, *The Female Malady: Women, Madness and English Culture, 1830–1980* (London: Virago Press, 1987).

Shuttleworth, Sally, *George Eliot and Nineteenth-Century Science: The Make Believe of a Beginning* (London, New York, New Rochelle, Melbourne and Sydney: Cambridge University Press, 1984).

Sinfield, Alan, *The Wilde Century: Effeminacy, Oscar Wilde and the Queer Moment* (New York: Cassell, 1994).

Slater, Michael, *An Intelligent Person's Guide to Dickens* (London: Duckbacks, 1999).

Smith, Bruce, 'Listening to the Wild Blue Yonder: The Challenges of Acoustic Ecology', in Veit Erlman ed. *Hearing Cultures: Essays on Sound, Listening and Modernity* (Oxford and New York: Berg, 2004), 21–41.

Smith, Charles Manby, 'Music-Grinders of the Metropolis', *Chambers's Edinburgh Journal*, new series, 17 (1852), 197–201.

Smith, Crosbie, *The Science of Energy: Cultural History of Energy Physics in Victorian Britain* (Chicago and London: Chicago University Press, 1999).

Smith, D. T., *Vibration and Life* (Boston: Gorham Press, 1912).

Smith, Mark M., *Sensory History* (Oxford and New York: Berg, 2007).

Smith, W., *A Dissertation upon the Nerves; Containing an Account: 1/ of the Nature of Man 2/ of the Nature of Brutes 3/ of the Nature and Connection of Soul and Body 4/ of the Threefold Life of Man 4/ of the Symptoms, Causes and Cure of all Nervous Diseases* (London, 1768).

Snow, Mary Lydia Hastings Arnold, *Mechanical Vibration* (2005), Early American Manual Therapy Version 5.0, accessed 17 June 2010, http://www.meridianinstitute.com/eamt/files/snow/mvch2.htm.

Sterne, Jonathan, *The Audible Past: Cultural Origins of Sound Reproduction* (Durham: Duke University Press, 2003).

Stewart, R., letter to the *Lancet* (7 August 1875), 232.

Stimson, Frederic, 'Dr. Materialismus', in *Future Perfect: American Science Fiction of the Nineteenth Century* (London, Oxford and New York: Oxford University Press, 1978), 169–87.

Strahan, S. A., 'Bicycle Riding and Perineal Pressure, Their Effect on the Young', *Lancet* (20 September 1884), 490–1.

'Subwoofer Cat', accessed 20 July 2009, www.youtube.com/watch?v=zmRTGR brATs.

Syson, Lydia, *Doctor of Love: James Graham and His Celestial Bed* (Richmond: Alma Books, 2008).

Taylor, George Henry, *An Illustrated Sketch of the Movement Cure: Its Principles, Methods and Effects* (New York, 1866).

—*Diseases of Women: Their Causes, Prevention, and Radical Cure* (Philadelphia, New York and Boston: Geo. MacLean, 1871).

—*Pelvic and Hernial Therapeutics* (New York: J. B. Alden, 1885).

—*Mechanical Aids in the Treatment of Chronic Forms of Disease* (New York: George W. Rodgers, 1893).

Taylor, W. G. Langworthy, *Katie Fox: Epochmaking Medium and the Making of the Fox-Taylor Record* (New York and London: G. P. Putman's Sons, 1933).

Tesla, Nikola, *Nikola Tesla, 1856–1943: Lectures, Patents, Articles*, (eds) Vojin Pović, Radoslav Horvat, and Nikola Nikolić (Beograd, Yugoslavia: Nikola Tesla Museum, 1956).

—*My Inventions: The Autobiography of Nikola Tesla*, ed. Ben Johnston (New York: Barnes and Noble, 1982).

Thompson, Robert, *The Pelican History of Psychology* (Harmondsworth: Penguin, 1968).

Thomson, James, *Complete Poetical Works of James Thomson*, ed. J. Logie Robertson (London: Oxford UP, 1951).

Thomson, William, *The Six Gateways of Knowledge* (Birmingham: Osborne and Son, 1883).

—'The Wave Theory of Light', *Popular Lectures and Addresses*, 2nd edn, 3 vols (London: Macmillan and Co., 1891), 1, 307–55.

Thurschwell, Pamela, *Literature, Technology and Magical Thinking, 1880–1920* (Cambridge: Cambridge University Press, 2001).

Todd, Janet, *Sensibility: An Introduction* (London and New York: Methuen, 1986).

Todorov, Tzvetan, *The Fantastic: A Structural Approach to a Literary Genre* (New York: Cornell UP, 1975).

Tomson, W. Bolton, 'The General Appreciation of Vibration as a Sense Extraordinary', *The Lancet* (14 June 1890), 1299.

Trimble, Michael, *Post-Traumatic Neurosis: from Railway Spine to Whiplash* (Chichester, New York, Brisbane and Toronto: John Wiley and Sons, 1981).

Trower, Shelley, 'Vibratory Movements', special issue of *Senses and Society* 3 (2008).

—'"Nerve-Vibration": Therapeutic Technologies in the 1880s and 1890s', in *Neurology and Modernity: A Cultural History of Nervous Systems, 1800–1950*, ed. Laura Salisbury and Andrew Shail (Basingstoke: Palgrave, 2010), 148–62.

Turner, Mark, 'Periodical Time in the Nineteenth Century', *Media History*, 8 (2002), 183–96.

Tyndall, John, *Sound: A Course of Eight Lectures* (London: Longmans, Green and Co., 1867).

—'Radiation', part 2, in *Fragments of Science: A Series of Detached Essays, Addresses, and Reviews*, 7th edn, 2 vols (London: Longmans, Green and Co., 1889), 2, 28–73.

Uvedale, Christian, *The Construction of the Nerves, and the Causes of Nervous Disorders, Practically Explained. With a Distinction of these Diseases into two Kinds, hitherto not sufficiently observed, though essential to their Cure. With Plain Directions for Nervous Patients, in regard to Management and Medicines; and a few useful Receipts* (London: R. Baldwin, 1758).

Vallins, David, *Coleridge and the Psychology of Romanticism: Feeling and Thought* (London: MacMillan Press, 2000).

Vickers, Neil, *Coleridge and the Doctors, 1795–1806* (Oxford: Clarendon Press, 2004).

Walkowitz, Judith, 'Science and Séance: Transgressions of Gender and Genre in Late Victorian London', *Representations*, 22 (1988), 3–29.

Wallian, Samuel Spencer, *Rhymotherapy: A Discussion of the Physiologic Basis and Therapeutic Potency of Mechano-Vital Vibration* (Chicago: The Ouellette Press, 1906).

Walmsley, Derek, 'The Primer: Dubstep', *The Wire*, 279 (May 2007), 44.

Ward, James, 'An Attempt to Interpret Fechner's Law', *Mind: A Quarterly Review of Psychology and Philosophy*, 1 (London and Edinburgh: Williams and Norgate, 1876), 452–66.

Watson, Thomas, *Exploring Life: The Autobiography of Thomas A. Watson* (New York: D. Appleton, 1926).

Wells, H. G., *The War of the Worlds* (London: Heinemann Educational Books, 1951).

—*The First Men in the Moon*, ed. Patrick Parrinder (London: Penguin, 2005).

—'The New Accelerator', in *The Country of the Blind and Other Selected Stories*, ed. Patrick Parrinder (London: Penguin, 2007), 296–310.

Wernicke, Hugo, 'Preface', *On Life After Death* (London: Searle and Rivington, 1882).

Wheeler, Katherine, *The Creative Mind in Coleridge's Poetry* (London: Heinemann, 1981).

Whytt, Robert, 'Observations on the Nature, Causes, and Cure of those Diseases which are Commonly called Nervous, Hypochondriac, or Hysteric; To which are prefixed some Remarks on the Sympathy of the Nerves', in *The Works of Robert Whytt* (Edinburgh: Balfour, Auld and Smellie, 1768), 487–713.

Widmer, Peter, 'A Misrecognised Object in Psychoanalysis: the Voice', trans. Hanjo Berressem, *Literature and Psychology*, 37 (1991), 1–8.

Wightman, W., 'Wars of Ideas in Neurological Science –from Willis to Bichat and from Locke to Condillac', in *The History and Philosophy of Knowledge of the Brain and its Functions* (Oxford: Blackwell Scientific Publications, 1958), 135–53.

Will, Barbara, 'Nervous Systems, 1880–1915', in Tim Armstrong ed. *American Bodies*, (Sheffield: Sheffield Academic Press, 1996), 86–100.

Williams, Keith, 'Alien Gaze: Postcolonial Vision in *The War of the Worlds*, in Steven McLean ed. *H. G. Wells: Interdisciplinary Essays* (Cambridge: Cambridge Scholars, 2008), 49–73.

Winslow, L. S. Forbes, 'Spiritualistic Madness', in Mike Jay and Michael Neve (eds), *1900: A Fin-de-Siècle Reader* (London: Penguin, 1999), 118–19.

Winter, Alison, 'The Construction of Orthodoxies and Heterodoxies in the Early Victorian Life Sciences', in Bernard Lightman ed. *Victorian Science in Context*, (Chicago and London: University of Chicago Press, 1997), 24–50.

—*Mesmerized: Powers of Mind in Victorian Britain* (Chicago and London: University of Chicago Press, 1998).

Wintle, Sarah, 'Horses, Bikes and Automobiles: New Woman on the Move', in Angelique Richardson and Chris Willis (eds), *The New Woman in Fiction and Fact* (Basingstoke: Palgrave, 2001), 66–78.

Wood, Jane, 'Scientific Rationality and Fanciful Fiction: Gendered Discourse in "The Lifted Veil"', *Women's Writing*, 3 (1996), 161–76.

—*Passion and Pathology in Victorian Fiction* (Oxford: Oxford University Press, 2001).

Wooley, Benjamin, *The Bride of Science: Romance, Reason and Byron's Daughter* (London: Macmillan, 1999).

Worth, Aaron, 'Imperial Transmissions: H. G. Wells, 1897–1901', *Victorian Studies* 52 (2010), 65–89.

Wosk, Julie, *Women and the Machine: Representations from the Spinning Wheel to the Electronic Age* (Baltimore and London: Johns Hopkins University Press, 2001).

Young, Allan, *The Harmony of Illusions: Inventing Post-Traumatic Stress Disorder* (Princeton: Princeton University Press, 1995).

Young, Thomas, 'Experiments and Calculations Relative to Physical Optics', in Henry Crew ed. *The Wave Theory of Light: Memoirs by Huygens, Young and Fresnel* (New York: American Book Company, 1900), 68–76.

Zittel, Karl Alfred von, *History of Geology and Palaeontology to the End of the Nineteenth Century*, trans. Maria Ogilvie-Gordon (London: Walter Scott, 1901).

INDEX

Abrams, M. H. 22–3, 32, 35
Aeolian harp 9, 10, 13–15, 19–26,
　32–6, 44, 62–3, 72, 91, 94, 141
aliens 80, 89, 90
Armstrong, Tim 98, 145
associationism 9, 13, 14, 15, 16, 19, 23,
　32, 40, 44, 75
automatic processes 15, 19, 23–4, 25,
　45, 48
　see also unconscious
automatons 84, 90–3

Babbage, Charles 108–13, 120
Barrett, William 39n. 9, 84–5
bass 1, 111, 153
Beach Boys 153
Beard, George 144
Beattie, James 34
Beddoes, Thomas 28, 30–1
Bell, Alexander Graham 78, 86
Beer, Gillian 4, 6–7, 39, 53, 99–100
Benjamin, Walter 3, 97, 98
Bennett, Jane 8
bicycle riding 12, 126–7, 134–7, 148
Bilz, Friedrich 143
Bissell, David 9
Bloomfield, Robert 34
bones 1, 17, 87, 105, 113
Brennan, Teresa 11n. 43
British Medical Journal 127, 132,
　133–4
Brown, Bill 6, 7, 8
Brown, Isaac Baker 133, 134
Brown, John 28, 30–1
Browning, Elizabeth Barrett 83, 129–30
Buckland, Adelene 6, 7, 115–16
Burke, Edmund 27–33, 57, 140

Carlyle, Thomas 111
Carpenter, William 67–8, 84, 85

Casson, Herbert 79–80
Coffin, Judith 133, 137
Cohen, William 5n. 22, 11, 65
Coleridge, Samuel Taylor 14, 15, 21,
　25, 28–30, 31, 50, 54, 56, 63, 74,
　81, 90, 91, 93, 94, 140
　'The Aeolian Harp' 9–10, 11,
　13–14, 15, 20–3, 25–6, 33, 34,
　62–3
　Biographia Literaria 15, 24, 30, 32
　'Dejection' 14, 15, 26–7, 31–4, 56,
　63, 94, 141
Collins, Wilkie 40, 54, 61–4, 66, 84,
　97
Connor, Steven 9, 69, 80, 87
Conrad, Joseph 123–4
conservation of energy 10, 38, 39–40,
　48–53, 66–7, 72, 74, 75, 96,
　112–13, 124, 146–8
counting 3, 11, 92–3, 96, 103–12,
　115–16, 119, 127
　see also frequencies
Crary, Jonathan 5n. 22, 14–15, 22–3,
　36, 43–4, 45, 48, 71–2, 104
Crookes, William 51, 68, 86, 92, 102,
　148–9

Daly, Nicholas 97, 127
Davy, Humphry 31
degeneration 107, 112, 120, 135–6,
　137
Deleuze, Gilles and Felix Guattari 9
Dickens, Charles 110, 111, 125, 152
　Bleak House 116
　Dombey and Son 99, 113–19,
　121–5, 129
　Household Words 114
　Martin Chuzzlewit 129
　'The Signalman' 125
　A Tale of Two Cities 123

'An Unsettled Neighbourhood' 120–1
Down, J. Langdon 132, 133
Du Maurier, George 61, 84

ear 5, 16–17, 18, 30, 33, 44–5, 46, 66–72, 80, 105
earthquakes 99, 114–16, 118, 119–20, 124, 125
Edison, Thomas 68–9, 78, 89, 91, 113
electricity 4, 18, 19, 23, 24, 35, 75–6, 78, 79, 82, 87–9, 91, 144–6
Eliot, George 60
    Adam Bede 60
    'The Lifted Veil' 40, 54–61, 66, 67, 69, 70, 71
    Middlemarch 55–6, 59, 60, 131
Ellenberger, Henri 50
Ellis, Havelock 130, 132, 136–7
Engels, Friedrich 120, 121, 122–3
Enns, Anthony 68, 74, 78, 81, 86n. 58
Erichsen, John 100
Erle, Sibylle and Laurie Garrison 10
ether 7, 16, 17, 24–5, 37, 53, 145

Fara, Patricia 82
Fechner, Gustav 38, 50, 74, 86, 102, 103, 140
    Elements of Psychophysics 38, 40–2, 44, 47, 49, 50, 57, 67
    On Life After Death 38, 47, 48, 49, 50, 52, 53, 57, 58, 67, 112, 146
    Nanna, or the Soul Life of Plants 47–8, 55
femininity 11–12, 29–30, 54–66, 67–8, 81–5, 136–8, 140, 141, 148–9
Finney, Gretchen 48, 63n. 91
Flint, Kate 6
Fox, Katie 12, 54–5, 96, 147–8
frequencies 2, 3, 4, 10, 38–40, 41–4, 49–53, 60, 68, 72, 92–3, 96, 99–112, 115, 119, 138–9, 141–4
Freud, Sigmund 45, 50, 98
Fulford, Tim 24–5

geology 6, 114–16
Gissing, George 127–8

God 11, 25–6, 27, 31, 35, 50, 73, 76, 78, 81, 87, 92
God's nerves 77, 82, 87
Goodman, Steve 155–6n. 11
Gouk, Penelope 4n. 12, 5n. 20, 16
Graham, James 31n. 68, 142
Granville, Joseph Mortimer 95, 139–43, 144, 148
Gurney, Edmund 51, 69, 77–8

hallucinations 69, 70, 71–2, 73, 74, 77–9, 80–1, 84, 86
Hardy, Thomas, *Far From the Madding Crowd* 130–1
Harrington, Anne 50, 81n. 33
Hartley, David, *Observations on Man* 9, 13, 14, 15–28, 32, 40–1, 75, 76, 88, 95, 140
Havergal, Frances Ridley 72
Helmholtz, Hermann 3, 4, 38, 50, 95
    'The Conservation of Force' 39, 47
    'The Facts of Perception' 43
    'The Origin of the Planetary System' 39
    'The Physiological Causes of Harmony' 3, 4, 38–9, 41–2, 99–100
    The Sensations of Tone 39–40, 43, 44–5, 75–6
Herschel, William 39
Hey, Hanson 52
horse-riding 28, 130, 138, 142
House, Humphrey 115

L'Isle-Adam, Villers de 68–9, 91

James, William 81

Kipling, Rudyard 70, 141–2
Kittler, Friedrich 5n. 22, 15, 45, 48, 59, 65, 71–2
Kircher, Athanasius 21
Kraepelin, Emil 77–8, 86

Lancet, The 100–8, 110, 113, 118–19, 121, 123, 127–9, 133–6, 139–43
Latour, Bruno 8, 9
Le Fanu, Sheridan 69–70

Ledger, Sally 128, 137–8
Levine, George 55
Lewes, George Henry 15, 55, 56
Lewis, Matthew, *The Monk* 28–9, 34
life 8, 9, 10, 12, 14, 30–1, 35–6, 38, 40,
     47, 70, 89, 90, 149, 152–3
light 4, 7, 10, 21–2, 31, 33, 37–40, 42,
     55–6, 87–8, 92, 108
     see also light waves
Locke, John 16, 40
Luckhurst Roger 51, 86
Lyell, Charles 114–15, 116

Maines, Rachel 130, 138, 143
Marconi, Guglielmo 86
Martineau, Harriet 83
Marvin, Carolyn 80, 88
Marx, Karl 120, 121, 122–3
Mason, Diane 134
Maudsley, Henry 84
McDonagh, Josephine 60
McLandburgh, Florence 40, 54, 66,
     91
McLuhan, Marshall 5, 79
medical vibrations 12, 14, 27–8, 29,
     30–6, 57, 95–6, 123, 126, 130,
     138–49, 152–3
     see also percuteur
Mersenne, Marin 4
Mesmer, Franz Anton 24–5
mesmerism 24–5, 50, 58–9, 62, 82–4
Miles, Robert,19, 25, 29
Miller, David 8
Morton, Timothy 20
Muller, Johannes 42, 44
music 1, 2, 3, 4, 9, 19, 30, 32, 34,
     38, 42, 43, 102, 110–11, 113,
     116–17, 141
musical strings 5, 9, 10, 13, 16, 17–19,
     24–5, 29, 34, 39, 44–8, 65, 92,
     140, 152
     see also aeolian harp, sympathetic
     vibration
Musselman, Elizabeth 76, 77

Nancy, Jean Luc 9
natural philosophy 4
nerves 4, 5, 9, 10, 11, 13–36, 37–8,

41–9, 54, 73, 75–7, 79–84, 92–3,
     94–5, 105, 138–40
nervous illness 3–4, 14, 28, 34, 54–66,
     69–70, 71–2, 73–4, 77–8, 81–5,
     91, 94, 111, 126, 140–8
Newton, Isaac 16, 21, 24, 40
Noakes, Richard 39n. 9, 67, 76
noise 3, 11, 32, 34, 59–60, 71–2, 73,
     74, 80–1, 89, 105, 109–13, 153
Nordau, Max 107, 120

Oppenheim, Janet, 50, 84n. 46,110n. 59
Otis, Laura 76, 77
Owen, Alex 64, 83

percuteur 2, 11, 138–43
     see also medical instruments
phonautograph 113
phonograph 68–9, 76, 113
piano, 3, 10, 44–5, 46
Pick, Daniel 120
Picker, John 111, 113
Pilgrim, Mauric 145–6
Porter, Roy 16n. 16, 158n. 38
Priestley, Joseph 18–19, 21, 30–1
psychophysics 38–9, 40–53, 55–6, 57,
     95, 104
     see also Fechner

radio 2, 7, 40, 71, 73, 85–6, 87, 88–91
railway 2, 3, 12, 94, 95, 98, 114–15,
     118–22, 124, 126–30, 148
railway spine 94–5, 98, 107, 126, 136,
     139
Richardson, Alan 14, 15
Roach, Joseph 17–18, 25
Roberts, Mark 73, 77
Rockwell, Alphonso 144
Ronell, Avital, 78, 80
Rousseau, G. S. 5n. 21, 9n. 38, 30, 95
Rudy, Jason R. 10n. 40
Ruston, Sharon 35
Rylance, Rick 15

salt 33
Sanders, Andrew 122–3, 124
Sarafianos, Aris 30, 31
Schiller, Friedrich 62–3

Schivelbusch, Wolfgang 96–7, 100, 106, 120
Schreber, Daniel Paul 11, 54–5, 71–2, 73–93, 95
Sconce, Jeffrey 85–6
screams 14, 33–4, 71, 110, 141
sensation novels 12, 29, 97
  see also Collins, Wilkie
Serres, Michel 8
sewing machines 12, 126–7, 132–4, 148
sexology 65–6, 130, 132–7
sextillions 92
sexual pleasure/excitement 82–3, 95–6, 109, 126–49, 152
Shelley, Mary 35, 144, 146
Shelley, Percy 34–5
shocks 1, 59–60, 94–109, 124–5, 126
Silverman, Robert and Thomas Hankins 19
Sinfield, Alan 65
siren 4, 41–2, 59, 99–100, 101, 104–5
Smith, W. 29–30
Snow, M. L. H. Arnold 143–4
Society for Psychical Research 49–50, 51, 54, 58
speakers 1, 2, 5
spiritualism 2, 10, 11–12, 38, 40, 47–72, 73–4, 76–9, 81–6, 91, 92, 96, 112, 146, 152–3
Spiritualists' National Union in Britain 52
Sterne, Jonathan 4n. 12, 5n. 20, 38
Stimson, Frederic 74, 91–2
Stoker, Bram 61
sublime 27–36, 57, 140, 141
sympathetic vibration 11, 16, 19, 25, 29, 39–40, 44–5, 51, 60, 63, 65, 79, 97, 140
sympathy 60–1

Taylor, George Henry 12, 95–6, 146–8
telegraph 75–6, 82,
telepathy 52–3, 54, 58–66, 78, 86, 127
telephone 11, 71, 73, 74, 76–81, 82
Tesla, Nikola 73–4, 87–91, 144

Thomson, James 13
Thomson, William 42, 43
Thurschwell, Pamela 11n. 44, 54, 61, 64–5, 91
trauma 97–8, 125, 126
Turner, Mark 102, 122
Tyndall, John 51, 55, 140
  'Visible and Invisible Radiation' 46
  Sound, 46–7 105, 106

unconscious/ness 3, 4, 10, 45, 97–8, 102, 104, 108–9
  see also automatic processes
universities 151–3

Verney Joseph Du 17–18
vibrancy 8, 9, 10, 89, 122–5, 151–3
  see also life
vibrator 2, 95, 137, 138, 149, 152–3
  see also percuteur and medical vibrations
Vickers, Neil 28, 31
voice 23–5, 56

Walkowitz, Judith 64, 83
war 89–90, 106–7
Watson, Thomas 78, 70, 86
waves
  brain 1, 48–53
  light and heat 4, 7, 10, 37, 38–40, 42–3, 53, 59–60, 105, 141
    see also light
  water 20, 53, 67
    see also radio
Wells, H. G. 73–4, 90, 93
Whytt, Robert 29
Widmer, Peter 77
Wilde, Oscar 54, 65–6, 84
Winter, Alison 82–4
Wood, Jane 57, 59, 63–4
Wordsworth, William 35
Wosk, Julie 120, 137

Young, Thomas 37, 141

x-rays 4, 40, 51, 86, 87, 101–2, 148